A. Glenn Mandeville's
Madame Alexander Dolls
3rd Collector's Price Guide

1953 Bible characters *Queen Esther, Joseph,* and *David. Mary Lee Stallings Collection. Photo by Ric Marklin.*

Published by | Hobby House Press | Hobby House Grantsville, MD 21536

D1451361

Dedication

This third edition of *A. Glenn Mandeville's Alexander Dolls Collector's Price Guide* is dedicated to Benita Schwartz. One could not ask for a better friend. Her love of Madame Alexander dolls, her commitment to perfection, and her willingness to share make her someone I am proud to know for longer than I care to admit! Thanks, Benita. You are what friendship and doll collecting are all about!

EA JA JRW

Alexander Dolls Collector's Price Guide is an independent study by the author A. Glenn Mandeville and published by Hobby House Press, Inc. The research and publication of this book was not sponsored in any way by the manufacturer of the doll, the doll costumes and the doll accessories featured in this study. Photographs of the collectibles were from dolls, costumes or accessories belonging to A. Glenn Mandeville, Marge Meisinger, Pamela Martinec, Benita Schwartz, Veronica Jochens, Sara Tondini, Tanya McWhorter, Karen Lynne and other collectors at the time the picture was taken unless otherwise credited with the caption.

The values given within this book are intended as value guides rather than arbitrarily set prices. The values quoted are as accurate as possible but in the case of errors, typographical, clerical or otherwise, the author and publisher assume no liability nor responsibility for any loss incurred by users of this book.

Additional copies of this book may be purchased at $11.95 (plus postage and handling) from
Hobby House Press, Inc.
1 Corporate Drive, Grantsville, MD 21536
1-800-554-1447
www.hobbyhouse.com
or from your favorite bookstore or dealer.
© 2000 A. Glenn Mandeville

Printed in the United States of America.

ISBN: 0-87588-560-8

Table of Contents

For four straight years in the early 1950s Madame Alexander won the prestigious Fashion Academy Award for Clothing Design. She is shown here in her office with three of her award-winning designs. *A. Glenn Mandeville Collection.*

Acknowledgements

This exciting new edition includes new information and exciting dolls – some shown for the first time ever! Thanks to Benita Schwartz, Joel Schwartz, Farin Schwartz, Karen Lynne, Tanya McWhorter, Mary Lee Stallings, Sara Tondini, Veronica Jochens, Donna Rovner, Dick Tahsin and photographers Ric Marklin and Carol J. Stover. The Sara Tondini doll photos were taken by Zehr Photography. Benita Schwartz collection photographed by A. Glenn Mandeville. A. Glenn Mandeville collection photographed by author.

If you want to learn more about a topic, just do a book on it and suddenly collectors come forward with unique information! Thanks again to individuals who made the second edition happen. They are Jan Lebow, Marge and Earl Meisinger, Pamela Martinec, Bernice Heister, Jean Bartenfeld, Jay Schwartz, Benita Schwartz and Chris Law.

The following collectors helped launch the first edition and their help will never be forgotten: Joe Carillo, Vivian Brady-Ashley, Ann Tardie, Pat Burns, Ann Rast, Neal Foster, Tanya McWhorter, Ira Smith and Beau James. Research on dates for all editions was done by Benita Schwartz, Judy Traina, Linda Collie and Donna Rovner.

Special thanks go to Mary Beth Ruddell, Virginia Heyerdahl, Pamela Martinec, and, of course, my wonderful editor Carolyn Cook.

The late Bob Gantz contributed more to any of my books than I could express in a listing. Thanks, Bob, for believing in me!

Without all these individuals and many more I could not have undertaken such a large project. Many, many thanks to all...A. Glenn Mandeville

Foreword

There are many exciting changes in this third edition! The wonderful world of Madame Alexander dolls has changed a great deal in the past several years.

The company is now under the able leadership of Herb Brown and with his unique ability to listen to what collectors are saying, The Alexander Doll Company has never looked better. Special editions *look* like they are special. The unusual costuming and the coloring of the vinyl are just breathtaking. Aside from that, the marketplace itself has taken several turns in just four short years.

Vintage Alexanders, those from the 1920s to late 1960s, are skyrocketing in price. You will be shocked, I am sure, at the values listed. Some dolls, like *Cissy*, are almost out of the reach of the average collector. Just about any mint condition hard plastic doll from 1947 to the mid-1950s is sometimes double what the old price used to be.

On the other hand, dolls made during the late 1970s and 1980s, when the factory was basically not making many changes to the line, have declined greatly in value with some notable exceptions.

The current dolls, many of which are reintroductions of past treasures like *Cissy*, are selling briskly and making instant collectibles as the edition numbers are very low compared to other manufacturers.

Collecting has taken on an entirely new face...that of a computer screen. Chat boards, on-line auctions and Internet newsgroups have allowed collectors to know about a new doll before the dealers do! Sales are easier than ever before, especially for those who are shut-ins or cannot travel to shows.

However, traditional auction houses and doll shows are still the primary way that sales of rare items occur. The new technology is growing, but nothing can replace examining a doll in person before buying it. I do see more on-line action becoming an increasing force in the hobby, but educated collectors and dealers will determine just how far the electronic collecting can go forward.

For the advanced collector, the listings in this edition have been broken down into almost minute detail. More breakouts are planned for the fourth edition. This way, even a novice can look up *Cissy* and not rely on a broad category such as "street dress." These breakouts will benefit everyone in buying and selling the creations of Beatrice Alexander and The Alexander Doll Company.

I hope you enjoy this third edition. If you have rare or unusual dolls, I would love to have photos of them for the next edition. Sharing and confirming knowledge is a wonderful part of the hobby.

Trust me when I say that collecting Madame Alexander dolls is a fast paced, ever changing and evolving hobby, but one that brings much satisfaction as well as friendships.

Speaking of friendships, they make doll collecting just a whole lot nicer. Please share and enjoy this book, for the dolls are worthy of the finest collections.

Collecting Madame Alexander dolls seems to make the world just a little bit nicer and that is something we can all agree is a joy forever!

A. Glenn Mandeville   December, 1999

The Magic of Collecting Madame Alexander Dolls

A mid 1930s *Princess Elizabeth* says it all. Traditions are what The Alexander Doll Company was and is all about. *Veronica Jochens Collection.*

There is indeed much magic, that elusive mystery and wonderment that comes from just looking at a Madame Alexander doll. In my opinion, no other doll can come close to the quality, workmanship and theme selections of the creations produced for over seventy years at The Alexander Doll Company.

During the "Golden Age" of the collectible dolls, namely the late 1940s until the mid-1960s, Madame Alexander dolls were the standard by which all other dolls were judged. It matters little if Madame was first with a new idea. When she entered the race, her version was always the best. Although Madame Alexander dolls cost much more than competitors' dolls, it was the quality and exquisite design that made Madame Alexander a legend.

The most overlooked fact is that Madame was not a doll artist but a clothing designer. She won the Fashion Academy Award for clothing design four straight years, 1951-1954. More astonishing is that the competition was not just doll clothing but *all* garments manufactured, period. This was, and still is, a large part of the magic of Madame Alexander dolls. Each perfectly tailored little garment could be made for a miniature person. If you were only eight inches tall, you'd have an entire playground realm – ball gowns, street wear, play clothes and more in your imaginary closet!

The dolls were rarely the stars because at The Alexander Doll Company the tradition is to take a face and use it to launch a thousand ships. To Madame, the dolls, for the most part, were merely the mannequins upon which she draped her dreams and her desire to educate those who would possess her creations.

Expensive and only available in "better" outlets, the dolls Madame created embodied her belief that today's child was underexposed to the great masters of art, literature and culture. It was through her dolls, that others became familiar with the histories of notables such as *Renoir* and *Mary Cassatt.*

A life of culture, often neglected even in the educated, became real as the same little 12-inch (31cm) doll became *Lord Fauntleroy, Napoleon* and *Josephine, Anthony* and *Cleopatra,* and even *Rhett* and *Scarlett*! One doll, one face, yet in the skillful hands of The Alexander Doll Company, magic was created as each new character came to life!

There is magic in collecting Madame Alexander dolls. For over 70 years, Madame Alexander and The Alexander Doll Company have provided us with a history and art that thrill to amaze us. They are proving that a thing of beauty is truly a joy forever.

What is My Alexander Doll Worth?

As a collector and appraiser of dolls, the most frequent question I am asked, at shows or by mail, is "What is my Alexander doll worth?"

The question, while seemingly simple, can be compared to asking a stranger you meet, "What is my car worth?" The person hearing the question would be shocked, as no further information is often given!

Some basic facts must be discussed. Antique dolls, defined as having a porcelain head and over 75 years old, are evaluated quite differently than Madame Alexander dolls.

With an antique doll, the value is primarily in the head of the doll. The mold number and the facial expression can add up to a doll head that is worth tens of thousands of dollars. The body can usually be "replaced" at a later date. "Period" clothing can always be found at a good doll show if it is missing, so basically the assigned value of the doll is contained from the neck up!

Madame Alexander dolls are another matter entirely; first, each doll is almost without exception like hundreds, even thousands of others. What makes the doll unique is the clothing, the wig, and the face painting. Thus a nude, wigless, Alexander doll has little, if any value, because the character of the doll is lost forever. Is it *Little Miss Muffet,* or maybe *Oliver Twist*? Could the nude, wigless little creature be a boy or a girl? An adult or a child?

The reader can quickly see that to bring top collector dollars, the doll must be complete with all the original accessories it was sold with.

Secondly, the condition of the doll is almost all the value. The same collectors who stared lovingly at the doll cases in John Wanamaker's in Philadelphia want that doll to look just as it did in 1957! After all, they remember it that way and waited over 30 years to own it! Certainly they are not interested in used children's toys. They want, and are willing to pay for, perfection. The collector wants to cheat time, as it were, and pretend that it is Christmas morning, 1957, and they are opening the dream doll they never received!

With Alexander dolls, the seller must realize the further you take the doll from crispy mint perfection, the lower the price goes. One has to understand that even with very rare dolls, the doll is either unplayed with and in mint condition, or it falls into the category of a used child's toy. Naturally, the played with doll has some value, often more sentimental than monetary, but the price drops drastically along with the condition.

Factors that add to the value of an Alexander doll are: Does the doll have original factory clothing, complete with all accessories? Is there a box? Does the doll have a booklet or wrist tag? Also, factors such as a good facial coloring and general eye appeal make for a superior doll.

There is much misunderstanding in the pricing of Alexander dolls. Some collectors will buy gently played with dolls and restore them, but they want the price to reflect the effort that they have to put forth to bring the doll up to another level. Other collectors simply will not look at a pale, badly played with doll and regard it as something that should be discarded or purchased for parts.

Sellers of dolls are becoming more educated to the fact that condition is the main ingredient in making an Alexander doll valuable. The dealer of today is more often a collector him/herself and thus very in tune to the factors that make an Alexander doll valuable.

Another question that I am often asked is, "How do I keep my collection from overtaking my house?" Many times a doll collector, myself included, loves <u>everything</u>! Naturally, if space and money were not a consideration, I suppose this would not be a problem, but I can offer the collector my favorite ten tips to make your collection award winning!

Ten Tips to Make Your Collection Award Winning!

Early 1930s 20-inch (51cm) *My Betty* is a very rare doll. *Veronica Jochens Collection.*

1. Decide on a focus for your collection. Stick to one particular size doll, or perhaps a theme such as fairy tale characters. By sticking to a category you can avoid the "I have to have everything they make" anxiety and strengthen your collection. What happens if you see an Alexander doll that is not in your category but that you must have? Well, like the person on a diet, you can splurge on that hot fudge sundae a few times, but not every day!

2. Buy the best you can afford and don't be afraid to upgrade if you see a better example. This is one area where you can be a bit obsessive! With older dolls, ask yourself if this doll is a better example than the one that you have at home. Sometimes new dolls have fabric variations. If you see one you like better, buy it and sell yours. The goal is always to have a strong collection in your chosen category.

3. If you are collecting a series, such as Americana dolls or foreign lands figures or anything similar, carry a small notebook with you to doll shows. That way you will remember what it is you need to complete a certain grouping.

4. Always note what accessories you need to make a doll go up a grade. Your notebook can list things like booklets, wrist tags, shoes, stockings, hats, etc., which can make a doll go from excellent to mint condition. It is possible to find these little things. I speak from experience, so note what it is you need.

5. Money is usually a factor with most collectors. If, at a show, you see a doll you need, inquire if the dealer has a layaway policy. Credit cards (a necessary evil in collecting) can be an option. When all else fails, at least get the name and phone number of the seller. Some dealers do only a couple of shows a year and it is possible that the item you are interested in will be available when you have the funds!

6. Assign each doll a code number. I use a letter code for the year and a number code for the item within that year. In other words, if 1993 is "A" and your first item is "1" this makes your code "A-1". Use a small self-stick label to put your code on the bottom of the doll's shoe. In a notebook record: the date of purchase, check number, receipt from the seller, etc. Insure your collection and photograph your dolls. Keep this information in duplicate in a place off the premises such as a safe deposit box or at a family member's home.

7. Enjoy your collection by taking the dolls out of the boxes. Rotate a display around a holiday theme or family tradition. Invest in built-in cabinets or curio cases. Having a doll out in the air for a month or so will not hurt it and will give the material a chance to "breathe." Remember, there are only a few precautions you need to follow: keep dolls out of direct sunlight or even brightly lit areas; avoid dust by using cases; and keep dolls away from small children and pets. I think it is better to risk a little wear and tear on your treasures than have them all packed away.

8. Read all you can on Alexander dolls. There are many excellent publications that can assist you. Company catalogs are invaluable, but sometimes changes and variations do exist as catalogs are often made up before the dolls are produced. They are a valuable research tool, but are not infallible. Also, clip the advertisements for the store specials that you buy and keep them in your notebook. They will be of great interest to you in the future. The more you know about Alexander dolls, the more you will enjoy collecting them.

This 21-inch (53cm) early 1950s is the essence of collecting.
Karen Lynne Collection.

9. Restoration has made many excellent dolls near mint. Study publications that show you how to revamp hair, textiles and fabrics. Never, however, practice on an expensive older doll. There are many opinions on how much, if anything, to do to "fix-up" an older doll. Listen to the options and opinions and then decide what your personal philosophy will be. It is your collection and it should reflect your ideals and standards.

10. Finally, don't overlook the fellowship and friendships that doll collecting offers. The doll show circuit is filled with people with the same interests you have. There are conventions devoted to Madame Alexander dolls, and ads placed by other collectors. One thing I have learned is that doll collectors seem to gravitate to each other. Lifestyles, age and wealth are not the barriers to doll relationships as they are in the outside world. Do reach out to just one collector and I'll bet within a month, you will find more new friends than you could ever imagine!

Yes, the world of doll collecting is a wonderful, fun-filled place. With a little effort, time and education, you can learn the history behind the beautiful dolls. Why not make your collection reflect the very best that life has to offer? Doll collecting, especially Madame Alexander dolls, makes life a great deal of fun! Start your collection today!

Alexander Doll Faces

The Alexander Doll Company has produced thousands of dolls over a span of 70 years! Known as a fashion designer and not a doll artist, Madame Alexander created most of her often award-winning characters out of a few basic doll faces. Some characters, especially celebrities like *Jane Withers, Sonja Henie,* and *Shari Lewis,* had a unique head designed for the company. Most of the never-ending parade of art and literary figures, storybook and nursery rhyme characters, and beloved dolls of royalty and film stars, were brought to life with the skilled use of a combination of clothing design, hairstyles and make-up. It is a cherished tradition that continues today.

Here in our photo gallery are some famous faces that have been used for three-quarters of a century. Look carefully at the faces, for while featured here, the next time you see it, that face may belong to a Prince, a Queen, a fairy tale character or even your favorite movie star!

It is not often important to identify an undressed Alexander doll. Frankly, as Madame would often say, "My figures (dolls) are merely the mannequins upon which I drape my dreams."

Clothing labels, wrist tags, (which are often dated) and research will tell more of a doll's history than a face alone.

Some generalizations with exceptions apply. Cloth dolls were unmarked, but jointed at the neck and used from the 1920s into the 1930s. Composition dolls (a mixture of sawdust and glue that is then painted) were the mainstay of doll making until the late 1940s. Hard plastic, especially on a larger doll, generally dates the doll from the 1950s. Soft vinyl plastic on a larger doll usually means the doll is more contemporary. One notable exception is the 8-inch (20cm) all hard plastic doll introduced as *Wendy Ann* in 1953. It still is being made today.

As with many doll companies, the date incised on the doll is the year the mold was made and not the particular date of the character that utilized that mold. As many as three decades can pass and a date will remain the same if that mold is still being used. As stated before, costuming and hairstyling are essential to identifying an Alexander doll.

The author would recommend the following grading system when buying, selling, or insuring your dolls.

MINT...a <u>very</u> overused term. In actuality, about 15% of older dolls advertised or shown for sale fit the definition of this word. A mint doll should look like it did when it left the factory, whether 70 minutes or 70 years ago! That "crisp" feeling to the clothing should be there. Facial coloring would be bright and fresh. The wig or rooted hairstyle must be undisturbed. This type of doll is not seen as often as one would expect with the overuse of this term. Naturally, an original box (a blessing to some collectors and a burden to others) would add more value, as would a catalog, wrist tag, hatbox, or any other accessory sold with the doll.

EXCELLENT...About 20% of dolls seen today, barring new releases, are in this condition. To some, "mint" and "excellent" mean the same. To the advanced collector they are not. These terms also do <u>not</u> apply to a doll with "replaced" anything. Avoid using the phrase, "excellent, but." They can't coexist! Your excellent dolls would have everything all original but perhaps lack that extra sparkle and crispness of a never handled doll.

GOOD...There is certainly nothing wrong with a doll in good condition. In my opinion, the bulk of dolls found today should be graded using this word. The term "good" as it applies to food is certainly not a negative and with an Alexander doll is should not be either. A constant source of conflict between buyer and seller is that the term "mint" has been used to describe a doll in really "good" condition. The collector of "mint" dolls generally is not looking for "good" condition dolls, even for a fair price. They would prefer a "mint" doll and should be willing to pay for it. Likewise, many collectors of "good" condition dolls do not want the expense or responsibility of a "mint" doll that must be carefully handled in order to keep its grading at "mint."

A "good" condition doll would have original clothing and shoes and maybe just need some surface cleaning. To be in good condition, an Alexander doll should not have badly laundered or replaced clothing, cut hair or missing important accessories. In reality, "good" dolls are quite desirable to many collectors.

Those who sell dolls would fair far better if price and condition matched each other. Once again, educating people that an intelligent grading system can work is the key.

FAIR...While many Alexander dolls are bought to be "shelf dolls" or just brought out on special occasions, many, many dolls were loved and cherished by countless children. Many collectors love "fair" condition dolls, and the low prices that they should have. At the very least, one half of the listed value is subtracted for a doll in "fair" condition. Once a stigma in collecting, skilled collectors often are quite thrilled to find a pre-loved doll and restore it to as close to mint condition as possible. The skill level of this group of collectors is astonishing! Dolls that once would be overlooked are getting a new lease on life and making a new owner proud! This classification, in my opinion, is the one that causes the most pricing problems. A used child's toy is <u>not</u> a coveted, mint condition art object and should be priced as such. Unless very rare, it would be hard to justify a price over $300 for a doll in pre-loved condition. As stated, don't overpay, whether for yourself or for resale, for many collectors would rather settle for no example of a doll than take a less than mint doll at any price. Once you have mastered this concept, you are on your way to a successful hobby or business. I have found that doll collectors are a special breed of people. Most are more than willing to share their knowledge!

POOR... This is an often overlooked category that affords the collector a great opportunity. Actually some dolls that are labeled in "poor" condition might have a fantastic wig or original shoes. This type of doll is usually bought for "parts" for a "good" or "fair" condition doll. If you are interested in "good" or "fair" condition dolls, don't overlook a doll graded as "poor." It just might have the missing accessory you have been searching for!

As you can see, grading an Alexander doll is really quite simple as long as you remain knowledgeable about a few facts!

1. You can never make a doll "mint." It can be skillfully restored to excellent condition but the very term "mint" implies seamless perfection. Do not decide to collect only "mint" dolls unless you are willing to pay top prices for the very best examples. The term "mint-reasonable" has no place in a doll wanted ad!

2. Learn all you can about the "tricks of the trade." Techniques such as using boiling water to restore hair sets and laundry methods that are state of the art can give you a very fine collection at an attractive price.

3. Do realize that "good" condition dolls are not the stepchildren of collecting. Just as some collectors want only mint dolls, others are turned off by dolls they feel they can never undress, handle or display. There is no right or wrong in a hobby, it is your choice.

4. Do try to convince anyone who will listen that pricing an Alexander doll is just like pricing a comic book or other collectible. The condition is everything. Certainly never pay a near-mint price for a played with doll.

The pressed cloth face shown here was the first doll face used by The Alexander Doll Company in the 1920s and into the early 1930s. Unmarked, it has a swivel neck. Most were hand painted by Madame and her sisters! *A. Glenn Mandeville Collection.*

5. While all price guides say that a guide is just that, do remember that many, many variables influence the price of a doll. Prices vary greatly throughout the country. A major doll convention in a particular area can also affect pricing. Special dolls vary greatly in price as the good time associated with the event sometimes gets added to the price. Remember that it is your money, your hobby and your life! Learn all you can about everything. Network with other collectors and I'll bet you will wind up with an outstanding collection, no matter what your taste and level of collecting may be.

Today is an exciting time for the collector of Madame Alexander dolls. There are all types of dolls, new and old, for just about any taste or budget. There are mint as new dolls, as well as some real "handyman's specials." Doll shows and events that feature Madame Alexander dolls occur just about every weekend! It's a doll's life out there! Why not get started today? With the popularity of Madame Alexander dolls, should your path change and you wake up one day thinking why are all my dolls blondes, or brides, or whatever, you can sell your dolls to eager collectors and go off in another direction. Doll collecting is one of the few areas of your life today where you are in total control! That's what makes it so much fun for "children" of all ages! In my experience, the friendships made while collecting dolls are long lasting and solid. There is a whole world of interesting people, places and dolls to see!

Above: A stunning *McGuffey Ana* shows yet another face used in the late 1930s and is usually marked with the "Princess Elizabeth" and Alexander name. This head mold was primarily used in the late 1930s and early 1940s on larger size dolls. *A. Glenn Mandeville Collection.*

This 7-inch (18cm) face was used on *McGuffey Ana,* as shown here, *Tiny Betty, Princess Elizabeth,* and dozens of dolls in a 7-inch (18cm) or 9-inch (23cm) size. For small dolls, it was the face used during the 1930s. The head is usually unmarked, but the body carries the Alexander name. *A. Glenn Mandeville Collection.*

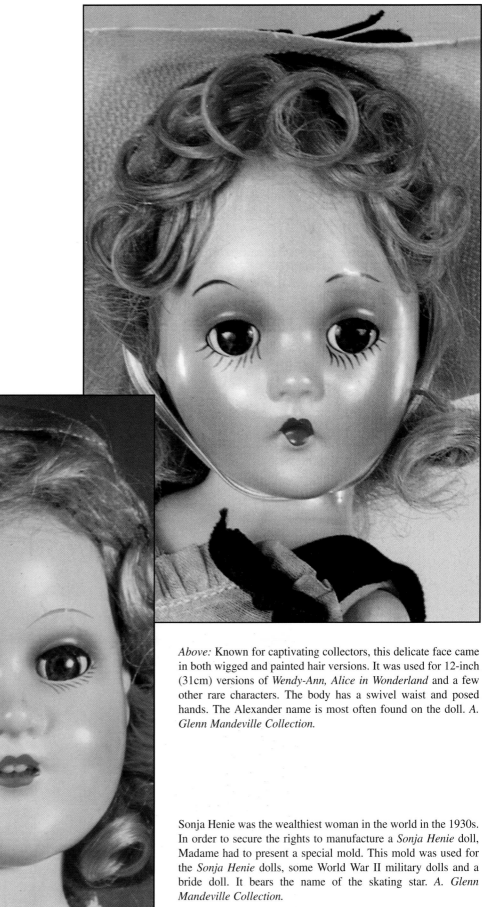

Above: Known for captivating collectors, this delicate face came in both wigged and painted hair versions. It was used for 12-inch (31cm) versions of *Wendy-Ann, Alice in Wonderland* and a few other rare characters. The body has a swivel waist and posed hands. The Alexander name is most often found on the doll. *A. Glenn Mandeville Collection.*

Sonja Henie was the wealthiest woman in the world in the 1930s. In order to secure the rights to manufacture a *Sonja Henie* doll, Madame had to present a special mold. This mold was used for the *Sonja Henie* dolls, some World War II military dolls and a bride doll. It bears the name of the skating star. *A. Glenn Mandeville Collection.*

13

Above: Margaret O'Brien was the child star of the new decade, the 1940s. Her likeness, usually marked ALEX on the head, was used in both composition and hard plastic from the 1940s into the early 1950s. It was a face that launched a thousand ships! *A. Glenn Mandeville Collection.*

Above: Virtually the same face, only in a larger size and in the new hard plastic, this face mold first used on the *Margaret O'Brien* dolls would become the standard of beauty for The Alexander Doll Company. *A. Glenn Mandeville Collection.*

An impish grin in hard plastic, 8-inch (20cm) style is *Maggie Mix-up* made in 1960-1961. While unmarked, this head became once again a collector favorite in the 1990s. Her smile was used on angels, devils and other assorted characters of fame and fable! The body has the Alexander Doll Company name. *A. Glenn Mandeville Collection.*

14

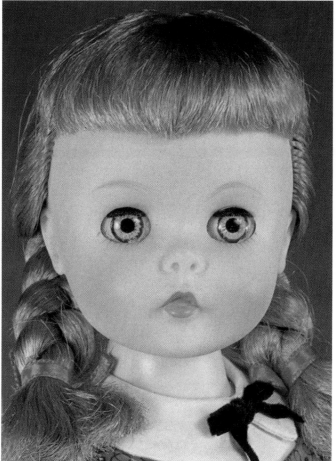

Above: Often unmarked, this full-cheeked unmistakable face was used in hard plastic in the early 1950s for Kate Smith's *Annabelle, Maggie Teenager, Peter Pan, Little Women, Little Men,* and many others such as brides and bridesmaids. Most of the larger size dolls used either this face or the mold first used on *Margaret O'Brien. A. Glenn Mandeville Collection.*

Often described as coy and cute, this vinyl face was used on several girl dolls of the late 1950s, such as *Marybell, The Doll Who Gets Well; Country Cousins; Kelly* and *Pollyanna.* She bears the Alexander marking on her head. *A. Glenn Mandeville Collection.*

Above: Cissy was Madame Alexander's entry into the world of high fashion. This face, which usually bears the Alexander Company markings, was used on child dolls such as *Binnie* and *Winnie Walker* and some of the early 1960s Portrait dolls. *Cissy* was a powerful presence in the Alexander line-up. *A. Glenn Mandeville Collection.*

15

Above: Another famous face is this mold that was originally used in 1957 on *Cissette,* a 10-inch (25cm) full figured doll, and then with heavy make-up for this *Jacqueline.* Friends such as *Margot, Gold Rush, Klondike Kate* and other worldly women were created from these enchanting molds. Still a popular favorite, this perky lady is the face used on the *Portrette Series,* both in the 1960s as well as the current line. The body bears the Alexander Company markings. *A. Glenn Mandeville Collection.*

Above: Often called "The Face," this 8-inch (20cm) darling is the masthead of the Alexander Star Fleet! Originally used in 1953, this face, in one form or another, is still the *Wendy That Loves Being Loved*! The head is unmarked but the body bears the Alexander Company name. *A. Glenn Mandeville Collection.*

Always a classic in hard plastic, this *McGuffey Ana* uses the face that collectors now call "Classic Lissy," meaning that the name *Lissy* was the nomenclature most often attached to this pursed-lip pretty! First used in 1956 as a demure little girl, the mold was retired in 1993. The head and body on this 12-inch (31cm) sweet girl is unmarked. *A. Glenn Mandeville Collection.*

Above: One of a long line of famous faces, this vinyl little girl first appeared in the mid-1960s and was retired in 1996. Always a 14-inch (36cm) size, she carries the Alexander Company markings on her neck. From *First Lady* to *McGuffey Ana*, *Alice* to *Little Orphan Annie*, this face is another Alexander doll star! *A. Glenn Mandeville Collection.*

The 21-inch (53cm) *Portrait* dolls started in the 1960s are the frosting on the cake for most collectors who would want more were it not for their imposing size. Marked on the back of the neck with the Alexander Company name, this doll was once *Jacqueline* of Camelot days, *Marie Antoinette* and enough classic characters to fill the finest of art galleries! *A. Glenn Mandeville Collection.*

Above: Introduced as a versatile 12-inch (31cm) vinyl young lady in the late 1960s, this face was utilized on the hard plastic body still in use today. From *Nancy Drew*, teen detective, to *Little Women*, this is indeed a famous visage! What other face could be *Scarlett* and *Rhett*, *Napoleon* and *Josephine*, *Antony* and *Cleopatra*, and *Lord Fauntleroy!* Marked with the Alexander Company markings on the neck, this face was another classic like the face used on the 8-inch (20cm) dolls. These faces were very versatile and chameleon-like in character creation. *A. Glenn Mandeville Collection.*

17

Preserving Your Alexander Dolls

Collectors of Alexander dolls have often been referred to as "perfectionists." In many cases this is true. The collector who has chosen to pay the price for mint-in-box dolls must, by definition, be somewhat of a perfectionist. And it would be necessary for that collector to keep being that way to maintain the "mint" grading of their dolls.

All this might sound pretty intimidating to the novice collector, or the casual reader of this book, but it is possible to maintain any Alexander doll collection at the purchase level with just some good advice and plain common sense.

My own Alexander collection is made up of a few perfect mint-in-box dolls that I must admit intimidate me a bit. We have been taught that the word "investment" implies perfection, but that is only true some of the time.

A couple of years ago, The Alexander Doll Company began a series of 8-inch (20cm) dolls dressed as angels. Casually titled "Tree Toppers," they were perfection itself. Speigel's has had exclusives and The Alexander Doll Company has issued some of its own.

When I got my first doll from Speigel's, the sheer wonder of that perfect little angelic tree topper in the box was awesome! It took me a week to get up the nerve to just remove the neck brace, which was stapled to the sides of the box. (If you don't understand any of this, then you are truly a new collector or a casual observer.)

Finally, when I removed that incredible creature and put her where she belonged, on top of my Christmas tree, I felt like a recovering "never take it from the box" collector! The happiness that doll brought to me, my family, my neighbors and friends would fill this book. My friends noticed my other dolls and even my family was spellbound by the majesty that this Tree Topper dealt from her lofty place.

After the holidays, I carefully returned my little angel to her box and, lo and behold, guess what? She had not suffered a bit! Her gown was still radiant; her halo angelic; and her pursed lips were still serene! I had broken the spell of the boxed doll! She had survived and so had I!

The moral of this story is that even the highest quality mint-in-box Alexander doll <u>can</u> be enjoyed out of its box and not suffer in the hands of a skilled collector. One has to remember that one does own the doll collection and not the other way around!

One of the nicer things about Alexander dolls for the most part is that they are not shrink wrapped and sealed in boxes. Unlike some other dolls (notably fashion dolls) they can be removed from their boxes, observed, photographed, gently handled and still not lose their "mint" grading. They are not held prisoner by cellophane and cardboard, but float loose in the box, to be set free by the new owner.

In one of my early encounters with Madame Alexander at a doll show in New England in the late 1970s, I asked Madame why her doll boxes did not portray the gorgeous artwork that fashion dolls, character dolls, and celebrity dolls did? Smiling, Madame said that the box was, and I quote, "merely the shipping carton for the doll to arrive safely from us to you. We are creating dolls, <u>not</u> boxes!" Well, I guess I knew from then on that an Alexander box is not the shrine that some collectors make it out to be!

How then can the collector who is buying a "mint" graded doll enjoy it without destroying it? Easy! There are just a few, simple rules!

Finally, don't you think that it's time we started enjoying our dolls more? I give programs all over the United States and I love photographing my own dolls, the dolls that come through my business, and my friends' dolls. Never once in 20 years has a doll suffered during a photo shoot. If anything, I examined the doll more closely before the photo and tamed a stray hair or fluffed up a dress. Like us, dolls seem to thrive on love and attention.

I guess the above mentioned topics will ruffle some feathers from the "don't touch" crowd, but as I stated, none of my dolls have ever suffered from careful display and handling, while I have had clothing disintegrate from acids in the box! The bottom line is, enjoy your dolls, and I think your doll collecting will be a whole lot more fun! I sure think so and I'll bet you will too!

ABBREVIATIONS

MADC = Madame Alexander Doll Club
LE = Limited Edition
FAD = Factory Altered Doll
EDH = Enchanted Doll House
CU = Collector's United
UFDC = United Federation of Doll Clubs
NECS = New England Collector's Society
S/A = Still Available
N/A = Information Not Available
AA = African American

Simple Rules to Preserve Alexander Dolls

1. If you do buy a mint-in-box Alexander doll, whether old or new, replace the tissue paper with acid-free tissue. This can be found at art supply houses, craft stores and even dry cleaners that specialize in wedding gown cleaning. This will prevent the acid in the tissue and cardboard from reacting with the fabric and the doll. Surprised? Yes, the box is often <u>not</u> the best place for your doll to be kept! If the original tissue captivates you, put it in a baggie and keep it in the box, which can be collapsed and stored.

2. Sunlight, even normal room light, is a real enemy of dolls. Fabrics fade gradually. Sometimes it isn't until you take a doll out of a cabinet years later that you notice the sun has faded the front of the doll's outfit. This does not mean that you can never have a doll on display in a "normal" room. Just be sure direct sunlight does not hit the doll and rotate the dolls in the room from time to time. Seasonal displays are one reason to collect dolls. Don't deny yourself the pleasure of a holiday display out of fear of harming your doll. Common sense is the password.

3. Children, pets and dolls do not mix. They can, but keep the dolls high and the rest low! Seriously, your five-year-old can't tell that your *Cissy* is over 30 years old. You can also be sure that the plastic still smells good to your "man's best friend," so prevention is the key. Don't mix the deadly triangle of pets, plastic and pretty children!

4. As mentioned above, enjoy your dolls. Why have them, if they are just listed in a notebook and stuffed in a closet? (Sometimes they don't even make a notebook!) Great that you went to Disney World® and stayed up all night to get that Alexander exclusive! Now what? Put the precious thing under a dome, or in a display and love it to death! That <u>is</u> why you bought it, isn't it?

5. Despite what some well meaning curators and gloom and doom "experts" say, sensible handling and displaying of your dolls will <u>not </u>make them lose a grade. For the collector of "good" condition dolls, this may be a chapter they think they can skip over. Not so! Any doll, if exposed to sunlight, insects, pets, extremes in temperature and ill handling (from the very young on up), can suffer greatly. I often think of a doll as a wonderful piece of jewelry. It enhances the owner's beauty, when worn and displayed, but does nothing in a safety deposit box except tarnish! It's the same with dolls!

Twenty Special Years of Special Dolls
By Benita Schwartz

YEAR	NAME OF DOLL & SIZE	PRODUCED FOR	OTHER INFORMATION
1980	Enchanted Doll 8"	Enchanted Dollhouse	3000 dolls made, lace trim
1981	Enchanted Doll 8"	Enchanted Dollhouse	3423 dolls made, eyelet trim
1983	Ballerina Trunk Set 8"	Enchanted Dollhouse	Blue or Pink Tutu
1984	Ballerina 8"	MADC Convention Doll	FAD of 360 dolls
1985	Cinderella Trunk Set 14"	Enchanted Dollhouse	Comes with Glass Slipper
1985	Happy Birthday Madame 8"	MADC Convention Doll	FAD of 450 dolls
1986	Scarlett 8"	MADC Convention Doll	FAD of 625, Red ribbon sash & hair bows
1987	CU Yugoslavia 8"	Collectors United Gathering	FAD
1987	Pussycat 18"	FAO Schwarz	
1987	Cowboy 8"	MADC Convention Doll	720 dolls made
1988	Miss Scarlett 14"	Belk Leggett Stores	
1988	Tippi 8"	Collectors United Gathering	800 dolls made
1988	Enchanted Doll 10"	Enchanted Dollhouse	5000 dolls made
1988	Brooke 14"	FAO Schwarz	Blonde or brunette
1988	Flapper 10"	MADC Convention Doll	FAD of 720 dolls
1989	Rachel 8"	Belk Leggett Stores	
1989	Miss Leigh 8"	Collectors United Gathering	800 dolls made
1989	Cinderella 10"	Disney World Doll & Teddy Bear Convention	250 dolls made
1989	Ballerina 8"	Enchanted Dollhouse	FAD of 320, Blue Tutu
1989	Diana & David 8"	FAO Schwarz	
1989	Samantha 14"	FAO Schwarz	
1989	Southern Belle 10"	My Doll House	Blonde or brunette
1989	Briar Rose 8"	MADC Convention Doll	804 dolls made, has Cissette head
1989	Jane Avril 10"	Marshall Fields	
1989	Victoria 14"	Lord & Taylor	FAD in pink
1989	Wendy 8"	MADC Club Doll	First Club Doll
1989	Noel 12"	New England Collector's Society	5000 dolls made, Porcelain
1989	Amy 12"	Sears	
1989	Beth 12"	Sears	
1989	Jo 12"	Sears	
1989	Meg 12"	Sears	
1989	Marme 12"	Sears	
1989	Laurie 12"	Sears	
1990	Nancy Jean 8"	Belk Leggett Stores	
1990	Shea 8"	Collectors United	800 dolls made
1990	Snow White 12"	Disney World Doll & Teddy Bear Convention	750 dolls made
1990	Bobbie Sox 8"	Disney Theme Parks	
1990	Lady Lee 8"	Doll Finders Fantasy Event	350 dolls made, FAD
1990	Vermont Maiden 8"	Enchanted Dollhouse	3600 dolls made, 2 hair colors
1990	Cissy By Scassi 21"	FAO Schwarz	
1990	Bessy Brooks 8"	CU Greenville Show	200 dolls made, FAD
1990	Halloween 8"	CU Greenville Show	200 dolls made, FAD

YEAR	NAME OF DOLL & SIZE	PRODUCED FOR	OTHER INFORMATION
1990	Cheerleader 8"	I. Magnin Stores	FAD-letter "S" on sweater
1990	Scarlett 8"	MADC Symposium Doll	800 dolls made
1990	Riverboat Queen 8"	MADC Convention Doll	825 dolls made
1990	Polly Pigtails 8"	MADC Club Doll	
1990	Queen Elizabeth I 10"	My Doll House	
1990	Madame Butterfly 10"	Marshall Fields	
1990	Joy 12"	New England Collector's Society	5000 dolls made, Porcelain
1990	Party Trunk 8"	Neiman Marcus	
1990	Angel Face 8"	Shirley's Dollhouse	3500 dolls made, 3 hair colors plus AA
1990	Beth 10"	Spiegel's	
1990	Sailor Boy 8"	UFDC Convention Luncheon Doll	260 dolls made
1991	Cameo Lady 10"	Collectors United	1000 dolls made
1991	Winter Wonderland Skater 8"	CU Nashville Show	200 dolls made, FAD
1991	Easter Bunny 8"	A Child at Heart	3000 dolls made, 3 hair colors
1991	Springtime 8"	MADC Premiere	1600 dolls made
1991	Sailor 8"	FAO Schwarz	
1991	Fannie Elizabeth 8"	Belk Leggett Stores	
1991	Autumn in New York 10"	New York Doll Club	260 dolls made, FAD
1991	Ring Master 8"	Collectors United Gathering	800 dolls made
1991	Queen Charlotte 10"	MADC Convention Doll	900 dolls made
1991	Miss Liberty 10"	MADC Club Doll	
1991	Pandora 8"	dolls n bearland	1800 dolls made, 3 hair colors
1991	David the Little Rabbi 8"	Celia's Dolls	3600 dolls made, 3 hair colors
1991	Mouseketeer 8"	Disney Theme Parks	
1991	Farmer's Daughter 8"	Enchanted Dollhouse	4000 dolls made, 3 hair colors
1991	Miss Magnin 10"	I. Magnin Stores	2500 dolls made
1991	Empress Elisabeth 10"	My Doll House	
1991	Merry Angel Tree Topper 10"	Spiegel's	
1991	Winter Sports 8"	Shirley's Dollhouse	975 dolls made, FAD
1991	Camelot in Columbia 8"	CU Columbia Show	400 dolls made, FAD
1991	Carnevale Doll 14"	FAO Schwarz	FAD
1991	Beddy Bye Brooke 14"	FAO Schwarz	FAD, 2 hair colors
1991	Little Huggums 12"	Imaginarium	2 hair colors plus bald
1991	Alice & White Rabbit 10"	Disney World Doll & Teddy Bear Convention	750 dolls made
1991	Miss Unity 10"	UFDC Convention Luncheon Doll	310 dolls made
1992	Nashville Skier 8"	CU Nashville Show	200 dolls made, FAD
1992	Wintertime 8"	MADC Premiere	1650 dolls made
1992	Spring Break 8"	Metroplex Doll Show	400 dolls made
1992	Prom Queen 8"	MADC Convention Doll	1100 dolls made
1992	Drucilla 14"	MADC	250 dolls made, FAD
1992	Faith 8"	Collectors United	800 dolls made
1992	Little Miss Godey 8"	MADC Club Doll	
1992	Round Up 8"	Disney Theme Parks	
1992	Little Miss Magnin 8"	I. Magnin Stores	3600 dolls made, 2 hair colors
1992	I. Magnin Baby & Cradle 12"	I. Magnin Stores	1500 dolls made
1992	Beddy Bye Brooke & Brenda Set 14" & 8"	FAO Schwarz	2 hair colors
1992	Beddy Bye Brenda 8"	FAO Schwarz	2 hair colors
1992	Susannah 8"	Dolly Dears	400 dolls made
1992	Suellen 12"	Jean's Dolls	192 dolls made, FAD, blonde hair
1992	My Little Sweetheart 8"	A Child at Heart	4500 dolls made, 4 hair colors and AA

YEAR	NAME OF DOLL & SIZE	PRODUCED FOR	OTHER INFORMATION
1992	Annabelle 8"	Belk Leggett Stores	3000 dolls made
1992	Mardi Gras 10"	Spiegel's	3000 dolls made
1992	Queen of Hearts 10"	Disney World Doll & Teddy Bear Convention	500 dolls made
1992	Alpine Twins 8"	The Christmas Shop	2000 sets made, 5 hair color combos
1992	Little Emperor 8"	UFDC Convention Luncheon Doll	400 dolls made
1992	Le Petit Boudoir 8"	Collectors United	700 dolls made, FAD
1992	Thoroughly Modern Wendy 8"	Disney Theme Parks	
1992	Joy Noel Tree Topper 10"	Spiegel's	3000 dolls made
1992	Bathing Beauty 10"	UFDC Regional Convention Doll	300 dolls made, FAD
1992	Oktoberfest 8"	CU Greenville Show	200 dolls made, FAD
1992	Oktoberfest Boy 8"	CU Greenville Show	6 dolls produced, FAD
1992	Farmer's Daughter 8"	Enchanted Dollhouse	1600 dolls made, FAD, 3 hair colors
1993	Anastasia 14"	MADC	375 dolls made, FAD
1993	Homecoming 8"	MADC Premiere	1800 dolls made
1993	Jack be Nimble 8"	Dolly Dears	288 dolls made, FAD
1993	Monique 8"	Disneyland Teddy Bear & Doll Classic	250 dolls made
1993	Bon Voyage Miss Magnin 10"	I. Magnin Stores	2500 dolls made, 3 hair colors
1993	Bon Voyage Lil Miss Magnin 8"	I. Magnin Stores	3600 dolls made, 3 hair colors
1993	Diamond Lil 10"	MADC Convention	876 dolls made
1993	Pussycat 14"	Horchow	
1993	Wendy-World Fair 8"	Shirley's Dollhouse	3600 dolls made, 3 hair colors
1993	Trick & Treat 8"	A Child at Heart	3000 sets made, 3 hair color combos
1993	Princess & the Pea 8"	Dolly Dears	2400 dolls made
1993	Princess & the Pea Mattress	Dolly Dears	1000 pieces made
1993	Hope 8"	Collectors United Gathering	800 dolls made
1993	Wendy Loves Being Best Friends 8"	MADC Club Doll	
1993	First Comes Love 8"	CU Nashville Show	200 dolls made, FAD
1993	Wendy Loves FAO 8"	FAO Schwarz	2 hair colors
1993	Annette 14"	Disneyana Convention	1000 dolls made
1993	Carol 8"	Saks Fifth Avenue	3 hair colors & AA
1993	Caroline 8"	Belk Leggett Stores	3600 dolls made
1993	Pamela Plays Dress Up at Grandma's 12"	Horchow	1250 trunk sets made
1993	Snow White 10"	Disney Theme Parks	2400 dolls made
1993	Wendy Loves Her ABC's 8"	ABC Productions	3200 dolls made, 3 hair colors
1993	Caroline's Storyland Trunk 8"	Neiman Marcus	1500 trunk sets made
1993	Alice & The Jabberwocky 12"	Disney World Doll & Teddy Bear Convention	500 sets made
1993	Shriner Doll 8"	Shriner's Convention	2000 dolls made
1993	Colombian Sailor 12"	UFDC Convention Luncheon Doll	
1993	Winter Angel 8"	Shirley's Dollhouse	1000 dolls made, FAD, 3 hair colors
1994	Wendy's Best Friend Maggie 8"	MADC Club Doll	2500 dolls made
1994	Navajo Woman 8"	MADC Convention Doll	835 dolls made
1994	Lil Miss Magnin Sponsors Arts 8"	I. Magnin Stores	1500 dolls made, 3 hair colors
1994	Captain's Cruise 8"	CU Nashville Show	250 trunk sets made, FAD
1994	Setting Sail for Summer 8"	MADC Premiere	1800 dolls made
1994	Love 8"	Collectors United Gathering	2400 dolls made
1994	America's Junior Miss 8"	Collectors United	Approx. 1000-1200 dolls made, 3 hair colors, AA and Asian

YEAR	NAME OF DOLL & SIZE	PRODUCED FOR	OTHER INFORMATION
1994	Wendy Starts her Collection 8"	Jacobsen's Department Stores	2400 dolls made
1994	Maypole Dance 8"	Shirley's Dollhouse	3000 dolls made, 3 hair colors
1994	Joy 8"	Saks Fifth Avenue	3 hair colors & AA
1994	Holly 8"	Belk Leggett Stores	2400 dolls made
1994	Shadow of Madame 8"	Doll & Teddy Bear Expo	500 dolls made
1994	Tweedledum & Tweedledee 8"	Disney World Doll & Teddy Bear Convention	750 sets made
1994	Secret Garden Trunk Set 8"	FAO Schwarz	
1994	Little Huggums 12"	FAO Schwarz	
1994	Caroline Travels the World 8"	Neiman Marcus	
1994	Anne Trunk Set 8"	Neiman Marcus	
1994	Wendy's Favorite Pastime 8"	Disney Theme Parks	
1994	Belle 8"	Disney Theme Parks	
1994	Little Women Set 8"	FAO Schwarz	500 sets made, also 700 of each doll sold separately
1994	Cinderella Gift Set I 14"	Disney Catalog	900 sets made, includes "poor" outfit
1994	Special Event Doll 8"	Various	Sash could be customized for event or store
1995	Goes Country 8"	CU Nashville Show	300 dolls made, FAD
1995	Snowflake 8"	MADC Premiere	1200 dolls made
1995	Frances Folsom 10"	MADC Convention	950 dolls made
1995	Flower Girl 8"	MADC Convention Companion Doll	950 dolls made
1995	Cinderella Gift Set II 14"	Disney Catalog	2 gowns in set
1995	Wendy Joins MADC 8"	MADC Club Doll	
1995	To Madame, With Love 8"	Doll & Teddy Bear Expo	750 dolls made
1995	Sleeping Beauty Gift Set 14"	Disney Catalog	
1995	Dian 8"	Collectors United	800 dolls made, 2 hair colors
1995	I Love Lucy Set 8"	FAO Schwarz	1200 sets made, also 1200 Lucy dolls sold separately
1995	Dick & Jane Set 8"	FAO Schwarz	1200 sets made
1995	Enchanted Princess Trunk Set 8"	FAO Schwarz	
1995	The Blue Fairy Tree Topper 10"	Disney Catalog	
1995	Mary Poppins 10"	Disney Catalog	
1995	Morgan LeFay 10"	Disney World Doll & Teddy Bear Convention	500 dolls made
1995	Easter of Yesteryear 8"	Collectors United	500 dolls made, FAD
1995	Mary Ann Dances for Grandma 14"	Horchow	
1995	Danielle Angel 8"	Belk Leggett Stores	
1995	Little Huggums 12"	Jacobsen's Department Stores	1800 dolls made
1995	Wendy Walks her Dog 8"	Jean's Dolls	500 dolls made, FAD
1995	America's Junior Miss-Fitness 8"	Collectors United	Approx. 500-700 dolls made
1996	Snow White Gift Set 14"	Disney Catalog	
1996	Belle 14"	Disney Catalog	
1996	Sunny 8"	CU Nashville Show	Approx. 300 dolls made, FAD
1996	Wendy Starts Her Travels 8"	MADC Premiere	Coat came in 3 different color combos
1996	Wendy Tours the Factory 8"	MADC Premiere Companion Doll	245 dolls made
1996	Cheshire Cat 8"	MADC Premiere Companion Doll	210 dolls made
1996	Bobby Takes a Picture 8"	MADC Premiere Companion Doll	215 dolls made
1996	I Dream of Jeannie 8"	FAO Schwarz	Less than 2000 sets made
1996	Grandma's Little Darling 8"	Shirley's Dollhouse	

YEAR	NAME OF DOLL & SIZE	PRODUCED FOR	OTHER INFORMATION
1996	Showgirl 10"	MADC Convention	Approx. 950 dolls made, came in 6 colors
1996	Maggie's First Doll 8"	Doll & Teddy Bear Expo	
1996	The Little Rascals 8"	FAO Schwarz	Less than 2000 sets made
1996	Singing in the Rain 8"	FAO Schwarz	Less than 2000 sets made
1996	Elizabeth Angel 8"	Belk Leggett Stores	
1996	Knave 8"	Disney World Doll & Teddy Bear Convention	500 dolls made
1996	Olympia 8"	Collectors United Gathering	2 hair colors, can have gym bag boxed separately
1996	America's Junior Miss-Interview 8"	Collectors United	Approx. 500-700 dolls made
1996	Boo 8"	MADC Fall Symposium	150 dolls made, FAD
1996	Wendy Honors Margaret Winson 8"	MADC Club Doll	
1996	America's Junior Miss-Talent 8"	Collectors United	Approx. 500-700 dolls made
1996	Greta 8"	CU Greenville Show	
1996	Alice 14"	Disney Catalog	1500 dolls made
1996	Home for the Holidays 8"	Lillian Vernon	
1997	Miss Tennessee Waltz 8"	CU Nashville Show	250 dolls made, FAD
1997	Belle in Winter Coat 14"	Disney Catalog	
1997	Wendy's Tea Party 8"	MADC Premiere	800 dolls made, 2 hair colors
1997	Cissette Coral & Leopard 10"	Bloomingdales	FAD
1997	Lucy & Ethel at the Chocolate Factory 8"	FAO Schwarz	Less than 2500 sets made
1997	From the Madame's Sketchbook 8"	MADC Club Doll	
1997	Little Bit Country 8"	MADC Convention	925 dolls made
1997	Toto 8"	Disney World Doll & Teddy Bear Convention	750 dolls made
1997	The Honeymooners 8"	FAO Schwarz	2000 sets made
1997	CU Salutes Broadway 8"	Collectors United Gathering	650 dolls made, can have fur stole boxed separately
1997	Winter Wonderland 8"	Lillian Vernon	
1997	United States 8"	TJ Maxx	FAD-slight fabric variations from original doll
1997	Cinderella 8"	TJ Maxx	FAD-slight fabric variations from original doll
1997	Miss Muffett 8"	TJ Maxx	FAD-slight fabric variations from original doll
1997	Alice 8"	TJ Maxx	FAD-slight fabric variations from original doll
1997	Little Bo Peep 10"	TJ Maxx	FAD-slight fabric variations from original doll
1997	Blue Angel 8"	Home Shopping Club	3000 dolls made
1997	Gardenia Cissy 21"	MADC	20 dolls made, FAD with blonde hair
1997	Valentine Prince & Princess 8"	Collectors United	Less than 200 sets made, FAD
1998	Diamond Pixie 8"	MADC Premiere	800 dolls made
1998	Sailing with Sally 8"	Collectors United	500 dolls made
1998	Cissy St John 21"	Neiman Marcus	750 dolls made
1998	Curly Locks 8"	Home Shopping Club	FAD-slight fabric variations from original doll
1998	Dolly 8"	Home Shopping Club	FAD-slight fabric variations from original doll
1998	Lady Lee 8"	Home Shopping Club	FAD-slight fabric variations from original doll
1998	Daisy 10"	Home Shopping Club	FAD-slight fabric variations from original doll
1998	Jasmine 10"	Home Shopping Club	FAD-slight fabric variations from original doll

YEAR	NAME OF DOLL & SIZE	PRODUCED FOR	OTHER INFORMATION
1998	Belle of the Ball 10"	Home Shopping Club	FAD-slight fabric variations from original doll
1998	Crystal Blue Enchantment 10"	Home Shopping Club	
1998	Wendy Goes to Summer Camp 8"	CU Nashville Show	250 dolls made, FAD
1998	All American Wendy 8"	TJ Maxx	
1998	Grease 10"	FAO Schwarz	2000 sets made
1998	Gabrielle 10"	UFDC Convention Luncheon	400 dolls made, comes with dress form
1998	Gary Green 8"	Collectors United	500 dolls made
1998	Polynesian Princess 8"	Collectors United Gathering	600 dolls made, can have grass skirt boxed separately
1998	The Rose Queen 8"	MADC Convention	910 dolls made
1998	Goldilocks & Baby Bear 8"	Disney World Doll & Teddy Bear Convention	350 sets made, bear made by Robert Raikes
1998	Undergarment Doll 8"	MADC	
1998	Margaret O'Brien 8"	MADC Convention Companion Doll	925 dolls made
1998	Princess Margaret Rose 15"	Ashton-Drake Galleries	2000 dolls made, porcelain
1998	Cheerleader 8"	Doll & Teddy Bear Expo West	75 dolls made with blue sweaters
1998	Cheerleader 8"	Doll & Teddy Bear Expo East	75 dolls made with green sweaters
1998	Skate with Wendy 8"	MADC Club Doll	1500 dolls made
1998	Summer Cherry Picker 8"	QVC	500 dolls made
1998	Home for the Holidays 10"	QVC	400 dolls made
1998	Southern Belle 8"	TJ Maxx	
1998	Mary Mary Quite Contrary 8"	TJ Maxx	
1998	Rebecca of Sunnybrook Farm 8"	TJ Maxx	
1998	Prom Queen 10"	TJ Maxx	
1998	Charleston Girl 10"	TJ Maxx	
1998	Pilgrim Girl 8"	QVC	500 dolls made
1998	Betsy Ross 8"	QVC	500 dolls made
1998	Heart of Dixie 8"	Elegant Doll House	289 dolls made
1998	Ice Princess 8"	Dolls & Ducks	300 dolls made
1998	Elegant Easter 8"	Elegant Doll House	300 dolls made
1998	Angel of Grace 10"	Matilda Doll & Bear Company	300 dolls made
1999	Maggie Visits Rockefeller Center 8"	MADC	350 dolls made
1999	Be Mine 8"	Lillian Vernon	
1999	Little Bo Peep 8"	QVC	700 dolls made
1999	Alice in Wonderland 8"	QVC	
1999	Lady Bug Garden 8"	QVC	
1999	Starlett Glamour 10"	MADC Premiere	700 dolls made
1999	Now I'm Nine 8"	CU Nashville Show	
1999	Blossom 8"	QVC	500 dolls made
1999	A Rose for You 8"	QVC	
1999	Kiss Me I'm Irish 8"	QVC	
1999	Spring Flowers 8"	QVC	
1999	Lavender Rose 10"	QVC	600 dolls made
1999	Pollyanna 8"	QVC	500 dolls made
1999	Investigator Wendy 8"	QVC	500 dolls made
1999	Faye Ray & King Kong 10"	FAO Schwarz	500 sets made, King Kong Manufactured by Steiff
1999	Love is in the Air 8"	Doll & Teddy Bear Expo West	100 dolls made

YEAR	NAME OF DOLL & SIZE	PRODUCED FOR	OTHER INFORMATION
1999	Holiday Magic 8"	Doll & Teddy Bear Expo East	100 dolls made
1999	Electra 8"	MADC Companion Doll	800 dolls made
1999	Electro 8"	MADC Club Doll	
1999	Summer Blossom 8"	MADC	300 dolls made
1999	Orange Blossom 10"	MADC Convention Doll	800 dolls made
1999	Lilly Pulitzer Cissy 21"	MADC Cissy Breakfast	25 dolls made
1999	Fortune Teller 8"	Collectors United Gathering	600 dolls made, can have scarves & rings boxed separately
1999	Fortune Teller Cissy 21"	Collectors United Gathering	180 dolls made
1999	Springtime Darling 8"	MADC	350 dolls made
1999	Carnival Queen 16"	CU Alexander Dinner	24 dolls made
1999	Coca Cola Carhop 12"	Danbury Mint	Porcelain doll
1999	Little Doll Collector 8"	Shirley's Dollhouse	1000 dolls made, 2 hair colors and AA
1999	Springtime Bride 10"	QVC	400 dolls made
1999	Fourth of July 8"	QVC	400 dolls made
1999	One Enchanted Evening 16"	UFDC Convention Dinner	310 dolls made
1999	Autumn Breeze 8"	QVC	
1999	Jane & Michael Banks 8"	Disney World Doll & Teddy Bear Convention	200 sets made
1999	Eloise 8"	FAO Schwarz	
1999	Eloise Rag Doll 16"	FAO Schwarz	
1999	Today I Feel Silly Rag Doll 16"	FAO Schwarz	
1999	Coca Cola Aviator 12"	Danbury Mint	Porcelain doll
1999	Arnold Scaasi Cissy 21"	Danbury Mint	2500 dolls made
1999	Sleeping Beauty 8"	Disney Store Gallery	1000 dolls made
1999	Golden Holiday Tree Topper 10"	Bloomingdales by Mail	1000 dolls made
1999	Christmas Morn' 8"	Collectors United	
1999	Fun at Halloween 8"	QVC	
1999	Miss Millennium 8"	Lillian Vernon	
1999	White Tree Topper 10"	QVC	
1999	Snow White 8"	Disney Store Gallery	1000 dolls made
1999	Silver Sensation Tree Topper 10"	Disneyland	300 dolls made
1999	Tanya 8"	Colonial Southwest, Inc.	550 dolls made
1999	Ariel 8"	Disney Store Gallery	1000 dolls made
1999	Jasmine 8"	Disney Store Gallery	1000 dolls made
1999	Cinderella 8"	Disney Store Gallery	1000 dolls made
1999	Belle 8"	Disney Store Gallery	1000 dolls made
1999	Mouseketeer Pair 8"	Disney Theme Parks	
1999	Golden Girl 10"	M. Pancner's House of Collectibles	25 dolls made, FAD has auburn hair
1999	Sock Hop 8"	M. Pancner's House of Collectibles	50 dolls made, FAD has brunette hair

One-Of-A-Kind Dolls

These dolls do not appear in the price guide.
The value of the dolls can not be determined since they were either auctioned or raffled,
and are one-of-a-kind dolls.

YEAR	NAME OF DOLL & SIZE	PRODUCED FOR
1989	Sleeping Beauty 21"	Disney World Doll & Teddy Bear Convention
1990	Christine, Phantom of the Opera 21"	Disney World Doll & Teddy Bear Convention
1991	Queen Isabella 21"	Disney World Doll & Teddy Bear Convention
1992	It's A Girl 21" with 8" doll in carriage	Disney World Doll & Teddy Bear Convention
1992	The Emperor and the Nightingale 26" Gund Bear holding 8" Alexander Doll	Disney World Doll & Teddy Bear Convention
1993	Cissy Bride 21" with 8" Flower Girl & Ring Bearer	Disneyland Teddy Bear and Doll Classic
1993	Women in the Garden 10"	Disney World Doll & Teddy Bear Convention
1993	Frog Prince & Princess 24" Steiff Bear with 8" Alexander Doll	Disney World Doll & Teddy Bear Convention
1993	Harmony 21" Porcelain Gunzel doll with 8" Alexander Doll	Disney World Doll & Teddy Bear Convention
1994	Romeo & Juliet 21" pair	Disney World Doll & Teddy Bear Convention
1994	Wendy Loves the Dionnes 8" set of 5	MADC Convention
1995	Cissette Bride 10"	Dolly Dears
1995	Sir Lancelot Du Lac and Queen Guinevere 21" pair	Disney World Doll & Teddy Bear Convention
1995	Ultimate Cissy 21"	MADC Convention
1996	Alice in Wonderland Chess Set 8-21" set of 35 dolls	Disney World Doll & Teddy Bear Convention
1996	Cissy Showgirl 21"	MADC Convention
1996	Josephine Baker 21"	Doll and Teddy Bear Expo West
1996	Miss Eliza Doolittle 21"	Doll and Teddy Bear Expo East
1997	Nashville Wendy 8"	MADC Convention
1997	Dorothy, Glinda, Wicked Witch 21" set plus 8" Toto	Disney World Doll & Teddy Bear Convention
1998	Cissy Diamond Beauty 21"	MADC Convention
1998	Goldilocks & the Three Bears 16" Porcelain Doll with Raikes Bears	Disney World Doll & Teddy Bear Convention
1999	Trapeze Artist 21"	Collectors United Gathering
1999	Electra & Electro 21" pair	MADC Convention
1999	Mary Poppins 21" plus 14" Jane & Michael Banks	Disney World Doll & Teddy Bear Convention
1999	A Night at the Belmont Ball 16"	Belmont Ball 1999

Active Miss
    18" (46cm) hard plastic, 1954 $900
Adams, Abigail
    14" (36cm) plastic/vinyl, 1st set, *First Ladies Series*,
    1976-1978 $100
Adams, Louisa
    14" (36cm) plastic/vinyl, 1st set, *First Ladies Series*,
    1976-1978 $100
Addams Family
    8" (20cm) and 10" (25cm) set of 4 dolls plus Thing,
    1997-1998 $350
    8" (20cm) Wednesday and Pugsley pair, 1997 $150
    10" (25cm) Morticia and Gomez pair, 1997 $175
    8" (20cm) Wednesday, 1998 $90
    8" (20cm) Pugsley, 1998 $90
    10" (25cm) Gomez, 1998 $90
    10" (25cm) Morticia, 1998 $90
Africa
    8" (20cm) hard plastic, bent knee, #766, 1966-1971
                                                     $275
    8" (20cm) hard plastic, straight legs, re-issued,
    1988-1992 $60

Agatha
    8" (20cm) hard plastic, black top and floral gown,
    straight leg non-walker, 1953-1954 $1,100
    18" (46cm) hard plastic, pink taffeta, *Me and My Shadow
    Series*, 1954 $1,700
    21" (53cm) *Portrait*, red gown, 1967 $550
    10" (25cm) *Portrette*, red velvet, #1171, 1968 $450
    21" (53cm) *Portrait*, rose gown with cape, 1974 $450
    21" (53cm) *Portrait*, blue with white sequin trim,
    1975 $350
    21" (53cm) *Portrait*, blue with white rick-rack trim,
    1976 $325
    21" (53cm) *Portrait*, lavender, 1979-1980 $225
    21" (53cm) *Portrait*, turquoise, 1981 $225
Agnes
    cloth, 1930s $825
Aladdin
    8" (20cm) hard plastic, *Storyland Dolls*, 1993-1994
                                                     $50
Alaska
    8" (20cm) hard plastic, *Americana Series*, 1990-1992
                                                     $50
Albania
    8" (20cm) hard plastic, straight legs, 1987 $65
Alcott, Louisa May
    14" (36cm) 1989-1990 $85
    8" (20cm) hard plastic, *Storyland Dolls*, 1992 $70
Algeria
    10" (25cm) hard plastic, 1996 $100

The 1990s saw many innovative ideas at The Alexander Doll Company. This little known set is *The Addams Family*, complete with *Thing*.

1953 8-inch (20cm) rare
Alexander-kin baby.
Veronica Jochens collection.

Alexander Rag Time Dolls

    cloth, 1938-1939 $950 up

Alexander-Kins

hard plastic (sometimes called Wendy, Wendy-Ann or Wendy-kins).

7-1/2-8" (19-20cm) straight leg non-walker, 1953-1954

Country Picnic, #376	$850
Garden Party, #347	$1,000
Little Southern Girl, #305	$800
Shopping with Auntie, #388	$575
Trousseau in Cardboard Dresser	$1,000
Wendy's Favorite Outfit, #342	$425
Baby in Christening Dress	$475
Coat, hat (dress)	$500
Cotton coat dress	$450
Cotton dress with cotton pinafore and hat or bonnet	$475
Cotton dress with organdy pinafore and hat or bonnet	$475
Day in Country long gown	$700
Easter doll (early version)	$1,000 up
Felt jacket with a pleated dress and cap	$575
Jumper (cotton or taffeta) with organdy or cotton bodysuit and hat or bonnet	$475
Nightgown	$350
Nude, perfect doll	$300
Organdy dress with apron and hat or bonnet	$475
Organdy dress with hat or bonnet	$525
Organdy dress and organdy pinafore with hat or bonnet	$475
Pajamas	$350
Raincoat and hat	$475
Red Coat with taffeta dress and leopard hat	$625
Robe	$350
Satin dress, pinafore, hat	$600
Sleeveless pinafore	$425
Sun suit	$350
Taffeta coat, dress and bonnet	$500
Taffeta dress with hat or bonnet	$575
Taffeta dress with velvet hat	$675
Taffeta dress with cotton pinafore and hat or bonnet	$600
Trousseau in trunk or case, FAO Schwarz exclusive	$1,000 up

7-1/2-8" (19-20cm) straight leg walker, 1954-1955

Ballet Lessons, white tutu, #454	$500
Basic doll in box, panties, shoes, socks, #400	$425
Beach Outfit, #427	$400
Birthday Party, #455	$500
Calls on Grandma, #459	$500
Dressed for a Summer Morning, #424	$425
Gabardine Coat, #451	$475
Garden Party gown, #488	$1,000
Goes Marketing, #423	$350
Goes to School, #460	$425
Goes to Sunday School, #457	$400
Goes to the Matinee, #463	$500
Goes Visiting, #462	$475

Helps Mummy in the Garden, #422	$400
Helps Mummy Serve Luncheon, #428	$475
In Another Smart School Outfit, #444	$400
In a Smart School Outfit, #441	$375
Likes a Rainy Day, #453	$475
Little Godey Lady, #491	$900
Loves Her White Cardigan, #467	$475
Loves Pinafores, #429	$450
Loves this School Dress, #442	$400
Loves to Waltz, #476	$800
Maypole Dance, #458	$650
Plane Trip, #452	$475
Plays in the Garden, #440	$425
Plays on the Beach, #403	$375
Simple Morning Dress, #412	$375
Swimming Outfit, #406	$375
Takes Her Dog for a Walk, #456	$425
Tea Party at Grandma's, #447	$400
Train Journey, #468	$475
Visitor's Day at School, #450	$425
Visits Auntie, #469	$450
Coat with dress and hat or bonnet	$450
Cotton dress	$325
Cotton dress and pinafore with hat or bonnet	$425
Cotton dress with hat or bonnet	$425
Felt jacket with skirt or dress	$475
Nightgown	$200
Nude, perfect doll	$300
Organdy dress with hat or bonnet	$400
Organdy gown	$650
Pajamas	$200
Robe and pajamas	$250
Sailor dress	$650
Sleeveless organdy dress	$325
Taffeta dress with cotton pinafore	$500
Taffeta dress with nylon pinafore and hat or bonnet	$500
Taffeta party dress with organdy pinafore and hat or bonnet	$525
Trousseau in trunk or case, FAO Schwarz exclusive	$900 up

Bent knee walker, 1956-1964

Adores a Cardigan Outfit, #575, 1956	$475
Always Likes Stripes, #384, 1957	$400
Another Smart School Outfit, #553, 1956	$400
At Home, #544, 1956	$425
Attending a House Party, #582, 1956	$425
Basque, #574, 1956	$575
Blue Cotton Dress with White Lace Yoke, #619, 1964	$550
Cabana Outfit, #520, 1958	$375
Calls on a School Friend, #594, 1956	$425
Candy Stripe Cotton Dress, #335, 1960	$375
Can Read, #390, 1957	$450
Charming Little Frock, #321, 1960	$375
Come Rain or Come Shine, #372, 1957	$500
Comes to Breakfast, #537, 1956	$400
Cotton Beach Robe and Swimsuit, #541, 1956	$425

Dozens of Blossoms, #366, 1957	$400
Dressed for a Hot Morning, #338, 1957	$375
Dressed for a Lovely Summer Day, #352, 1962	$400
Dressed for a Summer Day, #432, 1959	$475
Dressed in Another Party Dress, #571, 1958	$450
Everybody has a Car Coat, #371, 1957	$475
Feel so Grown-Up, #380, 1957	$450
First Long Dancing Dress, #606, 1956	$850
First Long Party Dress, #376, 1957	$750
Flowered Cotton Dress, #538, 1956	$425
Fond of Simple Morning Dresses, #345, 1957	$400
For a Sunny Day, #370, 1957	$400
Fun in the Pool, #362, 1957	$375
Fun in the Sun, #315, 1957	$375
Fussy About Her School Dress, #391, 1957	$400
Garden Party, #620, 1956	$675
Gay as a Buttercup, #325, 1957	$400
Gay as a Jonquil, #442, 1959	$450
Gay as the First Crocus, #584, 1958	$725
Gay Little Dress so Becoming, #433, 1959	$425
Gay Organdy Dress, #426, 1961	$450
Gay Suspender Dress, #392, 1957	$575
Gingham Dress, #450, 1963	$400
Goes Calling with Mother, #586, 1956	$425
Goes to the Carousel, #568, 1958	$425
Goes to Sunday School, #587, 1956	$500
Goes Walking, #581, 1956	$475
Going Calling, #387, 1957	$425
Going Shopping, #593, 1956	$425
Going to Grandmother's House for Tea, #575, 1958	
	$425
Going to the Ballet, #601, 1956	$625
Going to the Circus, #561, 1958	$425
Gold Taffeta Ball Gown, #623, 1956	$950
Grandma's Favorite Dress, #603, 1956	$550
Has New Separates, #375, 1957	$475
Has So Many, #531, 1958	$375
Invited a Guest to Luncheon, #542, 1956	$425
Is Off to School, #570, 1958	$400
It is May Day, #365, 1957	$425
Leotards and Pinafore, #413, 1959	$425
Let's Have a Tea Party, #344, 1957	$375
Let's Roll a Hoop, #346, 1957	$350
Looking as Sweet as a Lollipop, #326, 1957	$350
Looking Especially Pretty, #341, 1960	$400
Looking Very Well Dressed, #340, 1960	$400
Looks Cool and Summery, #530, 1958	$400
Looks so Sweet, #588, 1956	$475
Looks so Well Dressed, #444, 1959	$450
Loves Her Party Hairdo, #422, 1961	$425
Many School Frocks to Choose From, #368, 1957	
	$400
Most Becomingly Dressed, #569, 1958	$425
Mother May I Go Out to Play, #374, 1957	$550
Needs More than One Coat, #580, 1956	$475
No Doll Adores a Party, #566, 1958	$425
On a Shopping Jaunt, #595, 1956	$400
One of Wendy's Favorite Dresses, #385,1957	$400

Organdy Party Dress, #565, 1958	$425
Oriental Influence, #591, 1956	$550
Perky Hairdo, #539, 1956	$475
Pink A-Line Dress with Rose Applique, #673, 1964	
	$450
Pink Organdy Dress with Apron, #676, 1964	$400
Polka Dot Dress, #518, 1956	$375
Prettiest Girl You Know, #388, 1957	$400
Raincoat and Hat, #461, 1963	$475
Ready for any Weather, #572, 1956	$475
Ready for a Party, #679, 1964	$500
Reminds You of a Daffodil, #563, 1958	$425
Rosebuds and Ribbon, #394, 1957	$375
Sailor Dress, #576, 1956	$650
School Bell Rings at Nine, #383, 1957	$400
School Days for Dolls are Happy Days, #542, 1958	
	$400
Spectator Sports, #578, 1956; #393, 1957	$500
Spic and Span, #358, 1957	$400
Summer Afternoon, #584, 1956	$400
Summer Party Dress, #604, 1956	$650
Surely Looks Smart, #568, 1956	$450
Sweet Suggestion #386, 1957	$400
Taffeta Sun Suit, #515, 1956	$325
Takes a Basket of Fruit to Grandma, #566, 1956	
	$450
Terry Beach Robe and Swimsuit, #562, 1956	$400
Terry Beach Smock with Bloomers, #626, 1964	$375
Time for School, #359, 1957	$400
Trip to Market with Mommy, #382, 1957	$450
Trousseau Box Set, #495, 1963	$850 up
Velvet Party Dress, #389, 1957	$550
Very Becoming Hairdo, #353, 1962	$400
Visiting Her Cousins, #559, 1956	$425
Wardrobe in Metal Trunk, #690, 1956	$850 up
Wearing a Charming Ensemble, #625, 1956	$675
Who'll have a Soda, #340, 1957	$425
Basic doll in box, panties, shoes, socks, #500, 1956; #300, 1957; #500, 1958; #400, 1959; #300, 1960; #400, 1961; #300, 1962; #400, 1963; #600, 1964	
	$250
Car coat with slacks and hat or bonnet	$575
Coat and dress with matching hat or bonnet	$400
Cotton dress	$375
Cotton dress and apron with or without hat	$400
Cotton dress with cotton pinafore and hat or bonnet	
	$375
Cotton dress with hat or bonnet	$375
Cotton dress with organdy pinafore and hat or bonnet	
	$400
Cotton dress with pique pinafore and hat or bonnet	
	$400
Cotton dress with taffeta pinafore and hat or bonnet	
	$425
Cotton jumper with dotted swiss blouse	$400
Dotted swiss dress	$400
Felt jacket with pleated skirt or dress and matching hat	
	$450

Faux fur coat with hood	$375	Shoe and sock set	$125
Gabardine coat with dress or skirt and blouse and matching hat or bonnet	$400	Slacks with sweater or shirt and hat or cap	$425
Nightgown	$225	Sleeveless cotton dress with or without bonnet	$325
Nylon dress with hat or bonnet	$425	Sleeveless nylon dress with or without bonnet	$350
Nylon long dress with bonnet	$475	Sleeveless organdy dress with or without bonnet	$350
Nude, perfect doll	$150	Sundress	$325
Organdy dress	$425	Sweater with skirt set, pants set or dress	$425
Organdy dress with hat or bonnet	$425	Swimsuits, beach outfits	$375

Organdy dress with cotton pinafore and hat or bonnet — $400

Organdy dress with organdy pinafore and hat or bonnet — $425

Organdy dress with taffeta pinafore and hat or bonnet — $425

Pajamas — $225

Pique dress with hat or bonnet — $400

Robe — $225

Shirt and skirt set with hat or cap — $375

Taffeta coat with dress and matching hat or bonnet — $550

Taffeta dress — $425

Taffeta dress and hat or bonnet — $500

Taffeta dress with apron — $500

Taffeta dress with taffeta pinafore and hat or bonnet — $525

Taffeta gown — $625

Trousseau in trunk or case, FAO Schwarz exclusive — $900 up

Tulle gown — $725

Velvet coat and hat — $600

Velvet dress — $475

Bent knee, non-walkers, 1965
- Basic doll with panties, shoes, socks, #600 — $200
- Cotton dress — $325
- Doll in Easter Egg — $900 up
- Doll in Sewing Kit, exclusive for FAO Schwarz — $800 up
- Nude, perfect doll — $95
- Pink Organdy dress, #621 — $400
- Red Cotton dress, #622 — $450

Alex the Bellhop
- 8" (20cm) hard plastic, 1997-1998 — $80

Algeria
- 8" (20cm) hard plastic, straight leg, 1987-1988 — $65

Alice (sometimes called Alice in Wonderland)
- 16" (41cm) cloth, 1930s — $800
- 7" (18cm) composition, 1930s — $375
- 9" (23cm) composition, 1930s — $400
- 11-14" (28-36cm) composition, 1936-1940 — $450
- 13" (33cm) composition, swivel waist, 1930s — $435
- 14-1/2-18" (37-46cm) composition 1947-1949 — $500-$700
- 21" (53cm) composition 1948-1949 — $1,000
- 14" (36cm) hard plastic, 1950 — $650
- 14" (36cm) hard plastic with trousseau, 1951-1952 — $1,600 up
- 17-23" (43-58cm) hard plastic, 1949-1950 — $675-$800
- 18" (46cm) hard plastic, 1951 — $775 up
- 29" (74cm) cloth/vinyl, 1952 — $750
- 15" (38cm), 18" (46cm), 23" (58cm) hard plastic, 1951-1952 — $500-$750
- 14" (36cm) *Alice and Her Party Kit*, FAO exclusive, 1965 — $1,000
- 14" (36cm) plastic/vinyl, #1452, 1966-1973; #1552, 1974-1992 — $90
- 14" (36cm) plastic/vinyl, blue taffeta dress, 1996 — $90
- 14" (36cm) plastic/vinyl, Disney Catalog, 1996 *(see Special Dolls)* — $200

1953-1954 8-inch (20cm) *Alice. Marge Meisinger Collection.*

12" (31cm) cloth/vinyl, *Little Huggums*, 1997 $50
12" (31cm) Prom Party set, Lissy face doll, 1963
$1,000 up
18" (46cm) cloth, 1996, not produced
7-1/2-8" (19-20cm) hard plastic, straight leg walker or
non-walker, #365, 1953-1954 $700 up
8" (20cm) hard plastic, bent knee walker, #590, 1956
$700
8" (20cm) hard plastic, Disney Crest Colors, Disney
Theme Parks, 1972-1976 *(see Special Dolls)* $475
8" (20cm) hard plastic, 1990-1992 $60
8" (20cm) hard plastic, red trim, 1993-1994 $60
8" (20cm) hard plastic, lace trimmed pinafore,
1995-1996 $60
8" (20cm) hard plastic, party dress with crown and
calendar, 1996-1997 $70
8" (20cm) hard plastic, party dress with crown,
1998-present $70
8" (20cm) hard plastic, TJ Maxx, 1997
(see Special Dolls) $60
8" (20cm) hard plastic, QVC, 1999
(see Special Dolls) $75

Alice and the Jabberwocky
12" (31cm) 1993 Disney World Teddy Bear and Doll
Convention, *(see Special Dolls)* $300

Alice and the White Rabbit
10" (25cm) made for Disney World, 1991 *(see Special
Dolls)* $350

A Little Princess
14" (36cm) Trunk set, 1995 $250
8" (20cm) hard plastic, 1998-present $85

All American Wendy
8" (20cm) hard plastic, TJ Maxx, 1998 *(see Special Dolls)*
$65

All Star
8" (20cm) hard plastic, white, *Americana Series*,
(minor costume change in 1994) 1993-1994 $60
8" (20cm) hard plastic, African American, *Americana
Series*, 1993 $60

Allison
18" (46cm) cloth/vinyl, 1990-1991 $100

Alpine Christmas Twins
8" (20cm) made for Christmas Shoppe, 1992, *(see Special
Dolls)* $165

Altar Boy
8" (20cm) hard plastic, *Americana Series*, 1991 $60

Amanda
8" (20cm) hard plastic, bent knee walker, *Americana
Series*, #489, 1961 $1,800

American Babies
16"-18" (41-46cm) cloth, 1930s $300

American Beauty
10" (25cm) *Portrette*, 1991-1992 $80

American Farm Couple
8" (20cm) hard plastic, 1997 $125

American Girl
7-8" (18-20cm) composition, 1938 $400
9-11" (23-28cm) composition, 1937 $425

8" (20cm) hard plastic, bent knee walker,
#388, 1962-1963; #788, 1964 (called McGuffey Ana in
1965) $375

American Indian
9" (23cm) composition, 1938-1939 $325

American Tots
16-21" (41-53cm) cloth, dressed in children's fashions,
1930s $825

American Women's Volunteer Service (AWVS)
14" (36cm) composition, 1942 $825

America's Junior Miss
8" (20cm) hard plastic, Collector's United, 1994
(see Special Dolls) $90
Fitness 8" (20cm) hard plastic, Collector's United,
1995 *(see Special Dolls)* $70
Interview 8" (20cm) hard plastic, Collector's United,
1996 *(see Special Dolls)* $70
Talent 8" (20cm) hard plastic, Collector's United,
1996 *(see Special Dolls)* $70

Amish Boy
8" (20cm) hard plastic, bent knee, *Americana Series*,
#727, 1966-1969 $325

Amish Girl
8" (20cm) hard plastic, bent knee, *Americana Series*,
#726, 1966-1969 $325

Amy *(see Little Women)*

Anastasia
10" (25cm) *Portrette Series*, 1988-1989 $90
14" (36cm) MADC Convention Special 1993
(see Special Dolls) $175

Anatolia
8" (20cm) hard plastic, straight legs, 1987 $75

Angel
7 1/2-8" (19-20cm) hard plastic, in pink, blue, or white,
straight leg walker, Guardian Angel, has a harp,
#480, 1954 $800 up
7-1/2-8" (19-20cm) hard plastic, straight leg walker,
Baby Angel, #480, 1955 $800
8" (20cm) hard plastic, bent knee walker, Maggie smile
face, 1961 $750 up

Angel Face
8" (20cm) made for Shirley's Doll House, 1990
(see Special Dolls) $100

Angel Lace *(see Tree Topper)*

Angel of Grace
10" (25cm) Matilda Doll and Bear Company, 1998
(see Special Dolls) $110

Angel Tree Toppers *(see Tree Toppers)*

Angel with Musical Crèche
8" (20cm) hard plastic, 1997-present $250

Anna Ballerina
18" (46cm) composition, 1940 $825 up

Anna Karenina
21" (53cm) *Portrait*, 1991 $350
10" (25cm) hard plastic, doll only, 1998-present $120
10" (25cm) hard plastic, doll with trunk,
1998-present $260

Late 1930s 7-inch (18cm) *April*, composition, part of the *Months of the Year* collection. *Marge Meisinger Collection. Photo by Carol J. Stover.*

Annabelle

14-15" (36-38cm) hard plastic, 1951-1952	$550
14-15" (36-38cm) trousseau/trunk, 1952	$1600
18" (46cm) hard plastic, 1951-1952	$675
20-23" (51-58cm) hard plastic, 1951-1952	$800
29" (74cm) vinyl/cloth, 1952 (Barbara Jane)	$675
8" (20cm) made for Belk & Leggett, 1992 *(see Special Dolls)*	$75

Anna and the King of Siam

8" (20cm) hard plastic, 1996	$160 pair

Anne of Green Gables

14" (36cm) plastic/vinyl, 1989-1990	$125
14" (36cm) Anne Goes to School, with trunk, wardrobe, 1992-1993	$250
14" (36cm) Anne's Trunk Set, with trunk, wardrobe, 1994	$250
14" (36cm) Anne Arrives at Station, 1992-1993	$140
14" (36cm) Anne Arrives at Station, 1994-1995	$140
14" (36cm) Anne Becomes the Teacher, 1993	$125
Puff sleeve dress, 1992-1993	$40
White organdy dress, 1992-1993	$45
Winter Coat outfit, 1992-1993	$45
Winter coat, 1994, minor costume change	$45
Garden Dress, 1994, not produced	
8" (20cm) Anne at the Station, 1994-1995	$80

Anne's Puff Sleeve, 8" (20cm) hard plastic, 1994 — $80

Anne's Concert Dress, 8" (20cm) hard plastic, 1995 — $80

Anne's Trunk Set, 8" (20cm) hard plastic, 1995	$175
8" (20cm) hard plastic, floral dress, 1997-present	$80
Trunk set, 8" (20cm) Neiman Marcus, 1994 *(see Special Dolls)*	$195

Ann Estelle

8"(20cm) hard plastic, 1999	$70

Annette

14" (36cm) porcelain, 1993 *(see Special Dolls)*	$450

Annie Laurie

14" (36cm) composition, 1937	$625
17" (43cm) composition, 1937	$925

Annie the Artist

20" (51cm) plastic/vinyl, 1996, not produced

Antoinette

21" (53cm) composition, 1946	$2,100

Antony, Mark

12" (31cm) Portraits of History, 1980-1985	$75

A Place in the Sun

10" (25cm) hard plastic, 1996	$100

Apple Annie

8" (20cm) hard plastic, straight leg walker or non walker, 1953-1954	$1,000 up

Apple Pie
    14" (36cm) Classic Dolls, 1991 $85

Apple Tree
    8" (20cm) hard plastic, 1999 $80

April
    14" (36cm) Classic Dolls, 1990-1991 $95

April Showers Bring May Flowers
    8" (20cm) hard plastic, 1998-present $95

Aquarius
    8" (20cm) hard plastic, 1997-1998 $85

Argentine Boy
    8" (20cm) hard plastic, bent knee walker, #772, 1965
        $500
    8" (20cm) hard plastic, bent knee, #772, 1965-1966
        $500

Argentine Girl
    8" (20cm) hard plastic, bent knee walker, #771, 1965
        $200
    8" (20cm) hard plastic, bent knee, #771, 1965-1972
        $150
    8" (20cm) hard plastic, straight legs, "Alex Mold",
    #0771, 1973; #571, 1974-1975 $65
    8" (20cm) hard plastic, straight legs, 1976-1986 $60

Ariel
    8" (20cm) hard plastic, made for Disney Store Gallery,
    1999 (see Special Dolls) $80

Aries
    8" (20cm) hard plastic, 1997-1998 $85

Armenia
    8" (20cm) hard plastic, 1989-1990 $65

A Rose for You
    8" (20cm) hard plastic, QVC, 1999 (see Special Dolls)
        $75

Arriving in America
    8" (20cm) hard plastic, Americana Series, 1992-1993
        $65

Artie
    12" (31cm) plastic/vinyl, # 1150, 1963 $250
    In case with Smarty, FAO Schwarz exclusive, 1962
        $1,000

Artiste Wendy
    8" (20cm) hard plastic, 1997-present $80

Ashley
    8" (20cm) hard plastic, jacket, hat, Scarlett Series,
    1990 $70
    8" (20cm) hard plastic, Confederate Officer, Scarlett
    Series, 1991-1992 $70

Ashley's Farewell (see Scarlett)

Aster
    9" (23cm) vinyl, 1953 $125

Astrological Doll of the Month
    14-17" (36-43cm) composition, 1938 $485 each

Aunt Agatha
    8" (20cm) hard plastic, bent knee walker, #434, 1957
        $1,000

Aunt Betsy
    cloth/felt, 1930s $925

Auntie Em
    8" (20cm) hard plastic, 1995 $95

Aunt March
    8" (20cm) hard plastic, 1995-1996 $70

Aunt Pitty Pat
    14-17" (36-43cm) composition, 1939 $1,400
    8" (20cm) hard plastic, bent knee walker, #435, 1957
        $1,500
    8" (20cm) hard plastic, straight legs, Scarlett Series,
    1991-1992 $85

Australia
    8" (20cm) hard plastic, 1990-1991 $55

Austria
    8" (20cm) hard plastic, International Series, 1994
        $50

Austria Boy*
    8" (20cm) hard plastic, straight legs, "Alex Mold",
    #599, 1974-1975 $65
    8" (20cm) hard plastic, straight legs, #599,
    1976-1989 $60

Austria Girl*
    8" (20cm) hard plastic, straight legs, "Alex Mold",
    #598, 1974-1975 $65
    8" (20cm) hard plastic, straight legs, #598, 1976-1990
        $60

Autumn
    14" (36cm) Classic Dolls, 1993 $145

Autumn Breeze
    8" (20cm) hard plastic, QVC, 1999 (see Special Dolls)
        $75

Autumn Leaves
    14" (36cm) Classic Dolls 1994 $130

Autumn in NY
    10" (25cm) made for First Modern Doll Club, 1991
    (see Special Dolls) $200

Avril, Jane
    10" (25cm) made for Marshall Fields, 1989
    (see Special Dolls) $175

*Formerly Tyrolean Boy and Girl

Babbie
    cloth, inspired by Katherine Hepburn $1,300
    16" (41cm) cloth, 1934-1936 $750
    14" (36cm) hard plastic $800

Babette
    10" (25cm) *Portrette Series*, 1988-1989 $95

Babs
    20" (51cm) hard plastic, 1949 $800

Babsie Baby
    Composition/cloth, 1930s $550

Babsie Skater
    15" (38cm) composition, roller skater, 1941 $700

Babs Skater
    18" (46cm) composition $1,000
    15" (38cm) hard plastic, 1948-1950 $1,000
    17-18" (43-46cm) hard plastic $1,100
    21" (53cm) hard plastic $1,200

Baby Angel
    7 1/2-8" (19-20cm) hard plastic, straight leg walker,
    #480, 1955 $800

Baby Betty
    10-12" (25-31cm) composition, 1935-1936 $275

Baby Brother and Sister
    20" (51cm) cloth/vinyl, 1977-1979 $100 each
    14" (36cm) 1979-1982 $90 each
    14" (36cm) re-introduced 1989 $70 each

Baby Clown
    7 1/2-8" (19-20cm) hard plastic, straight leg walker,
    #464, 1955 $1,250

Baby Ellen
    14" (36cm) African American, 1965-1972 $145

Baby Genius
    11" (28cm) all cloth, 1930s $400
    11-12" (28-31cm) composition/cloth, 1930s-1940s
        $200
    14" (36cm) composition/cloth, 1930s-1940s $200
    16" (41cm) composition/cloth, 1930s-1940s $250
    18" (46cm) composition/cloth, 1930s-1940s $325
    20" (51cm) composition/cloth, 1930s-1940s $400
    22" (56cm) composition/cloth, 1930s-1940s $500
    24" (61cm) composition/cloth, 1930s-1940s $525
    15" (38cm) hard plastic head/vinyl limbs, 1949-1950
        $185
    18" (46cm) hard plastic head/vinyl limbs, 1949-1950
        $185
    21" (53cm) hard plastic head/vinyl limbs, 1952-1955
        $350
    8" (20cm) hard plastic/vinyl limbs, 1956-1962 (*see Little
    Genius*)

Baby Jane
    16" (41cm) composition, 1935 $900

Baby Lynn
    14" (36cm) cloth/vinyl, 1973-1976 $135
    20" (51cm) cloth/vinyl, 1973-1976 $150

Baby Madison
    14" (36cm) vinyl, with layette, 1999 $100

Baby McGuffey
    11" (28cm) composition/cloth, 1930s-1940s $250
    14" (36cm) composition/cloth, 1930s-1940s $375
    18" (46cm) composition/cloth, 1930s-1940s $425
    20" (51cm) composition/cloth, 1930s-1940s $425
    22-24" (56-61cm) composition, 1930s-1940s $475
    20" (51cm) cloth/vinyl, 1971-1976 $150
    14" (36cm) cloth/vinyl, 1972-1978 $150

Baby Precious
    14" (36cm) cloth/vinyl, 1975 $100
    21" (53cm) cloth/vinyl, 1974 discontinued 1976 $125

Baby Shaver
    12" (31cm) cloth, 1941-1943 $600

Bad Little Girl
    16" (41cm) cloth, blue dress, companion to *Good Little
    Girl*, #41, 1966 $200

Bali
    8" (20cm) hard plastic, *International Dolls*, 1993
        $65

Ballerina
    cloth, 1920s-1930s $450 up
    12-14" (31-36cm) composition, Tony Sarg marionette,
    1934-1940 $350 up
    7" (18cm) composition, 1940 $325
    9" (23cm) composition, 1935-1938 $350
    9" (23cm) composition, *Nina*, 1939-1941 $375
    11-14" (28-36cm) composition, 1936-1938 $450
    18" (46cm) composition, *Anna*, 1940 $825 up
    17" (43cm) composition, 1938-1941 $575
    15" (38cm) composition, pink tutu, *Karen*, 1946-1949
        $800
    18-21" (46-53cm) composition, pink tutu, *Karen* $1,000
    15-18" (38-46cm) hard plastic, pink tutu, *Karen*,
    1948-1949 $900
    14" (36cm) hard plastic, pink, yellow, or blue tutu, *Nina*,
    1949-1950 $550
    15" (38cm) hard plastic, pink, yellow, or blue tutu, *Nina*,
    1951 $625
    17" (43cm) hard plastic, pink, yellow, or blue tutu, *Nina*,
    1949-1950 $650
    18" (46cm) hard plastic, pink, yellow, or blue tutu, *Nina*,
    1949-1950 $700
    21" (53cm) hard plastic, white tutu, *Nina*, 1951 $775
    23" (58cm) hard plastic, pink, yellow, or blue tutu, *Nina*,
    1951 $850
    21" (53cm) hard plastic, white tutu, *Deborah*, 1949-1951
        $5,000 up
    15-18" (38-46cm) hard plastic, 1950-1952 $585
    15" (38cm) hard plastic, red, pink, or yellow tutu, *Treena*,
    1952 $775

18-21" (46-53cm) hard plastic, red, pink, or yellow tutu, *Treena*, 1952 $900

15-18" (38-46cm) hard plastic, red, yellow, white, pink or blue tutu, *Margot*, 1953-1955 $650-$800

15-18" (38-46cm) hard plastic/vinyl arms, red, yellow, white, pink or blue tutu, *Margot*, 1955 $650-$800

15" (38cm) hard plastic, *Binnie*, 1956 $400

18" (46cm) hard plastic, *Binnie*, 1956 $450

8" (20cm) hard plastic, straight leg non-walker, lavender, yellow, pink, 1953-1954 $800

blue (rare) $925

8" (20cm) hard plastic, str... leg walker, lavender, yellow, pink, blue, 1954-1955 $650

7-1/2"-8" (19-20cm) hard plastic, straight leg walker, white tutu, #454, 1955 $500

8" (20cm) hard plastic, bent knee walker, #564, rose tutu, 1956 $600

8" (20cm) hard plastic, rose tutu with wardrobe, 1956 $1,000 up

8" (20cm) hard plastic, yellow tutu, 1956 $600

8" (20cm) hard plastic, bent knee walker, pink or blue tutu, 1957 $475

8" (20cm) hard plastic, pink, 1958 $425

8" (20cm) hard plastic, gold, 1959 $600

8" (20cm) hard plastic, green, 1960 $800 up

8" (20cm) hard plastic, lavender, 1961 $650

8" (20cm) hard plastic, pink or blue tutu, 1960-1964 $300

8" (20cm) hard plastic, bent knee, yellow, pink, or blue tutu with sequin bodice, #620-1965 $400

8" (20cm) hard plastic, bent knee, blue or pink, #730, 1966-19_2 $150

8" (20cm) hard plastic, straight legs, pink tutu, "Alex Mold", #0730, 1973; #430, 1974-1975 $75

8" (20cm) hard plastic, straight legs, pink tutu, 1976-1989 (1985-1987 white face) $65

8" (20cm) hard plastic, *Tippi*, white tutu, CU Gathering, 1988 *(see Special Dolls)* $375

8" (20cm) hard plastic, white/gold, African American available, 1990-1991 $65

8" (20cm) hard plastic, pink, 1992-1995 $65

8" (20cm) hard plastic, *Red Shoes*, 1995 $70

8" (20cm) hard plastic, pink, African American, 1992 $65

8" (20cm) outfit only, pink tutu, 1996 $35

8" (20cm) *Diamond Pixie*, red tutu, made for MADC, 1998 *(see Special Dolls)* $150

8" (20cm) hard plastic, white lace tutu, 1997-1999 $80

8" (20cm) hard plastic, pink tutu, 1999 $80

8" (20cm) hard plastic, bent knees, blue tutu, 1999 $75

8" (20cm) hard plastic, bent knees, lilac tutu, 1999 $75

8" (20cm) hard plastic, bent knees, pink leotard, 1999 $70

8" (20cm) hard plastic, *Irish Dream*, 1999 $80

Late 1950s green ballerina. This is a very rare doll. *Benita Schwartz Collection.*

8" (20cm) accessory pack with ballet bag, leotard, slippers, 1999 $15

8" (20cm) ballerina trunk set, made for Enchanted Doll House, 1983 *(see Special Dolls)* $175

8" (20cm) hard plastic, Ballerina, MADC, 1984 *(see Special Dolls)* $250

8" (20cm) hard plastic, made for Enchanted Doll House, 1989 *(see Special Dolls)* $100

10" (25cm) hard plastic, pink or blue, #914, 1957; #813, 1960; #813, 1961; #735, 1962-1964 $450

10" (25cm) hard plastic, gold, #713, 1959 $475

10" (25cm) *Sugar Plum Fairy*, 1992-1993 $95

10" (25cm) *Violet*, 1994 $75

10" (25cm) hard plastic, white tutu, *Degas*, 1998-1999 $90

12" (31cm) hard plastic, jointed knees and elbows, pink, blue, white, or rose tutu, *Lissy*, #1242, 1956; #1214, 1958 $500

12" (31cm) plastic/vinyl toddler, pink, blue or yellow tutu, #1124, 1965 (*Janie*) $325

12" (31cm) *Muffin*, pink or blue tutu, 1989-1990 $70

12" (31cm) *Romance Collection*, 1990-1992 $80

12" (31cm) Ballerina, 1993 $95

14" (36cm) plastic/vinyl, pink tutu, #1410, 1963 *(Melinda)* $375

14" (36cm) plastic/vinyl, pink or blue tutu, 1965 *(Mary Ann)* $275

14" (36cm) plastic/vinyl, *Degas Dance Lesson*, 1994 $100

16-1/2" (42cm) hard plastic, pink, white, lavender, yellow, or blue, #1635, 1957 *(Elise)* $450 up

16-1/2" (42cm) hard plastic, white or pink tutu, #1725, 1958 *(Elise)* $500

16-1/2" (42cm) hard plastic, gold tutu, #1810, 1959 *(Elise)* $450

16-1/2" (42cm) hard plastic, pink or blue tutu, #1720, 1960 *(Elise)* $400

17" (43cm) plastic/vinyl, pink or blue tutu (upswept hairdo), #1825, 1961 *(Elise)* $400

17" (43cm) plastic/vinyl, pink or blue tutu, #1740, 1962 *(Elise)* $400

18" (46cm) blue or pink tutu, #1720-1963-1964 *(Elise)* $400

17" (43cm) plastic/vinyl, pink or blue tutu, #1725, 1965 *(Polly)* $275

17" (43cm) plastic/vinyl, pink, blue, yellow, or white tutu, 1966-1971 *(Leslie)* $275

17" (43cm) plastic/vinyl, pink, blue, yellow, silver or white, 1966-1989 *(Elise)* $150-175

17" (43cm) plastic/vinyl, *Firebird* and *Swan Lake*, 1990-1991 *(Elise)* $175

16" (41cm) plastic/vinyl, *Firebird*, 1997 $175

16" (41cm) plastic/vinyl, *Giselle*, 1997-1998 $185

16" (41cm) plastic/vinyl, *Swan Lake*, 1997-1998 $185

16" (41cm) plastic/vinyl, *Nutcracker*, 1998-1999 $190

16" (41cm) plastic/vinyl, *Classic*, 1999 $170

21" (53cm) vinyl, *Lilac Fairie Ballerina*, 1993-1994 (vinyl *Cissy*) $325

15" (38cm) porcelain, *Karen Ballerina*, 1999 $160

Barbara Jane
29" (74cm) cloth/vinyl, 1952 $500 up

Barbara Lee
8" (20cm) hard plastic, name given to *Wendy-Alexander-kins* by stores like FAO Schwarz, 1955 $450 up

Barton, Clara
10" (25cm) *Portrette Series*, 1989 $95

Baseball
8" (20cm) hard plastic, boy or girl doll, 1997 $60

Bathing Beauty
10" (25cm) UFDC Special Doll, 1992 *(see Special Dolls)* $250

Bears *(see Well Dressed Bears)*

Beast
8" (20cm) hard plastic *Storyland Dolls*, 1994-1995 $65

12" (31cm) *Romance Series*, 1992 $125

Beau Brummel
cloth, 1930s $775

Beauty
8" (20cm) hard plastic, *Storyland Dolls*, 1994-1995 $65

12" (31cm) *Romance Series*, 1992 $125

Beauty Queen
10" (25cm) hard plastic, 1961 *(see Cissette)*

Beaux Arts Dolls
18" (46cm) hard plastic, 1953 $1,800 up

Beddy-Bye Brenda
8" (20cm) made for FAO Schwarz, 1992 *(see Special Dolls)* $70

Beddy-Bye Brooke
14" (36cm) made for FAO Schwarz, 1991 *(see Special Dolls)* $125

Beddy-Bye Brooke & Brenda
14" (36cm) and 8" (20cm), made for FAO Schwarz, 1992 *(see Special Dolls)* $225

Belgium
7" (18cm) composition, 1935-1938 $300
9" (23cm) composition, 1930s $325
8" (20cm) hard plastic, bent knee, #762, 1972 $100
8" (20cm) hard plastic, straight legs, "Alex Mold", #0762, 1973; #562, 1974-1975 $70
8" (20cm) hard plastic, straight legs, 1976-1988 $65

Bell Display Jar
For 8" (20cm) doll, 1997-1998 $40
For 10" (25cm) doll, 1997-1998 $60

Belle
8" (20cm) hard plastic, Disney Theme Parks, 1994 *(see Special Dolls)* $110
14" (36cm) plastic/vinyl, Disney Catalog, 1996 *(see Special Dolls)* $155
14" (36cm) plastic/vinyl, Disney Catalog, wearing winter coat, 1997 *(see Special Dolls)* $160
8" (20cm) hard plastic, made for Disney Store Gallery, 1999 *(see Special Dolls)* $80

Belle
14" (36cm) plastic/vinyl, from Dicken's Christmas Carol, 1996 $125

Belle Brummel
cloth, 1930s $750

Belle of the Ball
10" (25cm) *Portrette Series*, 1989 $100
10" (25cm) hard plastic, Home Shopping Club, 1998 *(see Special Dolls)* $120

Belle Watling
10" (25cm) *Scarlett Series*, 1992 $100
21" (53cm) plastic/vinyl, 1995 $300

Bellow's Anne
14" (36cm) plastic/vinyl, *Fine Arts Series*, 1987 $100

Be Mine
8" (20cm) hard plastic, Lillian Vernon, 1999 *(see Special Dolls)* $75

Bernhardt, Sarah
21" (53cm) dressed in all burgundy, 1987 $300

Bessy Bell
14" (36cm) plastic/vinyl, *Classic Dolls*, 1988 $85

Bessy Brooks
8" (20cm) hard plastic, *Storyland Dolls*, 1988-1991 $70

Complete set of 1953 Herald House exclusive Bible characters. 8-inch (20cm) hard plastic.
Mary Lee Stallings Collection. Photo by Ric Marklin.

1957 8-inch (20cm) *Wendy* and *Bill* in riding habits. *Marge Meisinger Collection.*

Bessy Brooks Bride
    8" (20cm), Greenville Show, 1990 *(see Special Dolls)*
    $100

Best Man
    7 1/2-8" (19-20cm) hard plastic, straight let walker,
    #461, 1955 $700 up

Beth *(see Little Women)*

Beth
    10" (25cm) made for Spiegel, 1990 *(see Special Dolls)*
    $125

Betty
    12" (31cm) composition, 1936-1937 $375
    14" (36cm) composition, 1934-1942 $425
    16-18" (41-46cm) composition, 1934-1942 $425
    19-21" (48-53cm) composition, 1938-1941 $475
    14-1/2-17-1/2" (37-45cm) hard plastic, made for Sears
    in 1951 $525
    30" (76cm) plastic/vinyl, Cotton dress, #3105, 1960
    $425
    30" (76cm) plastic/vinyl, Cotton dress with white blouse,
    #3110, 1960 $425
    30" (76cm) plastic/vinyl, Dress with matching jacket,
    #3225, 1960 $450
    30" (76cm) plastic/vinyl, Organdy dress, #3111, 1960
    $450

Betty Bag
    all cloth, flat painted face, yarn hair, 1940s $350

Betty Blue
    8" (20cm) hard plastic, straight legs, *Storyland Dolls*,
    1987-1988 only $75

Betty Boop
    10" (25cm) hard plastic, 1999 $130

Bible Character Dolls
    8" (20cm) hard plastic, 1953-1954 $7,000

Bill or Billy
    7 1/2-8" (19-20cm) hard plastic, straight leg walker,
    groom, #466, 1955 $475
    8" (20cm) hard plastic, bent knee walker, riding habit,
    #373B, 1957 $475
    8" (20cm) hard plastic, bent knee walker, *Looks So
    Spic and Span*, #567, 1958 $450
    8" (20cm) hard plastic, bent knee walker, *The Boy Next
    Door*, #420, 1959 $450
    8" (20cm) hard plastic, bent knee walker, groom,
    #421, 1961 $400
    8" (20cm) hard plastic, bent knee walker, red jacket and
    blue shorts, #443, 1963; #643, 1964 $400

Billy in the Box
    8" (20cm) hard plastic head and torso, 1996 $100

Binnie or Binnie Walker
15-25" (38-64cm) hard plastic, 1954-1955
    15" (38cm) Black and White Striped Dress with Pinafore,
    #1522, 1954 $475
    18" (46cm) Black and White Striped Dress with Pinafore,
    #1822, 1954 $475
    25" (64cm) Black and White Striped Dress with Pinafore,
    #2522, 1954 $525
    18" (46cm) Blue Coat with Hat and Dress, #1856, 1955
    $475
    15" (38cm) Cotton Dress with Cardigan, #1527, 1955
    $450
    18" (46cm) Cotton Dress with Cardigan, #1827, 1955
    $450
    25" (64cm) Cotton Dress with Cardigan, #2527, 1955
    $475
    15" (38cm) Cotton Dress with Pinafore, #1528, 1955
    $425
    18" (46cm) Cotton Dress with Pinafore, #1828, 1955
    $450
    25" (64cm) Cotton Dress with Pinafore, #2528, 1955
    $475
    15" (38cm) Ice Skating Outfit, #1517, 1955 $550
    18" (46cm) Ice Skating Outfit, #1817, 1955 $650
    15" (38cm) Navy Taffeta Dress with Velvet Hat,
    #1523, 1954 $550
    18" (46cm) Navy Taffeta Dress with Velvet Hat,
    #1823, 1954 $600
    25" (64cm) Navy Taffeta Dress with Velvet Hat,
    #2523, 1954 $650
    25" (64cm) Pink Satin Gown, #2572, 1955 $675
    15" (38cm) Red Coat with Leopard Hat and Muff,
    #1525, 1954 $650
    18" (46cm) Red Coat with Leopard Hat and Muff,
    #1825, 1954 $650
    25" (64cm) Red Coat with Leopard Hat and Muff,
    #2525, 1954 $675
    15" (38cm) Striped Cotton Dress with Velvet Bodice,
    #1524, 1954 $650

18" (46cm) Striped Cotton Dress with Velvet Bodice,
#1824, 1954 $650
25" (64cm) Striped Cotton Dress with Velvet Bodice,
#2524, 1954 $675
15" (38cm) Striped Taffeta Dress, #1511, 1955 $575
18" (46cm) Striped Taffeta Dress, #1811, 1955 $600
25" (64cm) Striped Taffeta Dress, #2511, 1955 $650
15" (38cm) Taffeta Overdress with White Dotted Dress,
#1518, 1955 $475
18" (46cm) Taffeta Overdress with White Dotted Dress,
#1818, 1955 $500
25" (64cm) Taffeta Overdress with White Dotted Dress,
#2518, 1955 $525
15" (38cm) in suitcase with wardrobe, #350, 1954;
#218, 1955 $900 up
15" (38cm) in trunk set with wardrobe, #450, 1954;
#317, 1955 $900 up
18" (46cm) Toddler, plastic/vinyl, 1964 $325

Birds, The
10" (25cm) hard plastic, 1998, not produced

Birthday Dolls
7" (18cm) composition $350 each

Bitsey
11-12" (28-31cm) composition, 1942-1946 $275
11-16" (28-41cm) head hard plastic, 1949-1951 $200
12" (31cm) cloth/vinyl, 1965-1966 $155
19-26" (48-66cm) 1949-1951 $200-$250

Black Forest
8" (20cm) hard plastic, 1989-1990 $70

Blast Off 2000
8" (20cm) hard plastic, 1999 $70

Bliss, Betty Taylor
14" (36cm) plastic/vinyl 2nd set, *First Ladies Series*,
1979-1981 $100

Blossom
8" (20cm) hard plastic, QVC, 1999 *(see Special Dolls)*
    $75

Blue Angel
8" (20cm) hard plastic, Home Shopping Club, 1997
(see Special Dolls) $150

Blue Boy
16" (41cm) cloth, 1930s $700
7" (18cm) composition, 1936-1938 $375
9" (23cm) composition, 1938-1941 $400

12" (31cm) plastic/vinyl, *Portrait Children*, 1972-1983
    $75
In blue velvet, 1985-1987 $75
8" (20cm) hard plastic, 1997-1998 $70

Blue Danube Waltz
18" (46cm) hard plastic, blue taffeta, *Me and My Shadow
Series*, 1954 $1,600 up
7-1/2-8" (19-20cm) hard plastic, straight leg non-walker,
#351, 1954 $1,000 up

Blue Fairie
10" (25cm) *Portrette Series*, 1993-1994 $100
Tree Topper 10" (25cm) Disney Catalog, 1995 *(see
Special Dolls)* $165

Blue Moon
14" (36cm) *Classic Dolls*, 1991-1992 $170

Blue Zircon
10" (25cm) *Birthday Collection*, 1992 $90

Bobbie Sox
8" (20cm) hard plastic, made for Disney Theme Parks,
1990 *(see Special Dolls)* $150

Bobby
8" (20cm) hard plastic, bent knee walker, #347, 1957
    $550
8" (20cm) hard plastic, 1960 $550

Bobby Takes a Picture
8" (20cm) hard plastic, MADC, 1996 *(see Special Dolls)*
    $125

Bobby Q
16" (41cm) cloth, 1938-1942 $675

Bobo Clown
8" (20cm) hard plastic, 1991-1992 $65

Bohemia
8" (20cm) hard plastic, 1989-1991 $65

Bolivia
8" (20cm) hard plastic, bent knee walker, #386, 1963;
#786, 1964-1965 $400
Outfit only for 8" (20cm) doll, #0386, 1963 $125
8" (20cm) hard plastic, bent knee, #786, 1965-66
    $375

Bonnet Top Wendy
8" (20cm) hard plastic, 1995 $60

Bonnie (Baby)
11" (28cm) plastic/cloth, 1951 $125
16-19" (41-48cm) vinyl, 1954-1955 $125
24-30" (61-76cm) 1954-1955 $160-$200

Bonnie Blue
#1305, 14" (36cm) *Jubilee II*, 1989 $120
8" (20cm) hard plastic, 1990-1992 $95
8" (20cm) hard plastic, 1995 $85

Bonnie Goes to London
8" (20cm) hard plastic, *Scarlett Series*, 1993-1994
    $90

Bonnie Toddler
18" (46cm) cloth/hard plastic head, vinyl limbs, 1950-1951
    $150
19" (48cm) all vinyl, 1954-1955 $175
23"-24" (58-61cm) vinyl, 1954-1955 $220

Bon Voyage Little Miss Magnin
8" (20cm) made for I. Magnin, 1993 *(see Special Dolls)*
    $100

Bon Voyage Miss Magnin
10" (25cm) made for I. Magnin, 1993 *(see Special Dolls)*
    $125

Boo
8" (20cm) hard plastic, MADC, 1996 *(see Special Dolls)*
    $100

Boone, Daniel
8" (20cm) hard plastic, *Americana Series*, 1991 $75

Bo Peep, Little
7" (18cm) composition, *Storyland Dolls*, 1937-1941
    $350

9-11" (23-28cm) composition, 1936-1940	$375
7-1/2-8" (19-20cm) hard plastic, straight leg walker, #489, 1955	$650
8" (20cm) hard plastic, bent knee walker, #383, 1962-1963; #783, 1964-1965	$175
Outfit only for 8" (20cm) doll, #0383, 1962-1963	$100
8" (20cm) hard plastic, bent knee, #783, 1965-1972	$110
8" (20cm) hard plastic, straight legs, "Alex Mold", #0783, 1973; #483, 1974-1975	$70
8" (20cm) hard plastic, 1976-1987	$65
10" (25cm) *Portrette*, 1994	$90
10" (25cm) hard plastic, TJ Maxx, 1997 *(see Special Dolls)*	$80
8" (20cm) hard plastic, QVC, 1999 *(see Special Dolls)*	$75
14" (36cm) *Classic Dolls*, 1988-1989	$75
12" (31cm) porcelain, 1990-1992	$250
14" (36cm) re-introduced, 1992-1993	$125

Boy's Choir of Harlem

8" (20cm) hard plastic, 1997-1998	$75

Brazil

7" (18cm) composition, 1937-1943	$375
9" (23cm) composition, 1938-1940	$400
8" (20cm) hard plastic, bent knee walker, #773, 1965	$135
8" (20cm) hard plastic, bent knee, #773, 1965-1972	$100
8" (20cm) hard plastic, straight legs, "Alex Mold", #0773, 1973; #573, 1974-1975	$75
8" (20cm) hard plastic, straight leg, 1976-1988	$70
white face, 1985-1987	$65
8" (20cm) hard plastic, 1996-1997	$75

Brenda Starr

12" (31cm) hard plastic/vinyl, 1964, nude doll	$135
Basic doll wearing chemise #900 or green cotton dress #905	$225
Boxed chemise #0900 or green cotton dress only #0905	$30
Doll wearing floral print sheath #910	$225
Boxed outfit only #0910	$50
Doll wearing bathing suit with terry cloth cape #911	$275
Boxed outfit only #0911	$125
Doll wearing satin slacks with blouse #912	$275
Boxed outfit only #0912	$125
Doll wearing pink cotton dress with cluny lace trim #915	$225
Boxed outfit only #0915	$75
Doll wearing green evening gown with white lace bodice #920	$300
Boxed outfit only #0920	$150
Doll wearing blue cocktail dress with matching velvet cape #921	$350
Boxed outfit only #0921	$175
Doll wearing floral sheath with raincoat and hat #925	$300

Boxed outfit only #0925	$150
Doll wearing bridal gown #930	$300
Boxed outfit only #0930	$175
Doll in red sheath in gift set with extra wig #975	$450

Additional boxed outfits

Petti and step-ins #0950	$50
Pink nightgown #0955	$30
Pink robe #0956	$30
Slacks and sweater set #0957	$175
Red and white cotton dress #0958	$150
White floral print dress #0961	$150
Jersey sheath dress #0963	$175
Yellow dotted swiss dress #0966	$150
Taffeta #0971 or satin dress #0972	$175
Coral organza gown #0985	$150
Ivory and gold satin formal #0990	$200

Briar Rose

8" (20cm) hard plastic, MADC, 1989 *(see Special Dolls)*	$350
10" (25cm) hard plastic, 1995	$100

Bride

7" (18cm) composition, 1935-1939	$300
9-11" (23-28cm) composition 1936-1941	$350
13" (33cm), 14" (36cm), 15" (38cm) composition, 1935-1941	$400-$600
17-18" (43-46cm) composition, 1935-1943	$500 up
14" (36cm) composition, *Sally*, 1938-1939	$500
18-21" (46-53cm) composition, *Sally*, 1938-1939	$575-$700
14" (36cm) composition, *Lucy*, 1937-1940	$475
17" (43cm) composition, *Lucy*, 1937-1940	$575
21" (53cm) composition, *Lucy*, 1942-1944	$2,300
21" (53cm) composition, *June Bride*, 1939, 1946-1947	$2,100 up
21" (53cm) composition, *Royal Wedding Portrait*, 1945-1947	$2,100 up
21-23" (53-58cm) composition, 1942-1943	$800 up
15" (38cm) composition in trunk with trousseau	$1,600 up
14" (36cm) hard plastic, *Lucy*, 1949-1950	$625
17" (43cm) hard plastic, *Lucy*, 1949-1950	$650
18" (46cm) hard plastic, 1949-1955	$700
21" (53cm) hard plastic, 1949-1953	$1,000 up
15" (38cm) hard plastic, 1951-1955	$650
14-18" (36-46cm) hard plastic, *Peggy*, 1950-1951	$650
21" (53cm) hard plastic, *Peggy*, 1950	$850
17" (43cm) hard plastic, *Mary Rose*, 1951	$750
14" (36cm) hard plastic, *Godey*, 1950	$1,100
18" (46cm) hard plastic, *Godey*, 1950-1951	$1,300
21" (53cm) hard plastic, *Deborah*, 1949-1951	$5,000 up
14" (36cm) *Pink Bride*, 1950	$775
18" (46cm) *Pink Bride*, 1950	$850
21" (53cm) *Pink Bride*, 1950	$950
23" (58cm) hard plastic, 1949, 1952-1955	$750 up
15" (38cm) hard plastic, 1955-1956 *(Wendy)*	$625
18" (46cm) hard plastic, 1955-1956 *(Wendy)*	$800
25" (64cm) hard plastic, 1955 *(Wendy)*	$925
8" (20cm) hard plastic, *Quizkin*, 1953	$650

7-1/2-8" (19-20cm) hard plastic, straight leg walker, #475, 1954-1955 $575

8" (20cm) hard plastic, bent knee walker, #615, 1956; #410, 1957; #582, 1958; #480, 1961 $400-$600

8" (20cm) hard plastic, bent knee walker, pink gown, 1959 $650 up

8" (20cm) hard plastic, bent knee walker, #470, 1963 $350

8" (20cm) hard plastic, bent knee walker in ruffled dress, #670, 1964; #630, 1965 $350

8" (20cm) hard plastic, bent knee, #630, 1965 $250

8" (20cm) hard plastic, bent knee, #735, 1966-1972 $125

8" (20cm) hard plastic, straight legs, "Alex Mold", #0735, 1973; #435, 1974-1975 $70

8" (20cm) hard plastic, straight legs, 1976-1992 $60

8" (20cm) hard plastic, white face, 1985-1987 $60

8" (20cm), *Greenville Show*, 1990 *(see Special Dolls)* $100

8" (20cm) hard plastic, *Americana Series*, 1990-1996 $70

8" (20cm) hard plastic, *Scarlett Bride*, 1994 $70

8" (20cm) hard plastic, *Cake Top Bride*, 1996-1998 $95

8" (20cm) hard plastic, also available as African American, 1999 $80

8" (20cm) hard plastic, *Cinderella's Wedding*, 1999 $90

Cissy Brides

Lucille Ball *Forever Darling* Bride – Lace over-skirt with pleated underskirt, elaborate cap bridal veil decorated with flowers. (This doll was made the same year as the film "Forever Darling" with Lucille Ball and Desi Arnaz.) 1955 $3,000 up

Brocade gown appliqued bodice and skirt, *A Child's Dream Come True Series*, #2101, 1955 $900

Gown has lace bodice, tulle skirt, tulle Cap with veil, *Fashion Parade Series*, #2040, 1956 $775

White satin bodice, double train, tulle skirt, *Cissy Models Her Formal Gowns Series*, #2170, 1957 $700

Bridal Gown with wreath pattern at bottom of skirt, *Dolls to Remember Series*, #2280, 1958 $725

21" (53cm) doll has straight arms and short neck, nylon pleated tulle, #2170, 1959 $700

21" (53cm) doll has straight arms and short neck, beige lace overskirt, pleated tulle underskirt, 1962 $750

Cissette Brides

10" (25cm) hard plastic, gown tulle with short veil (pictured on front cover of Madame Alexander presents Cissette – promotion book that came with early dolls), # 970, 1957 $450

10" (25cm) hard plastic, gown tulle and bridal lace with tulle cap veil. (matches *Cissy* 1956 and *Lissy* 1957 Brides), #980, 1957 $450

10" (25cm) hard plastic, gown lace bridal wreath pattern. (matches *Cissy* and *Elise* Brides of same year), #876, 1958 $500

10" (25cm) hard plastic, gown tulle with puffed sleeves, #740, 1959; #840, 1960 $450

10" (25cm) hard plastic, pink gown, 1959 $750

10" (25cm) hard plastic, gown tulle with rhinestones on collar and veil, # 840, 1961 $450

10" (25cm) hard plastic, gown has lace on bodice and lace trim on skirt, long veil, #755, 1962 $400

10" (25cm) hard plastic, gown tulle with rows of lace at bodice and hem of skirt (matches *Elise* bride of same year), #755, 1963 $400

10" (25cm) hard plastic, in trunk, trousseau $1,000 up

Lissy Brides

12" (31cm) jointed knees and elbows, tulle gown, tulle cap, #1247, 1956 $475

12" (31cm) jointed knees and elbows, tulle gown with lace cap, #1160, 1957 $475

12" (31cm) jointed knees and elbows, dotted gown, #1235, 1958 $475

Elise Brides

dolls were jointed at ankle, knee, hip, elbow and shoulder

16-1/2" (42cm) hard plastic, gown nylon tulle, chapel length veil, #1650, 1957 $425

Early 1940s composition 21-inch (53cm) Bride, all original. *Benita Schwartz Collection.*

Late 1930s, early 1940s all composition 11-inch (28cm) Bridesmaid. *Veronica Jochens Collection.*

16-1/2" (42cm) hard plastic, gown tulle bridal wreath pattern on skirt, # 1750, 1958 $450

16-1/2" (42cm) hard plastic, pleated tulle dress, #1835, 1959 $450
16-1/2" (42cm) hard plastic, pink gown, 1959 $750
16-1/2" (42cm) hard plastic, satin gown, #1735, 1960 $425
17" (43cm) plastic/vinyl, tulle gown with puffed sleeves, #1835, 1961 $400
17" (43cm) plastic/vinyl, tulle gown with "cobwebby" lace, #1750, 1962 $400
18" (46cm) vinyl, gown tulle rows of lace at bodice and hem, #1755, 1963 $400
18" (46cm) hard plastic/vinyl, gown with tiers of lace, chapel length veil, #1740, 1964 $400
12" (31cm) hard plastic/vinyl, *Brenda Starr*, 1964 $300
Boxed outfit only for 12" (31cm) *Brenda Starr*, 1964 $175

12" (31cm) hard plastic/vinyl, *Yolanda*, 1965-1967 $375
17" (43cm) plastic/vinyl, white brocade gown, #1754, 1965 (*Polly*) $450
17" (43cm) plastic/vinyl, white tulle gown, #1765, 1965 (*Polly*) $325
17" (43cm) plastic/vinyl, several variations of tulle and lace, 1966-1971 (*Leslie*) $275
17" (43cm) plastic/vinyl, 1966-1988 (Elise) $150-$175
16" (41cm) plastic/vinyl, *Classic Bride*, 1999 $190
21" (53cm) *Portrait*, full lace, lace edge on veil, 1965 $950
21" (53cm) full lace overskirt, plain veil, 1969 $800
21" (53cm) plastic/vinyl, Bride, *Scarlett Series*, 1990-1993 $350
21" (53cm) Pearl Embroidered Lace bridal gown, 1996 (*Cissy*) $550
21" (53cm) *Peony* and *Butterfly* wedding gown, 1997 (*Cissy*) $375
14" (36cm) plastic/vinyl, 1973-1976 $100
14" (36cm) plastic/vinyl, *Classic Dolls*, 1987-1990 $110
14" (36cm) ecru gown, re-introduced 1992 $160
21" (53cm) porcelain, 1989-1990 $500
21" (53cm) porcelain, *Cissy Godey* Bride 1993-1994 $500
10" (25cm) *Portrette Series*, 1990-1991 $100
10" (25cm) hard plastic, *Portrette Series*, Victorian, 1992 $95
10" (25cm) hard plastic, 20s Bride, 1995 $95
10" (25cm) hard plastic, MADC, Frances Folsom, 1995 (*see Special Dolls*) $250
10" (25cm) hard plastic, *Amy the Bride*, 1995-1996 $90
10" (25cm) hard plastic, *Father of the Bride*, 1996 $110
10" (25cm) hard plastic, *Jackie* doll, 1996 $110
10" (25cm) hard plastic, *Jackie* with *John* the groom, 1996 $225
10" (25cm) hard plastic, *Victorian*, 1998-1999 $135
10" (25cm) hard plastic, *Rococo*, 1998-1999 $140
10" (25cm) hard plastic, *Empire*, 1998-1999 $135
10" (25cm) hard plastic, *Elizabethan*, 1999 $130
10" (25cm) hard plastic, *Renaissance*, 1999 $130
10" (25cm) hard plastic, *Roaring 20's*, 1999 $150
12" (31cm) porcelain, 1991-1993 $250
12" (31cm) vinyl, *Maria Bride*, 1992-1993 $125

Bridesmaid

9" (23cm) composition, 1937-1939 $355
11-14" (28-36cm) composition, 1938-1942 $375-$450
15-18" (38-46cm) composition, 1939-1944 $400-$500
20-22" (51-56cm) composition, *Portrait*, 1941-1947 $1,500 up
21-1/2" (55cm) composition, 1938-1941 $1,000
15-17" (38-43cm) hard plastic, 1950-1952 $600 up
18" (46cm) hard plastic, 1952 $700 up
19" (48cm) rigid vinyl, in pink, 1952-1953 $650
21" (53cm) hard plastic, 1950-1953 $750 up

15" (38cm) hard plastic, 1952	$500
15" (38cm) hard plastic, 1955	$375
18" (46cm) hard plastic, 1955	$450
25" (64cm) hard plastic, 1955	$525
7-1/2-8" (19-20cm) hard plastic, straight leg non-walker, 1953	$900 up
7-1/2-8" (19-20cm) hard plastic, straight leg walker, #478, 1955	$800
20" (51cm) hard plastic, blue tulle, #2030, 1956	$900
8" (20cm) hard plastic, bent knee walker, #621, 1956; #408, 1957; #583, 1958	$700 up
16-1/2" (42cm) hard plastic, pink dotted swiss gown, #1638, 1957	$500
16-1/2" (42cm) hard plastic, nylon gown, #1736, 1958	$550
16-1/2" (42cm) hard plastic, pleated gown, #1830, 1959	$550
17" (43cm) plastic/vinyl, tulle gown, #1830, 1961	$475
18" (46cm) plastic/vinyl, #1730, 1964	$475
10" (25cm) hard plastic, dotted tulle dress, #960, 1957	$500
10" (25cm) hard plastic, floral tulle dress, #852, 1958	$625
10" (25cm) hard plastic, pleated nylon dress, #741, 1959	$525
12" (31cm) hard plastic, jointed knees and elbows, pink or blue, #1248, 1956	$500
12" (31cm) hard plastic, jointed knees and elbows, pink, blue, lavender or yellow, #1161, 1957	$575
12" (31cm) hard plastic/vinyl, *Yolanda*, 1965	$425
17" (43cm) plastic/vinyl, *Leslie*, 1966-1971	$325
17" (43cm) plastic/vinyl, *Elise*, 1966-1987	$150-$250
8" (20cm) outfit only, Doll and Teddy Bear Expo West exclusive, 1999	$40

Brigitta
    11" (28cm) & 14" (36cm), *(see Sound of Music)*

Brinker, Gretel
12" (31cm) 1993	$125
8" (20cm) hard plastic, 1996	$60

Brinker, Hans
12" (31cm) 1993	$125
8" (20cm) hard plastic, 1996	$60

Brooke
    14" (36cm) made for FAO Schwarz, 1988 *(see Special Dolls)* $130

Bubbles Clown
    8" (20cm) hard plastic, *Americana Series*, 1993-1994 $65

Buck Rabbit
    cloth/felt, 1930s $675

Bud
16-19" (41-48cm) cloth/vinyl, 1952	$175
19" & 25" (48cm & 64cm) 1952-1953	$250

Bulgaria
    8" (20cm) hard plastic, 1985-1987 $65

Bumble Bee
    8" (20cm) hard plastic, *Americana Series*, 1992-1993

	$60

Bunny
18" (46cm) plastic/vinyl, Coat with Dress and Bonnet, #1820, 1962	$275
18" (46cm) plastic/vinyl, Dotted Swiss Dress, #1805, 1962	$275
Boxed Outfits for 18" (46cm), 1962	
Coat and Bonnet	$100
Dress with Bloomers	$110
Nylon Nightgown	$80
Nylon Robe	$80

Bunny Beau
    16" (41cm) cloth, 1930s $750

Bunny Belle
    16" (41cm) cloth, 1930s $750

Burma
    7" (18cm) composition, 1939-1943 $350

Butch
14-16" (36-41cm) composition/cloth, 1942-1946	$175
11-12" (28-31cm) composition/cloth, 1942-1946	$175
18" (46cm) composition/cloth 1942-1946	$200
11-16" (28-41cm) hard plastic, 1949-1951	$175
14" (36cm) cloth/vinyl head and limbs, 1950	$150
12" (31cm) cloth/vinyl, 1965-1966	$100

Butch McGuffey
    22" (56cm) composition/cloth, 1940-1941 $250

1957 10-inch (25cm) hard plastic *Cissette Bridesmaid. Marge Meisinger Collection.*

Cake Top Bride *(see Brides)*
Calamity Jane
    8" (20cm) hard plastic, *Americana Series*, 1994 $65
Camelot in Columbia
    8" (20cm) made for Columbia Show, 1991 *(see Special Dolls)* $100
Cameo Lady
    10" (25cm) CU, 1991 *(see Special Dolls)* $125
Camille
    21" (53cm) composition, 1938-1939 $3,000 up
Canada
    8" (20cm) hard plastic, bent knee, #760, 1968-1972 $100
    8" (20cm) hard plastic, straight legs, "Alex Mold",
    #0760, 1973; #560, 1974-1975 $70
    8" (20cm) hard plastic, straight legs, 1976-1988 $65
    8" (20cm) hard plastic, white face, 1986 $60
    8" (20cm) hard plastic, a.k.a. Team Canada 1998-1999 $90
Cancer
    8" (20cm) hard plastic, 1998 $85
Candy Kid
    11"-15" (28-38cm) composition, 1938-1941 $300-$425
Capricorn
    8" (20cm) hard plastic, 1997-1998 $85
Captain Hook
    8" (20cm) hard plastic, 1992-1993 $80
Captain's Cruise
    8" (20cm) hard plastic, CU Nashville, 1994 *(see Special Dolls)* $200
Captain Von Trapp *(see Sound of Music)*
Careen
    14-17" (36-43cm) composition, 1937-1938 $800
    8" (20cm) hard plastic, *Scarlett Series*, 1994 $70
    14" (36cm) plastic/vinyl, *Scarlett Series*, 1992-1993 $125
    8" (20cm) hard plastic, 1999 $80
Carmen
    7" (18cm) composition, 1938-1943 $345
    9-11" (23-28cm) composition, boy and girl, 1938-1943 $325
    11" (28cm) composition, sleep eyes, 1937-1942 $375
    14" (36cm) composition, 1937-1942 $500
    17" (43cm) composition, 1939-1942 $700
    21" (53cm) composition, 1939-1942 $1,200 up
    14" (36cm) plastic/vinyl, Opera Series, 1983-1986 $100
Carmen Miranda
    10" (25cm) hard plastic, 1993 $90

Carnivale Doll
    14" (36cm) made for FAO Schwarz, 1991 *(see Special Dolls)* $200
Carnival in Rio
    21" (53cm) porcelain, 1989-1990 $ 450
Carnival in Venice
    21" (53cm) porcelain, 1990-1991 $500
Carnival Queen
    16" (41cm) plastic/vinyl CU Alexander Dinner, 1999 *(see Special Dolls)* $175
Caroline
    15" (38cm) vinyl, 1961-1962
        Checked Cotton Dress, #1305, 1962 $375
        Corduroy Pants Set, #4930, 1961 $400
        Dotted Swiss Sleeveless Dress, #4920, 1961 $400
        Embroidered Organdy Dress, #1310, 1962 $425
        Organdy Party Dress, #4925, 1961 $425
        Riding Outfit, #1312, 1962 $450
        Sailor Dress, #1307, 1962 $450
        Boxed Outfits for 15" (38cm) Doll
        Angora Jacket and Bonnet, #14-12, 1962 $175
        Coat, #14-18, 1962 $125
        Crepe Robe, #14-13, 1962 $95
        Dress with Bloomers, #14-7, #14-8, #14-9, #14-15, 1962 $125
        Flannel Pajamas, #49-8, 1961 $95
        Flannel Robe, #49-9, 1961 $95
        Nylon Party Dress, #49-15, 1961 $150
        Organdy Dress, #14-21, 1962 $150
        Overalls with Sweater, #14-10, 1962 $135
        Pajamas, #14-5, 1962 $95
        Pique Sleeveless Dress, #49-5, 1961 $110
        Robe, #14-6, 1962 $95
        Sailor Dress, #14-16, 1962 $150
        Smock with Leotard, #49-4, 1961 $135
        Snowsuit, #14-20, 1962 $135
        Tricot Pajamas, #49-6, 1961 $95
        Tricot Robe, #49-7, 1961 $95
        White Slippers and Socks, #49-1, 1961 $35
        In boy hairstyle (possibly John Jr.), undressed $450
        In case/wardrobe $1,400 up
Caroline
    8" (20cm) hard plastic, made for Belk & Leggett, 1993 *(see Special Dolls)* $100
    8" (20cm) hard plastic, Storyland trunk set, Neiman Marcus, 1993 *(see Special Dolls)* $250
    8" (20cm) hard plastic, World travel trunk set, Neiman Marcus, 1994 *(see Special Dolls)* $225
Carriage *(see Cinderella's Magic Carriage)*
Carrot Kate
    14" (36cm) plastic/vinyl, 1995 $155
Carrot Top
    21" (53cm) cloth, #80, 1967 $150
Caterpillar
    8" (20cm) workshop kit, Disney World Doll and Teddy Bear Convention, 1994 $65
    8" (20cm) hard plastic, 1995-1997 $80
Cat on a Hot Tin Roof
    10" (25cm) hard plastic, 1996 $85

Cats
    16" (41cm) cloth animals, 1930s $375 up
Century of Fashions
    14" & 18" (36 & 46cm) hard plastic, 1954 $1,600 up
Champs-Elysées
    21" (53cm) hard plastic, black lace gown over pink slip
                                                        $4,000 up
Charity
    8" (20cm) hard plastic, bent knee walker, *Americana
    Series*, #485, 1961 $1,800
Charlene
    18" (46cm) cloth/vinyl, African American baby, 1991-1992
                                                        $105
Charleston Girl
    10" (25cm) hard plastic, TJ Maxx, 1998 *(see Special
    Dolls)* $70
Charming Silk Victorian
    8" (20cm) hard plastic, 1999 $75
Chatterbox
24" (61cm) hard plastic/vinyl, has talking mechanism, 1961
    Floral Romper, #7950 $300
    Pique Dress, #7955 $325
Additional Boxed Outfits
    Coat and Hat, #79-25 $110
    Dress, #79-12 $125
    Pajamas, #79-10 $100
    Robe, #79-14 $95
    Ruffled Party Dress,#79-15 $125

    Taffeta Petticoat and Panties, #79-5 $50
Cheerleader
    8" (20cm) hard plastic, made for I Magnin, 1990
    (see Special Dolls) $75
    8" (20cm) hard plastic, *Americana Series*, red and white
    outfit, 1990-1991 $60
    8" (20cm) hard plastic, African American or white, royal
    blue outfit, *Americana Series*, 1992-1993 $60
    8" (20cm) hard plastic, *Wendy's Special Cheer*, 1998-1999
                                                        $80
    8" (20cm) Doll and Teddy Bear Expo West, 1998
    (see Special Dolls) $100
    8" (20cm) Doll and Teddy Bear Expo East, 1998
    (see Special Dolls) $100
Chef Alex
    8" (20cm) hard plastic, 1997-1998 $85
Cherie
    18" (46cm) hard plastic, white satin gown, pink coat,
    Me and My Shadow Series, 1954 $1,500 up
Cherry Blossom
    14" (36cm) plastic/vinyl, 1995 $140
Cherry Girl
    8" (20cm) hard plastic, 1999 $70
Cherry Twins
    8" (20cm) hard plastic, bent knee walker, #388E, 1957
                                                        $1,000 each
    8" (20cm) hard plastic, bent knee, 1999 $130 pair

As part of the nostalgic line of dolls, The Alexander Doll Company reissued the bent-knee dolls with this set of *Cherry Twins* in 1999, first made in the late 1950s. *A. Glenn Mandeville Collection.*

1955 8-inch (20cm) hard plastic *Cinderella. Sara Tondini Collection. Photo by Zehr Photography.*

Cherub
9" (23cm) vinyl and latex, 1952	$225
18" (46cm) hard plastic head, cloth/vinyl, 1950s	$375
26" (66cm) hard plastic head, cloth/vinyl, 1950s	$400
12" (31cm) vinyl, 1960-1961	$300

Cherub Babies
cloth, 1930s	$475

Cheshire Cat
8" (20cm) hard plastic, MADC, 1996 *(see Special Dolls)*	$175
8" (20cm) hard plastic, 1996-1999	$60

Chess Board Quilt
cloth quilt made for *Alice in Wonderland Series*, 1998	$75

Child's Angel
8" (20cm) hard plastic, 1996	$70

Chile
8" (20cm) hard plastic, 1992	$65

China
7" (18cm) composition, 1936-1940	$300
9" (23cm) composition, 1935-1938	$325
8" (20cm) hard plastic, bent knee, #772, 1972	$110
8" (20cm) hard plastic, with *Maggie* smile face, bent knee, #772, 1972	$125
8" (20cm) hard plastic, straight legs, "Alex Mold", #0772, 1973; #572, 1974-1975	$75
8" (20cm) straight legs, 1976-1986	$70
8" (20cm) straight legs, 1987-1989	$70
8" (20cm) hard plastic, 1995	$70
8" (20cm) hard plastic, 1996-1997	$75

China Sun
10" (25cm) hard plastic, 1998-1999	$125

Chinese New Year
8" (20cm) hard plastic, pair of dolls, 1996-1998	$130
8" (20cm) hard plastic, set of 3 dolls with dragon, 1996-1998	$220

Christening Baby
11-13" (28-33cm) cloth/vinyl, 1951-1954	$100
16-19" (41-48cm)	$150

Christmas Angel *(see Tree Topper)*

Christmas Candy
14" (36cm) *Classic Dolls*, 1993	$120
8" (20cm) hard plastic, 1994	$65

Christmas Caroler
8" (20cm) hard plastic, 1997	$85

Christmas Caroling
10" (25cm) *Portrette Series*, 1992-1993	$120

Christmas Cookie
14" (36cm), 1992	$125

Christmas Eve
14" (36cm) *Classic Dolls*, 1994	$100
8" (20cm) hard plastic, 1995	$75

Christmas Morn'
8" (20cm) hard plastic, Collector's United, 1999 *(see Special Dolls)*	$70

Churchill, Sir Winston
18" (46cm) hard plastic, 1953	$1,700

Cinderella
7-8" (18-20cm) composition, 1935-1944	$295
9" (23cm) composition, 1936-1941	$375
13" (34cm) composition, 1935-1937	$400
14" (36cm) composition, 1939	$450
15" (38cm) composition, 1935-1937	$450
16-18" (41-46cm) composition, 1935-1939	$500 up
14" (36cm) hard plastic, ball gown, 1950-1951	$800
14" (36cm) hard plastic, "poor" outfit, 1950-1951	$650
18" (46cm) hard plastic, 1950-1951	$800
21" (53cm) hard plastic, 1950	$1,000
7-1/2-8" (19-20cm) hard plastic, straight leg walker, #492, 1955	$975
12" (31cm) hard plastic, *Lissy* face, "poor" outfit, #1230, 1966	$800
12" (31cm) hard plastic, *Lissy* face, ball gown, #1235, 1966	$800
12" (31cm) hard plastic, *Lissy* face, window box with ball gown and poor outfit, #1240, 1966	$1,300
14" (36cm) plastic/vinyl, "poor" outfit, 1967-1992	$85
14" (36cm) blue gown with velvet bodice, outfit only, FAO Schwarz exclusive, 1968	$250
14" (36cm) plastic/vinyl, dressed in pink, 1970-1983	$100
14" (36cm) plastic/vinyl, blue ball gown, 1984-1986	$100
14" (36cm) Trunk set, made for Enchanted Doll House, 1985 *(see Special Dolls)*	$275

14" (36cm) white or blue ball gown, *Classic Dolls*, 1987-1991 $140

14" (36cm) gift set with poor outfit, made for Disney Catalog, 1994 *(see Special Dolls)* $175

14" (36cm) gift set with two gowns, made for Disney Catalog, 1995 *(see Special Dolls)* $200

10" (25cm) Disney World®, 1989 *(see Special Dolls)* $700 up

10" (25cm) *Portrette Series*, 1990-1991 $95

8" (20cm) hard plastic, *Storyland Dolls*, 1990-1992 $70

8" (20cm) hard plastic, "poor" outfit, 1990-1991 $65

8" (20cm) hard plastic, "poor" outfit, in blue with black stripes, 1992 $65

14" (36cm) white, gold ball gown, 1992 $140

14" (36cm) white gown, 1996 $125

21" (53cm) plastic/vinyl, 1995 $350

8" (20cm) hard plastic, blue ball gown, 1992-1994 $70

8" (20cm) hard plastic, topsy turvy doll-poor and rich outfits, 1995 $130

8" (20cm) hard plastic, pink ball gown, 1995-1999 $70

8" (20cm) hard plastic, "poor" outfit, 1997-1998 $75

8" (20cm) hard plastic, TJ Maxx, 1997 *(see Special Dolls)* $70

8" (20cm) hard plastic, made for Disney Store Gallery, 1999 *(see Special Dolls)* $80

Cinderella's Footmouse
    8" (20cm) hard plastic, 1999 $100

Cinderella's Magic Carriage 1999 $175

Cinderella's Prince
    8" (20cm) hard plastic, 1997 $65

Cinderella's Wedding
    8" (20cm) hard plastic, 1999 $90

Cissette
Cissette introduced in 1957. 10" (25cm) tall, high heel feet Jointed at the knee, hips, shoulder and neck. Prices for pristine dolls in original costumes, including undergarments and shoes. Allow more for mint-in-box, those in rare costumes and those with fancy hairdos.

    Accessory Set, #0991, 1957 $125

    Aqua Cotton Dress with Lace Collar, #722, 1959 $375

    Aqua Taffeta Day Dress with Hat, #918, 1957 $425

    Basic Doll in Chemise, #900, 1957; #800, 1958; #700, 1959; #800, 1960; #700, 1962-1963 $300

    Basic Doll in Slip, #801, 1958; #701, 1959; #801, 1960 $325

    Beauty Queen with Trophy, #710, 1963 $350

    Black Sheath Gown with Tulle Skirt, #974, 1957 $600

    Black Skirt with Striped Blouse, #837, 1958 $425

    Black Velvet Fitted Gown, # 973, 1957 $600

    Black Velvet Sheath and Pink Hat, #842, 1958 $575

    Camellia Ball Gown and Cape, #873, 1958 $650

    Coat with Dress and Hat, #748, 1963 $375

1963 10-inch (25cm) *Cissette Gift Set* with wigs. Very hard to find complete with all accessories and wrist tag. *Marge Meisinger Collection.*

Corduroy Rain Coat with Dress and Hat, #851, 1958 $375

Cotton Dress with Square Neckline, #913, 1957 $350

Cotton Dress with Embroidered Ruffles, #822, 1958 $350

Cotton Dress with Pique Blouse, #811, 1961 $375

Cotton Floral Print Dress with Hat, #811, 1958 $375

Cotton Shirtwaist Dress and Hat, #930, 1957; #813, 1958 $375

Denim Pants Set, #731, 1963 $425

Gold Gown with Net Stole, #824, 1960 $725

Gold Net over Taffeta Gown, 1961 $750

Gold Tulle Dancing Gown, #979, 1957 $750

Houndstooth Suit, #746, 1963 $575

Jumper Dress with Contrasting Blouse, #919, 1957; #839, 1958 $450

Lace Cocktail Dress, #731, 1959 $600

Lace Ruffled Gown, pink, blue or yellow, #745, 1963 $600

Lavender Taffeta Dress and Jacket, #943, 1957 $425

Light Blue Cotton Dress with Braid Trim, #810, 1958 $475

Navy Taffeta Dress with Pink Organdy Stole, #820, 1958 $475

Navy Taffeta Dress with Pink Sleeves, #912, 1957 $450

Navy Taffeta Dress with White Cape, #941, 1957
$450

Pin Dot Cotton Dress with Hat, #909, 1957 $400

Pink Nylon Checked Dress, #723, 1959 $500

Pink Organdy Dress with Rhinestones on Bodice, 1959
$575

Pink Ruffled Tulle Gown, #831, 1960 $650

Pink Satin Gown with Tulle Cape, #732, 1959 $700

Pleated Cotton Dress with Veiled Hat, #830, 1958
$400

Red and White Sun Suit with Skirt, #806, 1961 $425

Red Cotton Skirt with Black Blouse, #815, 1958 $575

Red Taffeta Dress with Polka Dot Sleeves, #910, 1957
$400

Satin Gown with Sequin Bodice, #840, 1963 $650

Satin Theater Dress and Coat, #976, 1957 $575

Sheer Cotton Dress with Straw Cloche, #821, 1958
$475

Silk Gauze Dress with Flowered Hat, #838, 1958
$475

Skirt, Blouse and Shorts Set, #732, 1963 $425

Taffeta Bathing Suit, #800, 1961 $350

Taffeta Cocktail Dress with Hat, #940, 1957 $450

Taffeta Cocktail Dress with Jacket and Hat, #841, 1958
$475

Taffeta Dress with Puff Sleeves and Pleated Organdy Back Inset, #916, 1957 $475

Toreador Pants and Lace Blouse, #905, 1957; #807, 1958 $375

Trousseau Window Box with Extra Wigs, #790, 1963
$800 up

Tulle Ruffled Gown, #745, 1962 $650

White Coat with Taffeta Dress and Fur Hat, #875, 1958
$575

White Jacket with Red Pleated Skirt, #832, 1958 $450

Yachting Slacks Set, #808, 1958 $475

Yellow Satin and Tulle Gown, #830, 1961 $750

Yellow Striped Cabana Beach Outfit, #805, 1958
$425

Bathing Suit $350

Cotton Dress and Hat $425

Corduroy Coat and Hat $425

Dotted Sheer Organza Dress $450

Evening Gown $600 up

Felt Coat and Hat $375

Formals $600 up

Fur Coat with Hood $375

Lace Corselette $125

Lace Petticoat and Panties $50

Nightgown $75

Pant outfit $400

Queen (see Queen)

Rain Coat and Hat $375

Robe $75

Shorts Set with Jacket $400

Street dresses $375 up

Taffeta Dress $400 up

Wool Skirt with Silk Blouse $475

Trousseau set in fiberboard case, FAO Schwarz exclusive,

1958 $800 up

Trousseau set in plastic window case, FAO Schwarz exclusive, 1957 $800 up

Coral and Leopard travel ensemble, also available as African American, 1997-1998 $100

Coral and Leopard travel ensemble, made for Bloomingdales, 1997 (see Special Dolls) $100

Ebony and Ivory Houndstooth suit, also available as African American, 1997-1998 $100

Café Rose and Ivory cocktail dress, also available as African American, 1997-1998 $100

Onyx Velvet Lace gala gown and coat, also available as African American, 1997-1998 $100

Red Sequin gown, 1998 $150

Daisy Resort ensemble, 1998 $150

Tea Rose Cocktail ensemble, also available as African American, 1998 $150

Gardenia Gala ballgown, 1998 $140

Calla Lilly Evening column and bolero, 1998 $200

Barcelona ensemble, 1999 $160

Cissy

20-21" (51-53cm) introduced with mature fashion body, jointed elbows, knees and high heel feet in 1955. The Cissy face had been used previously on other dolls. Hundreds of outfits were produced for Cissy, not all appear in the catalog reprints. The Cissy doll body is subject to seam cracks on legs and neck, one should inspect the doll carefully before purchase. Many dolls have lost their cheek color. Prices are for mint dolls, with good face color in original costumes

Aqua Taffeta Dress with Ivory Satin Coat, #2021, 1956
$575

Black and White Checked Suit, #2027, 1956 $550

Black Taffeta Cocktail Dress with Lace, #2091, 1955
$625

Black Velvet Gown with Fur Stole, #2173, 1957 $800

Black Velvet Torso Gown, #2043, 1956 $775

Blue Satin Gown with Rhinestones, #2097, 1955
$1,000

Champagne Satin Gown with Muff, #2094, 1955
$1,000

Cotton Dress with Straw Hat, #2211, 1958 $475

Dotted Tulle Ball Gown, #2260, 1959 $850

Floral Print Cotton Dress, #2232, 1958; #2222, 1958
$425

Gold Lace Skirt with Green Blouse, #2115, 1959
$475

Gold Taffeta Gown with Matching Short Coat, #2098, 1955 $900

Heavy Faille Gown with Lace Overlay, #2172, 1957
$1,000

Lavender Skirt with Striped Shirt, #2114, 1957 $475

Lavender Tulle Ball Gown, 1961 $1,200

Mauve Taffeta Torso Gown with Multi-Colored Bow, #2100, 1955 $900

Moire Shirtwaist Dress, #2218, 1959 $475

Navy Taffeta Cocktail Dress with Jacket, #2084, 1955
$575

Navy Taffeta Cocktail Dress with White Organdy Cape, #2141, 1957 $475

This *Cissy* was never produced. The doll was made for this Yardley of London ad for women's magazines in the mid to late 1950s. *A. Glenn Mandeville Collection.*

Below: Late 1957 21-inch (53cm) all original *Cissy* dolls. Hatboxes are from the early 1950s. *A. Glenn Mandeville Collection.*

Nylon Dress with Lace Bodice, #2230, 1958 $500
Organdy Party Dress with Rosebuds and Hat,
#2035, 1956 $650
Pink Camellia Gown, #2283, 1958 $850
Pink Dotted Nylon Gown, #2160, 1957 $800
Pink Organdy and Pleated Nylon Gown, #2245, 1961
$875
Pink Tulle Ankle Length Dress, #2025, 1956 $850
Polished Cotton Dress with Lace Trim, #2130, 1957
$475
Purple Velvet Torso Gown, 1957 $900
Red Cotton Dress with Striped Blouse, #2083, 1955
$500
Red Dotted Organdy Dress and Hat, #2019, 1956
$525
Red Taffeta Gown with Tulle Stole, #2285, 1958
$950
Rose Taffeta Torso Gown, 1958 $900
Satin Ball Gown with Fur Stole, #2041, 1956 $950
Satin Cocktail Dress with Satin Stole, #2120, 1959
$550
Satin Cocktail Dress with Tulle Stole, #2252, 1958
$550
Shell Pink Torso Gown, #2036, 1956 $900
Striped Cotton Shirtwaist Dress, #2014, 1956 $500
Taffeta Cocktail Dress with Matching Jacket,
#2143, 1957 $550
Taffeta Cocktail Dress with Pillbox Hat, #2012, 1956
$575
Taffeta Cocktail Dress with Velvet Bolero, #2017, 1956
$600
Taffeta Dress with Cotton Sleeves, #2110, 1957 $550
Tulle Gown with Floral Appliques, #2282, 1958
$1,000
Velvet Sheath Dress, #2231, 1958 $600
White Organdy Gown Trimmed in Lace and Red Roses,
#2095, 1955 $1,200
Yachting Slacks Set, #2205, 1958 $600
Wool Chemise Dress, #2233, 1958 $550
Yellow Floral Dress, #2120, 1957 $475
Basic Doll Wearing Chemise, #2100, 1957; #2200,
1958 $350
Accessory Set $175
Coat and Hat $400 up
Cotton Dress $400 up
Gowns $700 up
Lingerie and Corsets $250 up
Overalls and Blouse $550
Nightgown $400
Pant Suits $375 up
Queen (see Queen)
Skirt Sets $450 up
Taffeta Dress $400 up
Trunk with wardrobe, FAO Schwarz exclusive, 1957
$1,500 up
Yardley Ads, 1956-1957 $15-$175
Coral and Leopard travel ensemble, 1996 $300
Ebony and Ivory Houndstooth suit, also available as
African American, 1996 $425

Café Rose and Ivory cocktail dress, also available as
African American, 1996 $400
Aquamarine evening column and coat, 1996 $300
Onyx Velvet Lace gala gown and coat, 1996 $375
Pearl Embroidered Lace bridal gown, 1996 $550
Red Sequin gown, 1996 $375
Daisy Resort ensemble, 1997 $350
Tea Rose Cocktail ensemble, also available as African
American, 1997 $275
Gardenia Gala ballgown, 1997 $275
Gardenia Gala, blonde hair, MADC, 1997 *(see Special
Dolls)* $350
Peony and Butterfly wedding gown, 1997 $375
Calla Lilly Evening column and bolero, 1997 $550
Secret Armoire trunk set, 1997-1998 $600
Paris ensemble, 1998 $450
Barcelona ensemble, also available as African American,
1998 $450
Milan ensemble, 1998 $450
Venice ensemble, 1998 $450
Budapest ensemble, 1998 $475
Cissy St. John, Neiman Marcus, 1998 *(see Special Dolls)*
$450

Jessica McClintock ensemble, 1999 $450
Fernando Sanchez ensemble, 1999 $450
Josie Natori ensemble, 1999 $450
Anna Sui ensemble, 1999 $450
Linda Allard for Ellen Tracy ensemble, 1999 $450
Dana Buchman ensemble, 1999 $450
James Purcell ensemble, 1999 $450
Badgley Mischka ensemble, 1999 $450
Carolina Herrera ensemble, 1999 $450
Mark Bouwer ensemble, 1999 $450
Madame Alexander ensemble, 1999 $450
Arnold Scaasi ensemble, Danbury Mint, 1999 *(see Special
Dolls)* $450
Lilly Pulitzer ensemble, MADC, 1999 *(see Special Dolls)*
$550

Dressed as a Fortune Teller, Collector's United, 1999
(see Special Dolls) $475
Holiday Cissy, 1999 $300
Accessory Pak, exclusive for MADC *Cissy* Breakfast,
1999 $45

Cissy Godey Bride
21" (53cm) porcelain, 1993-1994 $500
Cissy by Scaasi
21" (53cm) made for FAO Schwarz, 1990 *(see Special
Dolls)* $350
Civil War
18" (46cm) hard plastic, *Glamour Girls Series,* 1953
$1,400
Clara & The Nutcracker
14" (36cm) plastic/vinyl, 1992 $100
Clarabelle Clown
19" (48cm) 1951-1953 $475
29" (74cm) $650
49" (124cm) $900

A regal late 1950s
21-inch (53cm)
*Cissy Queen. A.
Glenn Mandeville
Collection.*

Lucky for collectors, *Cissy* made a
return in the late 1990s. Every detail
was perfect. She was still 21 inches
(53cm) tall, but this time had a vinyl
head. *A. Glenn Mandeville Collection.*

A stunning 1996 *Cissy* is ready for a day of shopping. Dog is by the Annalee Doll Company. *A. Glenn Mandeville Collection.*

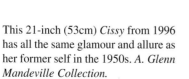

This 21-inch (53cm) *Cissy* from 1996 has all the same glamour and allure as her former self in the 1950s. *A. Glenn Mandeville Collection.*

A designer line of *Cissy* dolls were part of the exciting 1999 line. This doll is by Dana Buchman for The Alexander Doll Company. *A. Glenn Mandeville Collection.*

In 1998, *Cissy* took a ride on the Orient Express! *A. Glenn Mandeville Collection.*

Dealers were sent a special mailing about *Holiday Cissy* in late 1999. She was a spectacular doll that sold out quickly. *A. Glenn Mandeville Collection.*

Madame Alexander Doll Club former president Earl Meisinger was presented with this prototype 8-inch (20cm) Coca-Cola doll at the 1997 Premiere. *Marge Meisinger Collection.*

Clara's Party Dress
    8" (20cm) hard plastic, 1995 $65

Classic Riviera Day
    16" (41cm) outfit only, 1999 $50

Classic Riviera Night
    16" (41cm) plastic/vinyl, 1999 $170

Claudette
    10" (25cm) *Portrette Series*, 1988-1989 $95

Cleopatra
    12" (31cm) *Portraits of History Series*, 1980-1985
        $70
    10" (25cm) hard plastic, 1996 $100

Cleveland, Frances
    14" (36cm) plastic/vinyl, 4th set, *First Ladies Series*,
    1985-1987 $100

Clothing for Children
    Manufactured under the name Madame Alexander Tots,
    Inc., 1964-1966 $85-$150

Clover Kid
    7" (18cm) composition, 1935-1936 $350

Clown
    8" (20cm) hard plastic, painted face, *Americana Series*,
    1990-1992 $65
    Pin workshop kit, MADC exclusive, 1998 $15

Coca-Cola Celebrates American Aviation
    10" (25cm) hard plastic, 1998-1999 $165
    12" (31cm) porcelain, Danbury Mint, 1999 *(see Special*
    Dolls) $150

Coca-Cola Carhop
    10" (25cm) hard plastic, 1997-1999 $115
    12" (31cm) porcelain, Danbury Mint, 1999 *(see Special*
    Dolls) $150

Coca-Cola Fantasy
    10" (25cm) hard plastic, also available in African
    American, 1997-1998 $155

Coca-Cola Nostalgia
    16" (41cm) plastic/vinyl, 1999 $220

Coca-Cola Victorian Calendar Doll
    10" (25cm) hard plastic, 1998-1999 $165

Coca-Cola Winter Fun
    8" (20cm) hard plastic, 1998-1999 $100

Coco
    21" (53cm) plastic/vinyl, 1966 only, wearing floral print
    sheath #2010 $2,500 up
    Wearing blue and white striped dress #2015 $2,500 up
    Wearing black and orange suit #2020 $2,600 up
    Wearing black and white jumpsuit with yellow coat #2026
        $2,500 up
    Wearing pink brocade gown #2030 $2,400 up
Additional Boxed Outfits
    Pink, blue and green color block sheath #20-12 $550 up
    Red coat #20-13 $400 up
    Blue cotton dress with cape #20-14 $625 up
    Long sari dress #20-16 $600 up
    Black and white tweed suit #20-17 $550 up
    Plaid slack set with tan fur jacket #20-23 $650 up
    Blue formal gown with white fur jacket #20-27 $675 up

    10" (25cm) *Portrette Series*, 1989-1992 $75
    16" (41cm) plastic/vinyl, Travel Abroad Set with Dog,
    1997-1998 $200
    16" (41cm) plastic/vinyl, Ultimate Travel Wardrobe Set
    with Dog, 1997-1998 $400
    16" (41cm) outfit only, Capri Sightseeing, 1997-1998
        $100
    16" (41cm) outfit only, Cocktail Enchantment, 1997-1998
        $120
    16" (41cm) plastic/vinyl, Belle Epoque Set, 1998
        $300

Colleen
    10" (25cm) *Portrette Series*, 1988 $90

Colonial
    7" (18cm) composition, 1937-1938 $300
    9" (23cm) composition, 1936-1939 $325

Colonial Girl
    8" (20cm) hard plastic, bent knee walker, #389, 1962-1964
        $350
    Outfit only for 8" (20cm) doll, #0389, 1962-1963
        $150

Columbian Sailor
    12" (31cm) UFDC Luncheon, 1993 *(see Special Dolls)*
        $225

Columbine
    8" (20cm) hard plastic, 1995 $65

Columbus, Christopher
    8" (20cm) hard plastic, 1992 $125

Comedienne
    10" (25cm) hard plastic, 1996 $90

Computer Age Wendy
    8" (20cm) hard plastic, *Through the Decades Collection*,
    1999 $70

Confederate Officer
    12" (31cm) *Scarlett Series*, 1991-1992 $80

Congratulations
    8" (20cm) hard plastic, 1998 $80

Cookie
    19" (48cm) composition/cloth, 1938-1940 $600

Coolidge, Grace
    14" (36cm) plastic/vinyl, 6th set, *First Ladies Series*,
    1989-1990 $100

Coppertone Beach Set
    8" (20cm) hard plastic, 1998-1999 $130

Cornelia
    16" (41cm) cloth/felt, 1930s $725
    21" (53cm) dressed in pink with full cape, *Portrait Series*,
    1972 $425
    pink with 3/4-length jacket (green eyed), 1973 $350
    blue with black trim, 1974 $350
    rose red with black trim and hat, 1975 $325
    pink with black trim and hat, 1976 $300
    blue with full cape, 1978 $300

Cossack
    8" (20cm) hard plastic, 1989-1991 $70

Country Christmas
    14" (36cm) *Classic Dolls*, 1991-1992 $150
    8" (20cm) hard plastic, 1999 $75

Country Cousin
    10" (25cm) cloth, 1940s $600
    26" (63cm) cloth, 1940s $675
    30" (76cm) cloth, 1940s $800
    16-1/2" (42cm) vinyl, 1958 $400

Courtney and Friends
    8" (20cm) hard plastic with a 26" (66cm) porcelain Günzel
    doll, 1992 $750

Cousin Grace
    8" (20cm) hard plastic, bent knee walker, #632, 1956;
    #432-1957 $1,800

Cousin Karen
    8" (20cm) hard plastic, bent knee walker, #630, 1956
                                     $1,500

Cousin Marie
    8" (20cm) hard plastic, bent knee walker, #465, 1963
                                     $1,100

Cousin Mary
    8" (20cm) hard plastic, bent knee walker, #462, 1963
                                     $1,100

Cowardly Lion
    8" (20cm) hard plastic, *Wizard of Oz Series,* 1993-1999
                                     $70

Cowboy
    8" (20cm) hard plastic, bent knee, *Americana Series*,
    #732, 1967-1969 $400
    8" (20cm) hard plastic, MADC, 1987 *(see Special Dolls)*
                                     $400

Cowgirl
    8" (20cm) hard plastic, bent knee, *Americana & Storyland
    Dolls*, #724, 1966-1970 $400
    10" (25cm) *Portrette Series*, 1990-1991 $80

Crackle *(see Snap, Crackle, Pop)*

Crayola Blue
    8" (20cm) hard plastic, also available in African American,
    1999 $70

Crayola Green
    8" (20cm) hard plastic, also available in African American,
    1999 $70

Crayola Red
    8" (20cm) hard plastic, also available in African American,
    1999 $70

Crayola Yellow
    8" (20cm) hard plastic, also available in African American,
    1999 $70

Cream Lace *(see Tree Topper)*

Crete
    8" (20cm) hard plastic, straight legs, 1987 $70

Crockett, Davy (Boy or Girl)
    8" (20cm) hard plastic, 1955 $700

Croatia
    8" (20cm) hard plastic, *International Series*, 1994
                                     $65

Cry Dolly
    14-16" (36-41cm) vinyl, has layette, 1953 $200
    14" (36cm), 16" (41cm), 19" (48cm) swimsuit $125-$185
    16-19" (41-48cm) vinyl, dress or romper $150-$185

Crystal Blue Enchantment
    10" (25cm) Home Shopping Club, 1998 *(see Special
    Dolls)* $180

Cuba
    8" (20cm) hard plastic, 1995 $70

Cuddly
    10-1/2" (27cm) cloth, 1942-1944 $350
    17" (43cm) cloth, 1942-1944 $400

Cupid
    8" (20cm) hard plastic, 1997-1999 $80

Curly Locks
    7-1/2-8" (19-20cm) hard plastic, straight leg walker,
    #472, 1955 $900
    8" (20cm) hard plastic, straight legs, *Storyland Dolls*,
    1987-1988 $80
    8" (20cm) hard plastic, Home Shopping Club, 1998 *(see
    Special Dolls)* $80

CU Salutes Broadway
    8" (20cm) hard plastic, Collector's United, 1997 *(see
    Special Dolls)* $190

Cute Little Baby
    14" (36cm) cloth/vinyl, 1994-1995 $80-90
    Dressed doll with layette and basket, 1994-1995 $200

Cynthia
    15" (38cm) hard plastic, African American, #1530,
    1952; #1531, 1953 $800
    18" (46cm) hard plastic, African American, #1830,
    1952; #1831, 1953 $975
    23" (58cm) hard plastic, African American, #2330,
    1952; #2231, 1953 $1,225 up
    Outfit can be blue, pink, yellow or white on all of the
    above.

Cyrano
    8" (20cm) hard plastic, *Storyland Dolls*, 1994 $65

Czarina Alexandra
    8" (20cm) hard plastic, 1999 $80

Czechoslovakia
    7" (18cm) composition, 1935-1937 $275
    8" (20cm) hard plastic, bent knee, #764, 1972 $110
    8" (20cm) hard plastic, straight legs, "Alex Mold",
    #0764, 1973; #564, 1974-1975 $70
    8" (20cm) hard plastic, straight legs, 1976-1987 $60
    8" (20cm) hard plastic, white face, 1985-1987 $60
    8" (20cm) hard plastic, re-introduced 1992-1993 $60

Daffy Down Dilly
   8" (20cm) straight legs, *Storyland Dolls*, 1986 (Wendy
   Face) $75
   8" (20cm) *Storyland Dolls*, 1987-1989 (Maggie Face)
                                            $75

Dahl, Arlene *(see Pink Champagne)*
Daisy
   10" (25cm) *Portrette Series*, 1987-1989 $75
   10" (25cm) made for Home Shopping Club, 1998
   (see Special Dolls) $100
Danielle Angel
   8" (20cm) made for Belk Leggett Stores, 1995 *(see Special
   Dolls)* $100
Danish
   7" (18cm) composition, 1937-1941 $325
   9" (23cm) composition, 1938-1940 $350
Dare, Virginia
   9" (23cm) composition, 1940-1941 $425
Darlene
   18" (46cm) cloth/vinyl, 1991-1992 $105
David
   8" (20 cm) hard plastic, 1953-1954 Bible Children
                                            $7,000
David & Diana
   8" (20cm) made for FAO Schwarz, 1989 *(see Special
   Dolls)* $200
David Copperfield
   16" (41cm) cloth, Dicken's character, 1934 $835
   7" (18cm) composition, 1936-1938 $450
   14" (36cm) composition, 1938 $750
David Quack-A-Field
   cloth/felt, 1930s $750
David, The Little Rabbi
   8" (20cm) made for Celia's Dolls, 1991 *(see Special Dolls)*
                                            $80
David Twistail
   cloth/felt, 1930s $750
Day of Week Dolls
   7" (18cm) composition, 1935-1940 $325
   9-11" (23-28cm) composition, 1936-1938 $350
   13" (33cm) composition, 1939 $450
Dazzling Emerald
   16" (41cm) porcelain, 1998 $300
Dear America Dolls
   18" (46cm) vinyl, 1999 $80
Dearest
   12" (31cm) vinyl baby, 1962-1964 $140
Deborah Ballerina
   21" (53cm) hard plastic, 1949-1951 $5,000 up
Deborah Bride
   21" (53cm) hard plastic, 1949-1951 $5,000 up

Debutante
   18" (46cm) hard plastic, 1953 (*Maggie*) $1,250 up
December
   14" (36cm) Classic Dolls, 1989 $100
DeFoe, Dr.
   14" (36cm) composition, 1937-1939 $1,700
Degas
   21" (53cm) composition, Portrait, 1945-1946 $2,200
Degas Ballerina (aka The Star)
   10" (25cm) hard plastic, 1998-1999 $90
Degas Dance Lesson
   14" (36cm) plastic/vinyl, *Classic Dolls*, 1994 $100
Degas Girl
   14" (36cm) plastic/vinyl, *Portrait Children & Fine Art
   Series*, 1967-1987 $80
Delilah
   8" (20cm) hard plastic, 1995 $80
Denmark
   10" (25cm) hard plastic, #747, 1962 $700
   8" (20cm) hard plastic, bent knee, #769, 1970-1972
                                            $100
   8" (20cm) hard plastic, straight legs, "Alex Mold",
   #0769, 1973; #569, 1974-1975 $70
   8" (20cm) hard plastic, white face, 1985-1987 $60
   8" (20cm) hard plastic, re-introduced 1991 only $65
Devon Horse Show
   8" (20cm) hard plastic, bent knee walker, #541, 1958
                                            $750
Diamond Beauty
   21" (53cm) limited to 715 dolls, 1998 $1,000
Diamond Lil
   10" (25cm) MADC, 1993 *(see Special Dolls)* $325
Diamond Pixie
   8" (20cm) made for MADC, 1998 *(see Special Dolls)*
                                            $150
Diamond Princess
   10" (25cm) hard plastic, 1998 $150
Dian
   8" (20cm) hard plastic, made for Collectors United,
   1995 *(see Special Dolls)* $125
Diana's Sunday Social
   8" (20cm) *Anne of Green Gables Series*, 1995 $75
   14" (36cm) *Anne of Green Gables Series*, 1994 $110
Diana's Tea Dress
   14" (36cm) Anne of Green Gables Series, 1993 (doll and
   tea set) $125
Diana's Trunk Set
   Anne of Green Gables Series, 1993 (doll and wardrobe)
                                            $250
   Anne of Green Gables Series, 1994 (doll and wardrobe)
   costume change $250
   14" (36cm) Winter coat, 1993, pink $50
   14" (36cm) Nightgown, 1993 $50
   14" (36cm) Winter coat, 1994, purple $50
   14" (36cm) School outfit, 1994 $50
Dick and Jane
   8" (20cm) pair, made for FAO Schwarz, 1995 *(see Special
   Dolls)* $150

Late 1930s 16-1/2-inch (42cm) set of the *Dionne Quints*. All composition with sleep eyes and human hair wigs. *Marge Meisinger Collection.*

Dickinson, Emily
14" (36cm) *Classic Dolls*, 1989	$100

Dicksie & Ducksie
cloth/felt, 1930s	$675

Dilly Dally Sally
7" (18cm) composition, 1937-1942	$325
9" (23cm) composition, 1938-1939	$350

Ding Dong Dell
7" (18cm) composition, 1937-1942	$325

Dinner at Eight
10" (25cm) *Portrette Series*, 1989-1991	$70

Dinosaur
8" (20cm) *Americana Series*, 1993-1994	$55

Dion, Celine
10" (25cm) hard plastic, 1999	$130

Dionne Quints

Original mint or very slight crazing.

7-1/2-8" (19-20cm) composition toddlers, molded hair, painted eyes, 1935-1939 — $300 each / $1,225 set

7-1/2-8" (19-20cm) composition toddlers, wigs and painted eyes, 1938-1939 — $300 each / $1225 set

7-1/2-8" (19-20cm) composition babies, wigs or molded hair, 1935-1939 — $325 each / $1650 set

7-1/2" (19cm) composition baby, molded hair in individual wicker basket — $650 up

7-1/2" (19cm) composition babies in house with furniture, 1936 — $2,000 up

11" (28cm) composition toddlers, wigs and sleep eyes, 1935-1938 — $375 each / $1,900 set

11" (28cm) composition toddlers, molded hair and sleep eyes, 1937-1938 — $375 each / $1,900 set

11" (28cm) composition toddlers, wigs and sleep eyes, 1936 — $375 each / $1,900 set

11" (28cm) composition with wigs in wicker basket — $2,000 up

14" (36cm) composition toddlers, 1937-1938 — $475 each / $2,400 set

14" (36cm) cloth body, composition, 1938 — $525 each / $2,650 set

16" (41cm) all cloth, 1935-1936 — $875 each

16-17" (41-43cm) composition toddlers, 1937-1939 — $650 each / $3,300 set

17" (43cm) cloth body, composition, 1938 — $550 each / $2,800 set

19"-20"(48-51cm) composition toddlers, 1936-1939 — $725 each / $3,700 set

22" (56cm) cloth/composition, 1935-1936 — $700 each

24" (61cm) all cloth, 1935-1936 — $1,200 each

Furniture and accessories for 7-1/2-8" (19-20cm) dolls, 1930s
Basket for 5 dolls	$250
Bathtub with washcloths, soap and robes for 5 dolls	
	$375
Bed for 5 dolls	$275
Carousel for 5 dolls	$450
Chair for 5 dolls	$350
Crib for 1 doll	$125
Crib for 5 dolls	$325
Ferris Wheel for 5 dolls	$500
Glider for 5 dolls	$325
High Chair for 1 doll	$150
High Chair for 5 dolls	$375
Kiddie Car for 5 dolls	$300
Lawn Swing for 5 dolls	$325
Low Chair for 1 doll	$150
Playpen for 5 dolls	$325
Quint-O-Bile for 5 dolls	$325
Scooter for 5 dolls	$275
Seesaw for 5 dolls	$325
Table and chairs set	$325
Tricycle for 1 doll	$150
Wagon for 5 dolls	$375

8" (20cm) hard plastic, 1998, individual dolls $85
8" (20cm) hard plastic, 1998, all 5 dolls with carousel
$500

Dolls of the Month
7-8" (18-20cm) composition, 1936-1938 $375
Dolly
8" (20cm) *Storyland Dolls*, 1988-1989 $75
8" (20cm) hard plastic, made for Home Shopping Club, 1998 *(see Special Dolls)* $80
Dolly Dryper
11" (28cm) vinyl, 1952 with layette $325
Dolly Levi
10" (25cm) hard plastic, 1994 $85
Dominican Republic
8" (20cm) straight legs, 1986-1988 $65
Dormouse
8" (20cm) hard plastic, 1998-1999 $90
Dorothy
8" (20cm) hard plastic, Storyland, *Wizard of Oz Series*, 1991-present $60
8" (20cm) hard plastic (Emerald City), mid-year release, 1994 $150
14" (36cm) all blue, white check dress, 1990-1993
$85
14" (36cm) vinyl, 1996 $120
Dottie Dumbunnie
cloth/felt, 1930s $835
Dream Dance Blue
10" (25cm) hard plastic, 1999 $100

Dream Dance Pink
10" (25cm) hard plastic, 1999 $100
Dressed for the Opera
18" (46cm) hard plastic, 1953 $1,750
Dress Stand
for 10" (25cm), 1996-1998 $20
Dressed Like Daddy
8" (20cm), hard plastic, 1995-1997 $65
Dressed Like Mommy
8" (20cm), hard plastic, 1995-1998 $65
Drucilla
14" (36cm) MADC, 1992 *(see Special Dolls)* $185
Drum Majorette
7-1/2-8" (19-20cm) hard plastic, straight leg walker, #482, 1955 $925
Dude Ranch
7 1/2-8" (19-20cm) hard plastic, *Wendy Visits a Dude Ranch*, #449, 1955 $750
8" (20cm) hard plastic, bent knee walker, #570, 1956
$750
Dudley Do-Right & Nell
8" (20cm) hard plastic, 1999 $180 pair
Dumplin' Baby
20-24" (51-61cm) 1957-1958 $225
Dutch
7" (18cm) composition, 1935-1939 $325
9" (23cm) composition boy or girl, 1936-1941 $375
8" (20cm) hard plastic boy*, bent knee walker, #777, 1964-1965 $150
8" (20cm) hard plastic, bent knee, #777, 1965-1972
$95
8" (20cm) hard plastic, straight legs, "Alex Mold", #0777, 1973 $70
8" (20cm) hard plastic girl*, bent knee walker, #491, 1961; #391, 1962-1963; #791, 1964-1965 $150
Outfit only for 8" (20cm) doll, #0391, 1962-1963
$60
8" (20cm) hard plastic, bent knee walker, Maggie smile face, 1962-1963 $160
8" (20cm) hard plastic, bent knee, #791, 1965-1972
$95
8" (20cm) hard plastic, straight legs, "Alex Mold", #0791, 1973 $70
Dutchess
8" (20cm) hard plastic, 1996 $75
Dutchess Eliza
10" (25cm) hard plastic, 1996 $110
Dutch Lullaby *(see Wynken, Blynken and Nod)*

*Both became Netherlands in 1974.

Easter
7-1/2" (19cm) hard plastic, straight leg non-walker, 1953 $900
8" (20cm) hard plastic, also available as African American, 1996-1998 $65

Easter Bonnet
14" (36cm) 1992 $145
8" (20cm) hard plastic, also available as African American, 1995-1996 $65

Easter Bunny
8" (20cm) made for A Child At Heart, 1991 *(see Special Dolls)* $300

Easter Doll
8" (20cm) hard plastic, 1968 $1,000
14" (36cm) plastic/vinyl, 1968 $650

Easter of Yesteryear
8" (20cm) hard plastic, Collector's United, 1995 *(see Special Dolls)* $70

Easter Sunday
8" (20cm) hard plastic, also available as African American, 1993 $65
8" (20cm) hard plastic, also available as African American, 1998-1999 $90

Ecuador
8" (20cm) hard plastic, bent knee walker, #387, 1963; #787, 1964-1965 $375
Outfit only for 8" (20cm) doll, #0387, 1963 $125
8" (20cm) hard plastic, bent knee, #787, 1965-66 $375

Edith, the Lonely Doll
8" (20cm) hard plastic, 1958 $700
16" (41cm) plastic/vinyl, 1958-1959 $350
22" (56cm) 1958-1959 $375

Edith with Golden Hair
18" (46cm) cloth, 1940s $650

Edwardian
18" (46cm) "so-called" hard plastic, *Glamour Girl Series*, 1953 $1,500

Eisenhower, Mamie
14" (36cm) 6th set, *First Ladies Series*, 1989-1990 $100

Egypt
8" (20cm) straight legs, 1986-1989 $65
8" (20cm) hard plastic, 1998-1999 $100

Egyptian
7-8" (18-20cm) composition, 1936-1940 $350
9" (23cm) composition, 1936-1940 $375

Elaine
8" (20cm) hard plastic, matches 18" (46cm) 1954 $1,000

18" (46cm) hard plastic, blue organdy dress, *Me and My Shadow Series*, 1954 $1,500

Electra
8" (20cm) hard plastic, MADC, 1999 *(see Special Dolls)* $80

Electro
8" (20cm) hard plastic, MADC, 1999 *(see Special Dolls)* $80

Elegant Easter
8" (20cm) hard plastic, Elegant Doll Shop, 1998 *(see Special Dolls)* $70

Elise
16-1/2" (42cm) hard plastic/vinyl arms, jointed ankles and knees, 1957-1964
17" (43cm) vinyl head, fully jointed, 1961-1962
18" (46cm) bouffant hairstyle, 1963
Brocade Gown with Long Opera Coat, #1775, 1959 $700
Brown Jumper with Pink Blouse, #1632, 1957 $425
Brown Velvet Coat and Hat with Dress, #1640, 1957 $450
Checked Taffeta Dress, #1610, 1957 $400
Corduroy Skirt and Shorts Set, #1705, 1963 $425
Cornflower Blue Ball Gown, #1730, 1960 $800
Dotted Cotton Dress, #1710, 1958 $400
Nylon Shirtwaist Dress, #1718, 1958 $425
Pink Nylon Dress, #1815, 1959 $425
Riding Outfit, #1710, 1963 $400
Satin Print Skirt and Nylon Blouse, #1816, 1959 $450
Tulle Dancing Gown, #1730, 1958 $725
Basic Doll Wearing Lace Chemise, #1600, 1957; #1700, 1958; #1800, 1959 $250
Accessory Set $150
Coat and Hat $400 up
Cotton Dress $350 up
Evening Gown $650 up
Houndstooth Suit $450
Moire Dress $350 up
Nightgown $250
Organdy Dress $375 up
Peignoir Set $275
Queen (see Queen)
Robe $250
Skirt with Cardigan $375
Sleeveless Cotton Dress $350 up
Taffeta Dress $375 up
16-1/2" (42cm) hard plastic/vinyl, trunk set with trousseau, FAO Schwarz, 1958 and 1964 $700 up
17" (43cm) vinyl, Cotton Dress with Lace Trim, #1720, 1966 $275
17" (43cm) vinyl, Pleated Chiffon Formal, #1750, 1966 $350
17" (43cm) vinyl, Tulle Formal, 1967-1976 $200 up
17" (43cm) *Portrait*, 1972-1973 $225
17" (43cm) in trunk with trousseau, FAO Schwarz exclusive, 1966-1972 $700 up
17" (43cm) in wooden trunk with trousseau, Neiman

Late 1950s 8-inch (20cm) *Edith the Lonely Doll. Marge Meisinger Collection. Photo by Carol J. Stover.*

Late 1930s composition 4-inch (23cm) Eskimo. *Benita Schwartz Collection.*

Marcus exclusive, 1982 $2,500 up
Elsie Leslie
 14" (36cm) plastic/vinyl, 1988 $95
Eliza
 14" (36cm) *Classic Dolls*, 1991 $150
Elizabethan Bride
 10" (25cm) hard plastic, 1999 $130
Elizabeth Angel
 8" (20cm) made for Belk Leggett Stores, 1996 *(see Special Dolls)* $100
Eliza Doolittle
 10" (25cm) hard plastic, flower seller, 1995-1996
                                                                           $90
 10" (25cm) hard plastic, black and white ascot gown,

1995-1997 $90
 10" (25cm) hard plastic, white gown with red cape, 1996 $110
Eloise
 8" (20cm) hard plastic, FAO Schwarz, 1999 *(see Special Dolls)* $50
 16" (41cm) cloth, FAO Schwarz, 1999 *(see Special Dolls)*
                                                                           $45
Emerald City Dorothy *(see Dorothy)*
Emily
 cloth/felt, 1930s $725
Empire Bride
 10" (25cm) hard plastic, 1998-1999 $135
Empress Elisabeth
 10" (25cm) made for My Doll House, 1991 *(see Special Dolls)* $150
Enchanted Doll *(see Special Dolls)*
 8" (20cm) hard plastic, rick-rack pinafore, lace trim, 1980 $300
 8" (20cm) hard plastic, eyelet pinafore, eyelet trim, 1981 $300
 10" (25cm) hard plastic, 1988 $175
Enchanted Evening
 21" (53cm) *Portrait*, 1991-1992 (uses vinyl Cissy mold)
                                                                          $325
Enchanted Princess Trunk Set
 8" (20cm) hard plastic, FAO Schwarz, 1995 *(see Special Dolls)* $200
England
 8" (20cm) hard plastic, 1997-1999 $80
English Guard
 8" (20cm) hard plastic, bent knee, #764, 1966-1968
                                                                          $300
 8" (20cm) re-introduced 1989-1991 $65
Entertaining the Troops
 8" (20cm) hard plastic, 1999 $75
Eskimo
 9" (23cm) composition, 1936-1939 $350
 8" (20cm) hard plastic, bent knee, *Americana Series*, #723, 1966-1969 $350
 With Maggie smile face $375
Estonia
 8" (20cm) straight legs, 1986-1987 $85
Estrella
 18" (46cm) hard plastic, 1953 $1,350
Eva Lovelace
 7" (18cm) composition, 1935 $350
 23" (58cm) cloth, 1934 $625
Evangeline
 18" (46cm) cloth, 1930s $700 up
Evening Star
 15" (38cm) porcelain, 1999 $165
Evil Sorceress
 8" (20cm) hard plastic, 1997 $80

Fairy Godmother
　　14" (36cm) *Classic Dolls* 1983-1992　　$75-150
　　10" (25cm) *Portrettes*, 1993　　$85
　　8" (20cm) hard plastic, 1995　　$80
　　8" (20cm) hard plastic, 1997-1999　　$75

Fairy of Beauty
　　8" (20cm) hard plastic, 1997-1999　　$75

Fairy of Song
　　8" (20cm) hard plastic, 1997-1999　　$75

Fairy of Virtue
　　8" (20cm) hard plastic, 1997-1999　　$75

Fairy Princess
　　7" (18cm) composition, 1939-1943　　$350
　　9" (23cm) composition, 1939-1941　　$375
　　11" (28cm) composition, 1939-1943　　$395
　　15-18" (38-46cm) composition, 1939-1943　　$675
　　21-22" (53-56cm) composition, 1939-1946　　$950

Fairy Queen
　　14-1/2" (37cm) composition, 1940-1946　　$675
　　18" (46cm) composition, 1940-1946　　$775
　　14-1/2" (37cm) hard plastic, 1948-1950　　$775
　　18" (46cm) hard plastic, 1948-1950　　$975

Fairy Tales
　　Dumas 9" (23cm) composition, 1937-1941　　$350

Faith
　　8" (20cm) hard plastic, bent knee walker, *Americana Series*, #486, 1961　　$1,600
　　8" (20cm) hard plastic, CU Gathering, 1992 *(see Special Dolls)*　　$225

Fannie Elizabeth
　　8" (20cm) made for Belk & Leggett, 1991 *(see Special Dolls)*　　$75

Farmer's Daughter
　　8" (20cm) made for Enchanted Doll House, 1991 *(see Special Dolls)*　　$125

Farmer's Daughter Goes To Town
　　8" (20cm) made for Enchanted Doll House, 1992 *(see Special Dolls)*　　$90

Fashions of the Century
　　14-18" (36-46cm) hard plastic, 1954-1955　　$1,700 up

Father Christmas
　　8" (20cm) hard plastic, *Americana Series*, 1994　　$70

Father of the Bride
　　10" (25cm) hard plastic, 1996　　$110

Father of Vatican City
　　8" (20cm) hard plastic, 1999　　$80

Faye Wray and King Kong
　　10" (25cm) hard plastic, FAO Schwarz, 1999 *(see Special Dolls)*　　$500

Fillmore, Abigail
　　14" (36cm) plastic/vinyl, 3rd set, *First Ladies Series*, 1982-1984　　$100

Findlay, Jane
　　14" (36cm) plastic/vinyl, 2nd set, *First Ladies Series*, 1979-1981　　$100

Finland
　　8" (20cm) hard plastic, bent knee, #761, 1968-1972　　$110
　　8" (20cm) hard plastic, straight legs, "Alex Mold", #0761, 1973; #561, 1974-1975　　$70
　　8" (20cm) hard plastic, straight legs, 1976-1987　　$60

Finnish
　　7" (18cm) composition, 1935-1937　　$275

Firebird *(see Ballerinas)*

Firefighter Wendy
　　8" (20cm) hard plastic, 1997-1999　　$80

First Comes Love
　　8" (20cm) hard plastic, Collector's United, 1993 *(see Special Dolls)*　　$175

First Communion
　　8" (20cm) hard plastic, bent knee walker, #395, 1957　　$675
　　14" (36cm) *Classic Dolls*, 1991-1992　　$100
　　8" (20cm) hard plastic, 1994　　$70
　　8" (20cm) hard plastic, 1995　　$70
　　8" (20cm) hard plastic, 1995-1998, eyelet dress, also available in African American　　$75
　　8" (20cm) hard plastic, 1999　　$75

First Dance
　　8" (20cm) hard plastic pair, 1996　　$150

First Ladies
　　1st set, 1976-1978　　$800
　　2nd set, 1979-1981　　$650
　　3rd set, 1982-1984　　$650
　　4th set, 1985-1987　　$650
　　5th set, 1988　　$650
　　6th set, 1989-1990　　$600

First Recital
　　8" (20cm) hard plastic, 1996, also available in African American　　$65

Fisher Quints
　　"so-called" 7" (18cm) hard plastic/vinyl, 1964 set　　$450

Five Little Peppers
　　13" (33cm) & 16" (41cm) composition, 1936　　$675 each

Flapper
　　10" (25cm) *Portrette Series*, 1988-1991, red or white dress　　$65
　　10" (25cm) MADC, 1988 *(see Special Dolls)*　　$200
　　8" (20cm) hard plastic, 1995, rose dress　　$65

Flora McFlimsey
　　9" (23cm) composition, 1938-1941　　$375
　　12" (31cm) composition, 1944　　$900
　　14" (36cm) composition, 1938-1944　　$475
　　14" (36cm) composition trunk set　　$1,000 up
　　15-16" (38-41cm) composition, 1938-1944　　$550

Above: Late 1930s all composition 7-inch (18cm) *Fairy Princess.*
Veronica Jochens Collection.

The current trend toward nostalgia
is shown in this 1999 *Flower Child*!
A. Glenn Mandeville Collection.

16-17" (41-43cm) composition, 1936-1937 $550
22" (56cm) composition, 1938-1944 $750
15" (38cm) *Miss Flora McFlimsey*, vinyl head,
#1502, 1953 $625
14" (36cm) plastic/vinyl, 1995 $130

Florentine Angel Tree Topper *(see Tree Topper)*

Flower Child
8" (20cm) hard plastic, *Through the Decades Collection*,
1999 $50

Flower Girl
16-18" (41-46cm) composition, 1939, 1944-1947
    $575
20-24" (51-61cm) composition, 1939, 1944-1947
    $800
15" (36cm) hard plastic, 1954 $600
18" (46cm) hard plastic, 1954 $550
25" (64cm) hard plastic, 1954 $750
31" (79cm) *Mary Ellen*, 1954 $600
8" (20cm) hard plastic, bent knee walker, #602, 1956;
#398, 1957; #445, 1959 $750 up
10" (25cm) *Portrette Series*, 1988-1990 $80
8" (20cm) hard plastic, African American, 1992 or white
doll, 1992-1993 $65
8" (20cm) hard plastic, MADC, 1995 *(see Special Dolls)*
    $100
8" (20cm) hard plastic, 1999 $80

Folsom, Frances
10" (25cm) hard plastic, MADC, 1995 *(see Special Dolls)*
    $250

Footmouse *(see Cinderella's Footmouse)*

Forever Friends
14" (36cm) vinyl dolls with painted eyes, exclusive for
Toys 'R Us, 1994-1995 $75 each

Forrest
8" (20cm) hard plastic, 1998 *(see also Watchful Guardian
Angel)* $80

Fortune Teller
8" (20cm) hard plastic, Collector's United, 1999 *(see
Special Dolls)* $175
21" (53cm) Collector's United, 1999 *(see Special Dolls)*
    $475

Fourth of July
8" (20cm) hard plastic, QVC, 1999 *(see Special Dolls)*
    $75

French (France)
7" (18cm) composition, 1936-1943 $300
9" (23cm) composition, 1937-1941 $325
8" (20cm) hard plastic, bent knee walker, #490, 1961;
#390, 1962-1963; #790, 1964-1965 $125
Outfit only for 8" (20cm) doll, #0390, 1962-1963
    $60
8" (20cm) hard plastic, bent knee, #790, 1965-1972
    $100

8" (20cm) hard plastic, straight legs, "Alex Mold",
#0790, 1973; #590, 1974-1975 $75
8" (20cm) hard plastic, white face, 1985-1987 $65
8" (20cm) hard plastic, straight legs, 1976-1995 $65
8" (20cm) hard plastic, *International Series*, 1994-1995
    $60
8" (20cm) hard plastic, can-can dancer, 1996-1998
    $80

French Aristocrat
10" (25cm) *Portrette*, 1991 $110

French Flower Girl
8" (20cm) hard plastic, bent knee walker, #610, 1956
    $800

Friar Tuck
8" (20cm) hard plastic, 1989-1990 $60

Friends Around the Country
8" (20cm) outfit only, MADC Friendship Luncheon
exclusive, 1997 $35

From the Madame's Sketchbook
8" (20cm) hard plastic, MADC, 1997 *(see Special Dolls)*
    $75

Frou-Frou
40" (101cm) all cloth, yarn hair, ballerina in green, lilac,
1951 only $750

Fun at Halloween
8" (20cm) hard plastic, QVC, 1999 *(see Special Dolls)*
    $80

Funny
18' (46cm) cloth, #50, 1963-1977 $85

Funny Maggie
8" (20cm) hard plastic, *Storyland Dolls*, 1994 $55

Furniture
Available for 8"-10" (20cm-25cm) dolls, 1950s-1960s
    Black Wooden Chair $125
    Blue Wood Clothing Rack (also made for larger dolls)
    $100
    Brass Armchair with Velvet Cushion $145
    Brass Bed with Linens $200 up
    Brass Side Chair with Velvet Cushion $140
    Brass Table and Chairs Set $200
    Brass Vanity Set $175 up
    Linen Set $100
    Rocking Chair $125
    Velvet Chair with Braid Trim $125
    Velvet Sofa with Braid Trim $175
    White Wood Bed with Linens $150
    White Wood Clothing Rack $140
    White Wood Table and Chairs Set $175
    White Wood Vanity and Bench $165
    Cradle for baby dolls, 1996 $40
    Blue Wood Armoire for 8" (20cm), 1997-1998 $50
    Blue Wood Bed for 8" (20cm), 1997-1998 $35
    Piano for 8" (20cm), 1997 $40

G

Gabrielle
10" (25cm) hard plastic, UFDC Convention, 1998
(see Special Dolls) $300

Gainsborough
10" (25cm) pink, full dress, hat, #961, 1957 $650
20" (51cm) hard plastic, taffeta gown, picture hat, *Models Formals Series*, #2176, 1957 $1,500
21" (53cm) hard plastic/vinyl arms, blue with white lace jacket, 1968 $700
21" (53cm) bright blue with full ecru overskirt, 1972 $600
21" (53cm) pale blue, scallop lace overskirt, 1973 $500
21" (53cm) pink with full lace overdress, 1978 $400
10" (25cm) hard plastic, 1995 $100

Garden Party
18" (46cm) hard plastic, 1953 $1,550
7-1/2-8" (19-20cm) hard plastic, straight leg walker, #488, 1955 $1,200
20" (51cm) hard plastic, 1956-1957 $1,100

Garden Rose
10" (25cm) hard plastic, 1998-1999 $130

Garfield, Lucretia
14" (36cm) plastic/vinyl, 4th set, *First Ladies Series*, 1985-1987 $100

Gemini
8" (20cm) hard plastic, also available in African American, 1998 $170 pair

Genius Baby
21-30" (53-76cm) plastic/vinyl, flirty eyes, 1960-1961 $175-$225
Little, 8" (20cm) hard plastic head/vinyl, 1956-1962
(see Little Genius)

Geppetto
8" (20cm) *Storyland Dolls*, 1993-1994 $65

Geranium
9" (23cm) early vinyl toddler, red organdy dress and bonnet, 1953 $135

German (Germany)
8" (20cm) hard plastic, bent knee, #763, 1966-1972 $90
8" (20cm) hard plastic, straight legs, "Alex Mold", #0763, 1973; #563, 1974-1975 $70
8" (20cm) hard plastic, white face, 1985-1987 $60
8" (20cm) hard plastic, straight legs, 1976-1991 $60
8" (20cm) hard plastic, *International Series*, 1994 $60

Get Well
8" (20cm) hard plastic, also available in African American, 1998-1999 $80

Get Well Wishes
8" (20cm) hard plastic, 1995 $65

Ghost of Christmas Past
8" (20cm) hard plastic, 1996 $65

Ghost of Christmas Present
14" (36cm) plastic/vinyl in set with 8" (20cm) Want and Ignorance pair, 1996 $300

Gibson Girl
16" (41cm) cloth, 1930s $825
10" (25cm) hard plastic, eye shadow, striped blouse, #760, 1962 $800
10" (25cm) hard plastic, plain blouse without stripes, #760, 1963 $800
10" (25cm) hard plastic, *Portrette Series*, 1988-1990 $80
10" (25cm) hard plastic, *Through the Decades Collection*, 1999 $120

Gidget
14' (36cm) plastic/vinyl, black and white check jumper, #1415, 1966 $275
Floral cotton formal, #1420, 1966 $350
White nautical dress and hat, #1421, 1966 $300

Gigi
14" (36cm) *Classic Dolls*, 1986-1987 $95
14" (36cm) plastic/vinyl, 1996 $130
8" (20cm) hard plastic, 1998-1999 $80

Gilbert
8" (20cm) hard plastic, *Anne of Green Gables Series*, 1994-1995 $60

Gingerbread Man
8" (20cm) outfit only, Doll and Teddy Bear Expo East exclusive, 1999 $35

Girl on the Flying Trapeze
40" (101cm) cloth, FAO exclusive, 1951 $900

Giselle *(see Ballerinas)*

Glamour Girls
18" (46cm) hard plastic, 1953 $1,500 up

Glinda the Good Witch
8" (20cm) *Wizard of Oz Series*, 1992-1995 $80
14" (36cm) plastic/vinyl, 1994 $100
10" (25cm) hard plastic, 1997-1999 $115

Glistening Angel Tree Topper *(see Tree Topper)*
Glorious Angel Tree Topper *(see Tree Topper)*
Godey
21" (53cm) composition, 1945-1947 $2,000 up
21" (53cm) hard plastic, 1951 $2,000
14" (36cm) hard plastic, 1950-1951 $1,500 up
18" (46cm) hard plastic, *Glamour Girls Series*, 1953 $1,700
21" (53cm) hard plastic/vinyl straight arms, lavender and pink, 1961 *(Cissy)* $1,400
21" (53cm) hard plastic/vinyl straight arms, orange, 1962 *(Cissy)* $1,400
21" (53cm) dressed in all red, blonde hair, 1965 $775

21" (53cm) plastic/vinyl, red with black short jacket and hat, 1966 $2,400
21" (53cm) hard plastic/vinyl arms, dressed in pink & ecru, 1967 $625
10" (25cm) hard plastic, pink with ecru lace, #1172, 1968 $400
10" (25cm) yellow with bows, #1172, 1969 $425
21" (53cm) red with black trim, 1969 $575
10" (25cm) pink lace dress, #1183, 1970 $475
21" (53cm) pink with burgundy short jacket, 1970 $365
21" (53cm) pink, black trim, short jacket, 1971 $400
21" (53cm) ecru with red jacket and bonnet, 1977 $325

Godey Bride
14" (36cm) hard plastic, 1950 $1,100
18" (46cm) hard plastic, 1950-1951 $1,300
Godey Groom
14" (36cm) hard plastic, 1950 $950
18" (46cm) hard plastic, 1950-1951 $1,500
Godey Lady
14" (36cm) hard plastic, 1949 $1,000
18" (46cm) hard plastic, 1950-1951 $1,500
Goes Country
8" (20cm) hard plastic, CU Nashville, 1995 (see Special Dolls) $100
Golf Boy
8" (20cm) hard plastic, 1997-1998 $75
Golf Girl
8" (20cm) hard plastic, 1997-1998 $75
Gold Rush
10" (25cm) hard plastic, #762, 1962 $1,500
Golden Girl
10" (25cm) hard plastic, *Through the Decades Collection*, 1999 $120
10" (25cm) M. Pancner's House of Collectibles (see *Special Dolls*) $120
Golden Holiday Tree Topper
10" (25cm) Bloomingdales by Mail, 1999 (see *Special Dolls*) $120
Goldfish
8" (20cm) *Americana Series*, 1993-1994 $70
Goldilocks
18" (46cm) cloth, 1930s $800
7-8" (18-20cm) composition, 1938-1942 $325
18" (46cm) hard plastic, 1951 $900
14" (36cm) plastic/vinyl, satin dress, *Classic Dolls*, 1978-1979 $120
14" (36cm) cotton dress, 1980-1983 $95
8" (20cm) *Storyland Dolls*, 1990-1991 (1991 dress is different plaid) $65
14" (36cm) long side curls, *Classic Dolls*, 1994 $95
8" (20cm) hard plastic, *Storyland Dolls*, 1994-1995 $65
Goldilocks and Baby Bear
8" (20cm) Disney World Doll and Teddy Bear Convention, 1998 (see *Special Dolls*) $200

Three Bears House Backdrop workshop kit, exclusive for convention, 1998 $50
Gone with the Wind (see Scarlett)
Good Fairy
14" (36cm) hard plastic, 1947-1949 $700
Good Little Girl
16" (41cm) cloth, wears pink dress, mate to *Bad Little Girl*, #40, 1966 $200
Goya
8" (20cm) hard plastic, 1953 $1,000
21" (53cm) hard plastic/vinyl arms, multi-tier pink dress, 1968 $575
21" (53cm) maroon dress with black Spanish lace, 1982-1983 $275
Graduation
8" (20cm) hard plastic, bent knee walker, #399, 1957 $875
12" (31cm) hard plastic, 1957 $850
8" (20cm) white doll, *Americana Series*, 1990-1992 $65
8" (20cm) white or African American doll, 1991-1992 $65
8" (20cm) white or African American doll, 1995 $65
Grandma Jane
14" (36cm) plastic/vinyl, 1970-1972 $250
Grandma's Little Darling
8" (20cm) hard plastic, Shirley's Dollhouse, 1996 (see *Special Dolls*) $75
Grand Ole Opry
8" (20cm) hard plastic, boy and girl pair, 1996 $175
8" (20cm) hard plastic, boy only, 1996 $75
8" (20cm) hard plastic, girl only, 1996 $80
Grant, Julia
14" (36cm) plastic/vinyl, 3rd set, *First Ladies Series*, 1982-1984 $100
Grave, Alice
18" (46cm) cloth, 1930s $750
Grayson, Kathryn
20" (51cm) hard plastic, 1949 $5,000 up
Grease
10" (25cm) hard plastic, FAO Schwarz, 1998 (see *Special Dolls*) $250
Great Britain
8" (20cm) hard plastic, straight legs, #558, 1977-1988 $60
Great Gatsby
10" (25cm) hard plastic, pair, 1997 $190
Greece
8" (20cm) hard plastic, boy doll, 1992-1993 $60
Greek Boy
8" (20cm) hard plastic, bent knee walker, #769, 1965 $375
8" (20cm) hard plastic, bent knee, #769, 1965-1968 $350
Greek Girl
8" (20cm) hard plastic, bent knee, #765, 1968-1972 $100

8" (20cm) hard plastic, straight legs, "Alex Mold",
#0765, 1973; #565, 1974-1975 $70
8" (20cm) hard plastic, straight legs, 1976-1987 $65
Green, Gary
8" (20cm) hard plastic, Collector's United, 1998
(see Special Dolls) $75
Greta
8" (20cm) hard plastic, CU Greenville Show, 1996
(see Special Dolls) $150
Gretel
7" (18cm) composition, 1935-1942 $300
9" (23cm) composition, 1938-1940 $325
7-1/2-8" (19-20cm) hard plastic, straight leg walker,
#470, 1955 $600
18" (46cm) hard plastic, 1948 $950
8" (20cm) hard plastic, bent knee, *Storyland Dolls*,
#754, 1966-1972 $110
8" (20cm) hard plastic, straight legs, "Alex Mold",
#0754, 1973; #454, 1974-1975 $75
8" (20cm) hard plastic, straight legs, 1976-1986 $65
8" (20cm) hard plastic, *Storyland Dolls*, re-introduced,
1991-1992 $60
Gretl *(see Sound of Music)*
Groom
18-21" (46-53cm) composition, 1946-1947 $950
14-16" (36-41cm) hard plastic, 1949-1951 $775
18-21" (46-53cm) hard plastic, 1949-1951 $800
7-1/2-8" (19-20cm) hard plastic, straight leg non-walker,
Quiz-kin, 1953-1954 $475
7-1/2-8" (19-20cm) hard plastic, straight leg walker,
#466, 1955 $475
8" (20cm) hard plastic, bent knee walker, #577, 1956;
#377, 1957; #572, 1958; #421, 1961; #442, 1963
                                       $400

8" (20cm) hard plastic, *Americana Series*, 1989-1991
                                       $65
8" (20cm) hard plastic, 1993 $65
8" (20cm) hard plastic, also available in African American,
1996-1999 $65
Groovy Girl
8" (20cm) hard plastic, *Through the Decades Collection*,
1999 $75
Guardian Angel
7-1/2-8" (19-20cm) hard plastic, in pink, blue, or white,
straight leg walker, has a harp, #480, 1954 $800 up
10" (25cm) hard plastic, *Anniversary Collection*, 1995
                                       $140
10" (25cm) hard plastic, floral dress, 1997-1999 $110
Guardian Angel of Harmony
10" (25cm) hard plastic, 1996-1997 $110
Guardian Angel of Hope
10" (25cm) hard plastic, 1996 $110
Guardian Angel of Love
10" (25cm) hard plastic, 1995-1996 $110
Guatemala
8" (20cm) hard plastic, 1999 $80
Guinevere
10" (25cm) *Portrette Series*, 1992 $125
8" (20cm) hard plastic, in set with Lancelot, *Anniversary
Collection*, 1995 $200
8" (20cm) hard plastic, 1999 $80

Above: The 1999 *Groovy Girl* even has a tattoo. She is very retro '70s
with her bean bag chair. *A. Glenn Mandeville Collection.*

1954 8-inch (20cm) hard plastic *Guardian Angel.*
Marge Meisinger Collection. Photo by Carol J. Stover

Halloween
8" (20cm) made for Greenville Show, 1990 *(see Special Dolls)* $100

Hamlet
12" (31cm) *Romance Collection,* Nancy Drew Face, 1992 $95
12" (31cm) #1312, Lissy Face, 1993 $110

Hansel
7" (18cm) composition, 1935-1942 $300
9" (23cm) composition, 1938-1940 $325
18" (46cm) hard plastic, 1948 $950
8" (20cm) hard plastic, straight leg walker, #445, 1955 $600
8" (20cm) hard plastic, bent knee, *Storyland Dolls,* #753, 1966-1972 $110
8" (20cm) hard plastic, straight legs, "Alex Mold", #0753, 1973; #453, 1974-1975 $75
8" (20cm) hard plastic, straight legs, 1976-1986 $65
8" (20cm) hard plastic, *Storyland Dolls,* re-introduced, 1991-1992 $60

Happy
20" (51cm) cloth/vinyl, 1970 $200

Happy Birthday
8" (20cm) hard plastic, African American or white, *Americana Series,* 1992-1993 $60
8" (20cm) hard plastic, white only, *Americana Series,* fabric change, 1994 $60
8" (20cm) hard plastic, 1995 $65
8" (20cm) hard plastic, African American available, 1999 $70
14" (36cm) *Classic Dolls,* 1994 $90
14" (36cm) outfit only, 1996 $50

Happy Birthday Billy
8" (20cm) hard plastic, African American available, 1993 $65

Happy Birthday Maggie
8" (20cm) hard plastic, African American available, 1995-1998 $65

Happy Birthday Madame
8" (20cm) MADC, 1985 *(see Special Dolls)* $300

Happy Birthday Wendy
8" (20cm) hard plastic, African American available, 1995-1996 $65

Happy Chanukah
8" (20cm) hard plastic, 1995-1999 $75

Happy the Clown
8" (20cm) hard plastic, 1996 $65

Harding, Florence
14" (36cm) plastic/vinyl, 5th set, *First Ladies Series,* 1988 $100

Harlequin
8" (20cm) hard plastic, 1995 $65

Harley-Davidson
8" (20cm) hard plastic, black leather jacket, boy or girl, 1996-1997 $100
10" (25cm) hard plastic, boy or girl, 1997 $125
10" (25cm) hard plastic, black leather dress, 1998 $175
NOTE: All the dolls that appear in the 1996 catalog were not produced.

Harmony and Cherub
8" (20cm) doll with a 21" (53cm) porcelain Günzel doll, 1993 $750

Harrison, Caroline
14" (36cm) plastic/vinyl, 4th set, *First Ladies Series,* 1985-1987 $100

Hawaii
8" (20cm) *Americana Series,* 1990-1991 $65

Hawaiian
7" (18cm) composition, 1937-1944 $325
9" (23cm) composition, 1937-1944 $350
8" (20cm) hard plastic, bent knee, *Americana Series,* #722, 1966-1969 $375

Hayes, Lucy
14" (36cm) plastic/vinyl, 4th set, *First Ladies Series,* 1985-1987 $100

Heart of Dixie
8" (20cm) hard plastic, Elegant Doll Shop, 1998 *(see Special Dolls)* $75

Heather
18" (46cm) cloth/vinyl, 1990-1993 $95
8" (20cm) hard plastic, 1998 *(see also Watchful Guardian Angel Set)* $90

Heavenly Angel Tree Topper *(see Tree Topper)*

Heidi
7" (18cm) composition, 1938-1939 $300
14" (36cm) plastic/vinyl, *Classic Dolls,* 1969-1988 $90
8" (20cm) hard plastic, *Storyland Dolls,* 1991-1992 $65
8" (20cm) hard plastic, 1997-1999 $80
NOTE: 14" (36cm) pictured in 1995 catalog was not produced.

Hello Baby
22" (56cm) 1962 $185

Henie, Sonja
7" (18cm) composition, 1939-1942 $450
9" (23cm) composition, 1940-1941 $550
11" (28cm) composition $600
13-15" (33-38cm) composition, 1938-1942 $650
14" (36cm) composition $650 up
14" (36cm) in case, wardrobe $1,600 up
17-18" (43-46cm) composition, 1938-1942 $900 up
20-23" (51-58cm) composition 1938-1942 $1,000 up
13-14" (33-36cm) composition, jointed waist $750
15-18" (38-46cm) hard plastic/vinyl, no extra joints, 1951 only $875 up

23" (58cm) hard plastic/vinyl, no extra joints, 1951 only $875 up

Her Lady and Child
 21" (53cm) porcelain and 8" (20cm) hard plastic set,
 1993-1994 $500

Hershey's Kisses Doll
 8" (20cm) hard plastic, 1999 $75

Hiawatha
 18" (46cm) cloth, early 1930s $750
 7" (18cm) composition $300
 8" (20cm) hard plastic, bent knee, *Americana Series*,
 #720, 1967-1969 $400

Hickory Dickory Dock
 8" (20cm) hard plastic, 1998-1999 $85

Highland Fling
 7-1/2-8" (19-20cm) hard plastic, *Wendy Does the
 Highland Fling*, #484, 1955 $725

Holiday, Billie
 10" (20cm) hard plastic, 1997 $100

Holiday Magic
 8" (20cm) Doll and Teddy Bear Expo East, 1999
 (see Special Dolls) $100

Holiday on Ice
 8" (20cm) hard plastic, 1992 (some tagged, "Christmas on
 Ice") $85

Holland
 7" (18cm) composition, 1936-1943 $325

Holly
 10" (25cm) *Portrette Series*, 1990-1991 $95
 8" (20cm) hard plastic, Belk Leggett Stores, 1994
 (see Special Dolls) $85

Hollywood Glamour
 10" (25cm) hard plastic, *Through the Decades Collection*,
 1999 $100

Hollywood Trunk Set
 8" (20cm) hard plastic with wardrobe, 1997 $240

Homecoming
 8" (20cm) hard plastic, MADC, *1993 (see Special Dolls)*
                                                              $150

Home for the Holidays
 14" (36cm) plastic/vinyl, 1995 $100
 8" (20cm) hard plastic, Lillian Vernon, 1996 *(see Special
 Dolls)* $100
 10" (25cm) hard plastic, QVC, 1998 *(see Special Dolls)*
                                                              $110

Honey-Bea
 14" (36cm) vinyl, 1963 $175
 14" (36cm) layette set or window box gift set, 1963
                                                              $300

Honeybun
 18-19" (46-48cm) cloth/vinyl, 1951-1952 $225
 23-26" (58-66cm) 1951-1952 $275

Honeyette Baby
 7" (18cm) composition, little girl dress, 1934-1937
                                                              $300
 16" (41cm) composition/cloth, 1941-1942 $250

Honeymooners
 8" (20cm) hard plastic, FAO Schwarz, 1997 *(see Special
 Dolls)* $350

Hoover, Lou
 14" (36cm) plastic/vinyl, 6th set, *First Ladies Series*,
 1989-1990 $100

Hope
 8" (20cm) hard plastic, CU Gathering, 1993 *(see Special
 Dolls)* $180

Howdy Doody
 8" (20cm) hard plastic, marionette, 1999 $100

Huckleberry Finn
 8" (20cm) hard plastic, *Storyland Dolls*, 1989-1991
                                                              $65

Huggable Huggums
 12" (31cm) vinyl/cloth with bean bag body, African
 American available, 1998-1999 $40-$50
 12" (31cm) vinyl/cloth with bean bag body, *75th
 Anniversary Special Edition*, 1998 $80

Huggums, Big
 25" (64cm) Lively, knob moves head and limbs, 1963
                                                              $150
 25" (64cm) boy or girl, 1963-1979 $125

Huggums, Little
 12" (31cm) rooted hair, 1963-1982, 1988, 1996, 1999
                                                              $55
 12" (31cm) molded hair, (African American available
 1995-1998), 1963-1999 $40-$60
 Christening dress, 12" (31cm), 1993-1999 $75
 14" (36cm) molded hair, 1986 $50
 12" (31cm) made for Imaginarium Shop, 1991 *(see Special
 Dolls)* $55
 12" (31cm) made for I. Magnin, includes cradle, 1992
 (see Special Dolls) $130
 12" (31cm) made for FAO Schwarz, 1994 *(see Special
 Dolls)* $60
 12" (31cm) made for Jacobsen's, 1995 *(see Special Dolls)*
                                                              $60
 Boxed Outfits for 12" (31cm), 1996 $50

Hug Me Pets
 12" (31cm) vinyl/cloth, bunny, kitty or teddy, African
 American available, 1995-1996 $55

Hulda
 14" (36cm) hard plastic, African American doll, 1948-1949
                                                              $1,300 up
 18" (46cm) hard plastic, African American doll, 1949
                                                              $1,600 up

Humpty Dumpty
 8" (20cm) hard plastic and cloth, 1996-1998 $70

Hungarian (Hungary)
 8" (20cm) hard plastic, bent knee walker, metal crown,
 #397, 1962-1963; #797, 1964-1965 $175
 Outfit only for 8" (20cm) doll, #0397, 1962-1963
                                                              $90
 8" (20cm) hard plastic, bent knee, metal crown, #797,
 1965-1972 $125
 Without metal crown $100
 8" (20cm) hard plastic, straight legs, "Alex Mold",
 #0797, 1973; #597, 1974-1975 $75
 8" (20cm) hard plastic, straight legs, 1976-1986 $70
 8" (20cm) hard plastic, re-introduced, 1992-1993
                                                              $60
 8" (20cm) hard plastic, 1995 $60

Hyacinth
 9" (23cm) vinyl, 1953 $160

I

Ibiza
8" (20cm) hard plastic, 1989 $75

Ice Capades
20"-21" (51-53cm) *Cissy* or *Jacqueline*, 1950s-1960s
$1,500 up

Ice Princess
8" (20cm) hard plastic, Dolls and Ducks, 1998 *(see Special Dolls)* $70

Ice Skater
8" (20cm) bent knee walker, #555, 1956; #378, 1957; #540, 1958; #451, 1963 $600 up
8" (20cm) *Americana Series*, 1990-1991 $65
8" (20cm) hard plastic, boy doll, 1997 $55
8" (20cm) hard plastic, girl doll, 1997-1998 $60

Iceland
10" (25cm) hard plastic, #746, 1962 $750 up

I Dream of Jeannie
8" (20cm) hard plastic, FAO Schwarz, 1996 *(see Special Dolls)* $200

Ignorance *(see Ghost of Christmas Present)*

I'll Love You Forever
8" (20cm) hard plastic, 1999 $75

I Love Lucy
8" (20cm) hard plastic, set of four dolls, FAO Schwarz, 1995 *(see Special Dolls)* $600
8" (20cm) hard plastic, Lucy doll alone, FAO Schwarz, 1995 *(see Special Dolls)* $150

I Love You
8" (20cm) hard plastic, 1995 $65

India
8" (20cm) hard plastic, bent knee walker, dark skin, #775, 1965 $175
8" (20cm) hard plastic, bent knee, dark skin, #775, 1965-1972 $100
8" (20cm) hard plastic, bent knee and bent knee walker, white skin, #775, 1965-1972 $200
8" (20cm) hard plastic, straight legs, "Alex Mold", #0775, 1973; #575, 1974-1975 $75
8" (20cm) hard plastic, straight legs, 1976-1988 $65
8" (20cm) hard plastic, straight legs, 1996-1997 $65

Indian Boy
8" (20cm) hard plastic, bent knee, *Americana Series*, #720, 1966 $400

Indian Girl
8" (20cm) hard plastic, bent knee, *Americana Series*, #721, 1966 $425

Indonesia
8" (20cm) hard plastic, bent knee, #779, 1970-1972
$100

8" (20cm) hard plastic, with *Maggie* smile face, bent knee, #779, 1970-1972 $150
8" (20cm) hard plastic, straight legs, "Alex Mold", #0779, 1973, #579, 1974-1975 $75
8" (20cm) hard plastic, straight legs, 1976-1988 $65

Ingalls, Laura
14" (36cm) plastic/vinyl, *Classic Dolls*, 1989-1991
$85
14" (36cm) plastic/vinyl, 1995 $95
8" (20cm) hard plastic, 1998-1999 $70

Ingres
14" (36cm) plastic/vinyl, *Fine Arts Series*, 1987 $100

Inky
14" (36cm) cloth, poodle, 1954 $375

Innocent Silk Victorian
8" (20cm) hard plastic, 1999 $70

Investigator Wendy
8" (20cm) hard plastic, QVC, 1999 *(see Special Dolls)*
$80

Iris
10" (25cm) hard plastic, 1987-1988 $85

Irish (Ireland)
8" (20cm) hard plastic, bent knee walker, #778, 1964-1965 $175
8" (20cm) hard plastic, bent knee, #778, 1965-1972
$100
8" (20cm) hard plastic, straight legs, "Alex Mold", #0778, 1973; #578, 1974-1975 $75
8" (20cm) hard plastic, straight legs, 1976-1985 $60
8" (20cm) hard plastic, straight legs, 1985-1987 $60
8" (20cm) hard plastic, straight legs, short dress, 1988-1992 $60
8" (20cm) hard plastic, straight legs, 1994 $60

Late 1960s 8-inch (20cm) *Indian Boy* and *Indian Girl*. Also named *Hiawatha* and *Pocahontas*. *Marge Meisinger Collection*.

8" (20cm) hard plastic, straight legs, 1996-1998 $60
8" (20cm) hard plastic, straight legs, 1998-1999 $85

Irish Dream
8" (20cm) hard plastic, 1999 *(see also Ballerinas)*
$80

Irish Lass
8" (20cm) hard plastic, 1995 $65

Isolde
14" (36cm) Opera Series, 1985-1986 $100

Israel
8" (20cm) hard plastic, bent knee walker, #768, 1965
$155
8" (20cm) hard plastic, bent knee, #768, 1965-1972
$110
8" (20cm) hard plastic, straight legs, "Alex Mold",
#0768, 1973; #568, 1974-1975 $70
8" (20cm) hard plastic, straight legs, 1976-1988 $65

J

Jabberwocky
8" (20cm) hard plastic, 1999 $75

Jack and Jill
7" (18cm) composition, 1938-1943 $300 each
9" (23cm) composition, 1939 $325 each
8" (20cm) hard plastic, straight legs, *Storyland Dolls*,
1987-1992 $60 each
8" (20cm) hard plastic, only sold as a pair, 1996 $110 pair

Jack Be Nimble
8" (20cm) hard plastic, made for Dolly Dears, 1993
(see Special Dolls) $150

Jackson, Sarah
14" (36cm) plastic/vinyl, 2nd set, *First Ladies Series*,
1979-1981 $100

Jackie
10" (25cm) hard plastic, pink knit suit, 1995 $100
10" (25cm) hard plastic, bridal outfit, 1996 $110
10" (25cm) hard plastic, bridal outfit with groom doll
(John), 1996 $225
10" (25cm) hard plastic, pink linen suit, 1997-1998
$110
10" (25cm) hard plastic, opera coat and gown, 1998
$125
10" (25cm) hard plastic, cocktail dress, 1998 $125
21" (53cm) plastic/vinyl, doll with luggage and wardrobe,
1997 $600

Jacqueline
21" (53cm) hard plastic/vinyl arms, 1961-1962
Brocade Ball Gown with Crimson Full Length Coat,
#2140, 1962 $850

Italian
8" (20cm) hard plastic, bent knee walker, #493, 1961;
#393, 1962-1963; #793,1964 $165
Outfit only for 8" (20cm) doll, #0393, 1962-1963
$95
8" (20cm) hard plastic, bent knee, #793, 1965-1972
$110
8" (20cm) hard plastic, straight legs, "Alex Mold",
#0793, 1973; #593, 1974-1975 $75
8" (20cm) hard plastic, straight legs, 1975-1984 $65
8" (20cm) hard plastic, white face, 1985-1987 $60
8" (20cm) hard plastic, straight legs, 1988-1991 $65
8" (20cm) hard plastic, straight legs, 1992-1994 $65
8" (20cm) hard plastic, straight legs, 1995 $ 70
8" (20cm) hard plastic, straight legs, 1997-1998 $70

Ivory Lace *(see Tree Topper)*

White Brocade Ball Gown with Jacket, #2130, 1962
$875
Brocade Ball Gown with Rose Side Panels,
#2125, 1962 $900
Riding Outfit, #2117, 1962 $650
White Satin Gown with Long Coat, #2210, 1961 $700
Additional Boxed Outfits
Evening Gown, #22-30, 1962 $350
Evening Gown with Jacket, #22-35, 1962 $375
Jacket with Pillbox Hat, #22-15, 1962 $350
Nightgown, #22-17, 1962 $200
Riding Outfit, #22-25, 1962 $300
Robe, #22-18, 1962 $200
Skirt and Blouse, #22-10, 1962 $350
Wool Suit and Hat, #22-20, 1962 $375
In trunk with wardrobe, 1962 *(see Miss Judy)*
10" (25cm) hard plastic, 1962 only
Pink satin evening gown, #885 $700
Satin evening gown with matching long stole, #886
$600
Slacks and sweater set, #865 $625
Two piece suit with nylon blouse and matching hat, #894
$650
Wool coat and sheath dress, #895 $650
NOTE: Above outfits for 10" (25cm) Jacqueline were also
sold as boxed outfits. Deduct $180 from the price of the
dressed dolls.

Jamaica
8" (20cm) hard plastic, straight legs, 1986-1988 $65

Jane and Michael Banks
8" (20cm) Disney World Doll and Teddy Bear Convention,
1999 *(see Special Dolls)* $200

Janie
12" (31cm) toddler, 1964-1966
A-Line Linen Dress with Lace Trim, #1130, 1966
$325
Ballerina, pink, blue or yellow tutu, #1124, 1965 $325
Navy Coat and Hat, #1162, 1964 $300

Pink Cotton Dress with Rose Applique, #1170, 1964
$300
Pink Organdy Dress with Lace Trim, #1121, 1965
$325
Red School Dress with Applique, #1125, 1965 $325
Smock with Leotard, #1134, 1966 $350
White Cotton Dress with Red Sleeves, #1157, 1964
$325
White Linen Dress with Applique, #1158, 1964 $325
White Organdy Dress, #1156, 1964 $300
Yellow Dotted Cotton Dress, #1122, 1965 $300
14" (36cm) baby, 1972-1973 $85
20" (51cm) baby, 1972-1973 $95

Japan
8" (20cm) hard plastic, bent knee, #770, 1968-1972
$100
With *Maggie* smile face, 1968-1972 $125
8" (20cm) hard plastic, straight legs, "Alex Mold",
#0770, 1973; #570, 1974-1975 $75

8" (20cm) hard plastic, straight legs, 1976-1986 $65
8" (20cm) hard plastic, 1987-1990 $65
8" (20cm) hard plastic, painted white face, 1992-1993
$65
Jasmine
10" (25cm) *Portrette Series*, 1987-1988 $80
10" (25cm) hard plastic, Home Shopping Club, 1998
(see Special Dolls) $120
8" (20cm) hard plastic, made for Disney Store Gallery,
1999 *(see Special Dolls)* $80
Jeannie Walker
13-14" (33-36cm) composition, 1940s $700
18" (46cm) composition, 1940s $725
Jennifer's Trunk Set
14" (36cm) doll and wardrobe, 1990 $260
Jessica
18" (46cm) cloth/vinyl, 1990 $140
Jingles the Juggler
8" (20cm) hard plastic, 1996 $65

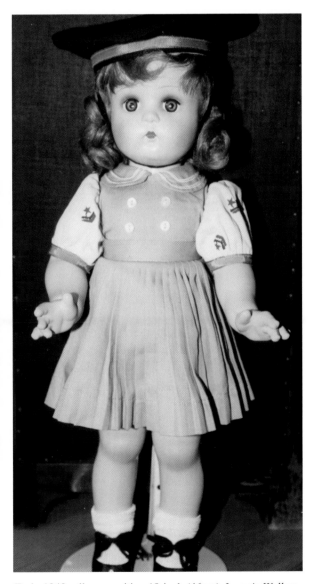

Early 1940s all composition 18-inch (46cm) *Jeannie Walker*.
Veronica Jochens Collection

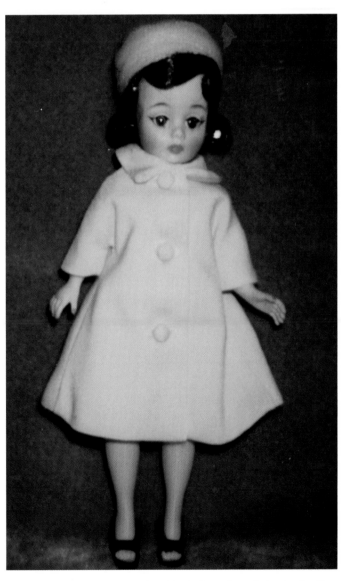

1962 10-inch (25cm) *Jacqueline*. The doll was intended to be the First
Lady. *Marge Meisinger Collection.*

Jo *(see Little Women)*
Joanie
 36" (91cm) plastic/vinyl, Cotton dress, #3510, 1960
  $500
 36" (91cm) Nurse, all white with black band on cap,
 1960 $450
 36" (91cm) Nurse, colored dress, all white pinafore and
 cap, #3610, 1961 $450
 36" (91cm) plastic/vinyl, Organdy dress with cotton
 pinafore, #3516, 1960 $500
 36" (91cm) plastic/vinyl, Organdy dress with organdy
 pinafore, #3520, 1960 $500
Jocko
 composition hand puppet, 1930s $200
John
 8" (20cm) hard plastic, *Storyland Dolls*, 1993 $65
John Power's Models
 14" (36cm) hard plastic, 1952 $1,550
 18" (46cm) hard plastic, 1952 $1,800
Johnson, Lady Bird
 14" (36cm) plastic/vinyl, *First Ladies Series*, 1994
  $100
Jolly Old Saint Nick
 16" (41cm) plastic/vinyl, 1997 $195
Jones, Casey
 8" (20cm) hard plastic, *Americana Series*, 1991-1992
  $65
Joseph and His Coat of Many Colors
 8" (20cm) hard plastic, *Bible Children Series*, 1953-1954
  $7,000
Josephine
 12" (31cm) *Portraits of History*, 1980-1986 $70
 21" (53cm) hard plastic/vinyl, *Portrait Series*, 1994
  $350

Joseph the Dream Teller
 8" (20cm) hard plastic, 1995 $80
Joy
 12" (31cm) porcelain, New England Collectors Society,
 1990 *(see Special Dolls)* $250
 8" (20cm) hard plastic, Saks Fifth Avenue, 1994 *(see
 Special Dolls)* $125
Joy Noel Tree Topper
 10" (25cm) hard plastic, made for Spiegel's, 1992
 (see Special Dolls) $125
Judy
 21" (53cm) composition, 1945-1947 $3,000 up
 21" (53cm) hard plastic/vinyl arms, 1962 *(see Miss Judy)*
Judo-Slav
 7" (18cm) composition, 1935-1937 $275
Juliet
 18" (46cm) composition, 1937-1940 $1,300
 21" (53cm) composition, *Portrait Series*, 1945-1946
  $2,000 up
 7-1/2-8" (19-20cm) hard plastic, straight leg walker,
 #473, 1955 $1,000
 12" (31cm) plastic/vinyl, *Portrait Children Series*,
 1978-1987 $70
 12" (31cm) *Romance Collection*, re-introduced,
 1991-1992 $90
 8" (20cm) hard plastic, *Storyland Collection*, mid-year
 release, 1994 $100
June Bride
21" (53cm) composition, *Portrait Series*, 1939, 1946-1947
  $2,100 up
June Wedding
 8" (20cm) hard plastic, 1956 $750

Karen Ballerina
 15" (38cm) composition, 1946-1949 $800
 18-21" (46-53cm) composition, late 1940s $1,000
 15-18" (38-46cm) hard plastic, 1948-1949 $900
 15" (38cm) porcelain, 1999 $160
Kate Greenaway
 16" (41cm) cloth, 1936-1938 $925
 7" (18cm) composition, 1938-1943 $375
 9" (23cm) composition, 1936-1939 $400
 13-15" (33-38cm) composition, 1938-1943 $700
 16"-18" (41-46cm) composition, 1938-1943 $750
 20" (51cm) composition, 1938-1943 $825
 24" (61cm) composition, 1938-1943 $875
 14" (36cm) Classic Dolls, 1993 $100
Kathleen Toddler
 23" (58cm) rigid vinyl, 1959 $160

Kathy
 17-21" (43-53cm) composition, 1939-1946 $750 up
 15-18" (38-46cm) hard plastic, has braids, 1949-1951
  $600-$800
 23" (58cm) hard plastic, braids, 1949-1951 $850
Kathy Baby
 13-15" (33-38cm) vinyl, rooted or molded hair, 1954-1956
  $80-$135
 11" (28cm) vinyl, molded hair, with trousseau, 1955-1956
  $140
 11-13" (28-33cm) vinyl, rooted or molded hair, 1955-1956
  $75-$135
 18-21" (46-53cm) rooted or molded hair, 1954-1956
  $125-$150
 21" (53cm) 1954 $175
 21" (53cm) and 25" (64cm) 1955-1956 $175-$200
 13" (33cm) layette in wicker basket, FAO Schwarz
 exclusive, 1954 $250
Kathy Cry Dolly
 11-15" (28-38cm) vinyl, 1957-1958 $75-$100
 18" (46cm), 21" (53cm), 25" (64cm) $100-$150
 11" (28cm) layette in window box, 1958-1959 $175

Kathy Skater
15" (38cm), 18" (46cm), 23" (58cm) hard plastic,
1949-1951 $650 up

Kathy Tears
11" (28cm), 15" (38cm), 17" (43cm) vinyl, closed mouth,
1959-1962 $75-$100
19" (48cm), 23" (58cm), 26" (66cm) 1959-1962
                                             $125-$175
12" (31cm), 16" (41cm), 19" (48cm) vinyl, 1960-1961
                                             $80-$100

Katie
12" (31cm) hard plastic, made for FAO Schwarz 100th
Anniversary, 1962 $1,300
12" (31cm) plastic/vinyl, African American, *Janie* Face,
Aqua Cotton Dress, #1155, 1965 $325
12" (31cm) plastic/vinyl, African American, *Janie* Face,
Pink Organdy Dress, #1156, 1965 $300
12" (31cm) plastic/vinyl, 1999 $55

Keane, Doris
cloth, 1930s $850
9-11" (23-28cm) composition, 1936-1937 $300

Kelly
12" (31cm) hard plastic, 1959 $500 up
15-16" (38-41cm) 1958-1959 $325-$400
16" (41cm) in trunk with wardrobe, FAO Schwarz
exclusive, 1959 $900
18" (46cm) 1958-1959 $325-$400
22" (56cm) 1958-1959 $475-$500
15" (38cm) vinyl, 1998-1999 $75-$100
18" (46cm) vinyl, 1997-1998 $125
20" (51cm) vinyl, 1998-1999 $100-$130

Kennedy, Jacqueline
14" (36cm) plastic/vinyl, 6th set, *First Ladies Seri*es,
1989-1990 $175

King
21" (53cm) composition, 1942-1946 $2,500 up

King Arthur
8" (20cm) workshop kit, Disney World Doll and Teddy
Bear Convention, 1995 $100

King of Hearts
8" (20cm) hard plastic, 1996 $65

Kiss Me, I'm Irish
8" (20cm) hard plastic, QVC, 1999 *(see Special Dolls)*
                                             $70

Kitten
24" (61cm) rooted hair, 1961-1963 $100
14-18" (36-46cm) cloth/vinyl, 1962-1963 $50-$95
20" (51cm) nurser, doesn't wet, cryer box, 1968 $100
20" (51cm) dressed in pink, 1985-1986 $95
8" (20cm) vinyl, 1998 $65

Kitten Kries
20" (51cm) cloth/vinyl, pink or blue dress, 1967 $100

Kitten, Lively
14" (36cm), 18" (46cm), 24" (61cm) knob moves head
and limbs, 1962-1963 $125-$185
14" (36cm) layette in suitcase, 1962 $225

Kitten, Mama
18" (46cm) same as *Lively* but also has cryer box, 1963
                                             $150 up

Kitty Baby
21" (53cm) composition, 1941-1942 $200

Klondike Kate
10" (25cm) hard plastic, #761, 1962 $1,600 up

Knave
8" (20cm) Disney World Doll and Teddy Bear Convention,
1996 *(see Special Dolls)* $150
8" (20cm) hard plastic, 1996-1998 $75

Korea
8" (20cm) hard plastic, bent knee, # 772, 1968-1970
                                             $225
8" (20cm) hard plastic, re-introduced 1988-1989 $70

Kukla
8" (20cm) hard plastic, 1995 $65

Kurt Von Trapp *(see Sound of Music)*

Kwanzaa
10" (25cm) hard plastic, 1995-1997 $100

L

Ladybird
8" (20cm) Storyland, 1988-1989 $75

Lady Bug Garden
8" (20cm) hard plastic, QVC, 1999 *(see Special Dolls)*
                                             $75

Lady Churchill
18" (46cm) hard plastic, 1953 $1,200 up

Lady Hamilton
18" (46cm) composition, 1940s $1,200 up
10" (25cm) hard plastic, pink silk gown, picture hat,
#975, 1957 $625
20" (51cm) hard plastic/vinyl arms, *Models Formal Series*,
#2175, 1957 $1,000
21" (53cm) #2182, beige lace over pink gown, 1968
                                             $500
12" (31cm) vinyl, *Portraits of History*, 1984-1986
                                             $65

Lady in Red
21" (53cm) red taffeta, *Cissy*, 1958 $950 up
10" (25cm) *Portrette Series*, 1990 $85

Lady in Waiting
7-1/2-8" (19-20cm) hard plastic, straight leg walker,
#487, 1955 $1,500 up

1955 8-inch (20cm) *Lady in Waiting. Marge Meisinger Collection. Photo by Carol J. Stover.*

Lady Lee
 8" (20cm) hard plastic, *Storyland Dolls*, 1988 $65
 8" (20cm) hard plastic, made for Doll Finders Fantasy Event, 1990 *(see Special Dolls)* $150
 8" (20cm) hard plastic, Home Shopping Club, 1998 *(see Special Dolls)* $80

Lady Lovelace
 cloth/felt, 1930s $675

Lady Valentine
 8" (20cm) hard plastic, *Storyland Dolls*, 1994 $60

Lady Windermere
 21" (53cm) composition, 1945-1946 $2,000 up

Lancelot
 8" (20cm) hard plastic, in set with Guinevere, *Anniversary Collection*, 1995 $200
 8" (20cm) hard plastic, 1999 $80

Lane, Harriet
 14" (36cm) plastic/vinyl, 3rd set, *First Ladies Series*, 1982-1984 $100

Laos
 8" (20cm) hard plastic, straight legs, 1987 $75

Lapland
 8" (20cm) hard plastic, *International Dolls*, 1993 $60

Lassie
 8" (20cm) hard plastic, 1995 $60

Latvia
 8" (20cm) hard plastic, straight legs, 1987 $70

Laughing Allegra
 cloth, 1932 $725

Laurie, Little Men
 8" (20cm) hard plastic, bent knee, #755, 1966-1972 $125
 Check pants, straight legs $65
 8" (20cm) hard plastic, straight legs, "Alex Mold" #0755, 1973; #416, 1974-1975 $70
 8" (20cm) hard plastic, straight legs, 1976-1992 $60
 8" (20cm) hard plastic, 1995-1996 $70
 12" (31cm) all hard plastic, 1966 only $500
 12" (31cm) plastic/vinyl, 1967-1988 $75
 12" (31cm) plastic/vinyl, made for Sears, 1989-1990 *(see Special Dolls)* $100

Laurie, Piper
 14" (36cm), 21" (53cm) hard plastic, 1950 $2,500 up

Lavender Rose
 10" (25cm) hard plastic, QVC, 1999 *(see Special Dolls)* $85

Lazy Mary
 7" (18cm) composition, 1936-1938 $300

Le Petit Boudoir
 10" (25cm) made for CU, 1992 *(see Special Dolls)* $125

Lemonade Girl
 8" (20cm) 1998-1999 $85

Lena *(see River Boat)*

Leo
 8" (20cm) hard plastic, 1998 $85

Leslie (African American *Polly*)
 17" (43cm) plastic/vinyl, wearing green cotton ruffled dress, #1615, 1965 only $275
 Wearing white lace dress with pink lining, #1624, 1965 only $275
 Wearing pink satin and velvet gown, #1632, 1965 only $450
 Wearing yellow tulle formal, #1651, 1965 only $400
 Wearing pink or aqua dress with lace trim and shawl, #1620, 1966 only $375
 Wearing pink pleated formal, #1650, 1966 only $300
 Wearing formal of tulle and lace, several variations, pink, blue or yellow, 1967-1971 $325
 Dressed as a bride, several variations of tulle and lace, 1966-1971 $275
 Dressed as a ballerina, pink, blue, yellow, or white tutu, 1966 –1971 $275
 Trunk set with wardrobe, FAO Schwarz exclusive, 1966 $700 up

Letty Bridesmaid
 7" (18cm) composition, 1938-1940 $300

Lewis, Shari
 14" (36cm) gold lace dress, #1430, 1959 $750

14" (36cm) yellow blouse with green skirt, #1433, 1959
$750

14" (36cm) shirtwaist dress, available in yellow, aqua, or green, 1959 $775

14" (36cm) theater dress and coat, #1440, 1959 $800

21" (53cm) gold lace dress, #2430, 1959 $850

21" (53cm) yellow blouse with green skirt, #2433, 1959
$850

21" (53cm) shirtwaist dress, available in yellow, aqua, or green, 1959 $875

21" (53cm) theater dress and coat, #2440, 1959 $900

Liberace
8" (20cm) hard plastic, 1997 $110

Libra
8" (20cm) hard plastic, 1998 $85

Liesl (see Sound of Music)

Li'l Christmas Cookie
8" (20cm) hard plastic, Americana Series, 1993-1994
$65

Li'l Clara & Nutcracker
8" (20cm) hard plastic, 1993-1994 $60

Li'l Miss Genius
7" (18cm) vinyl, 1993-1994 $40

Li'l Miss Magnin Sponsors the Arts
8" (20cm) I. Magnin, 1994 (see Special Dolls) $125

Li'l Sir Genius
7" (18cm) vinyl, 1993-1994 $40

Lila Bridesmaid
7" (18cm) composition, 1938-1940 $300

Lilac Fairie Ballerina
21" (53cm) plastic/vinyl, Portrait, 1993-1994 $325

Lilibet
16" (41cm) composition, 1938 $775

Lily
10" (25cm) hard plastic, 1987-1988 $75

Lily of the Valley
10" (25cm) hard plastic, 1998-1999 $130

Lincoln, Mary Todd
14" (36cm) plastic/vinyl, 3rd set, First Ladies Series, 1982-1984 $165

Lind, Jenny
10" (25cm) hard plastic, pink gown, #1171, 1969 $625

10" (25cm) hard plastic, pink gown with lace trim, #1184, 1970 $650

14" (36cm) plastic/vinyl, pink gown with lace trim, #1491, 1970 $400

21" (53cm) plastic/vinyl, pink gown, #2191, 1969
$1,300

21" (53cm) plastic/vinyl, pink gown with lace trim, #2181, 1970 $1,350

Lind, Jenny and Her Listening Cat
14" (36cm) plastic/vinyl, #1470, 1969-1971 $325

Linens
Pillow, blanket and sheet set for 8" (20cm) doll, 1950s
$125

Pillow and sheet set for Little Genius, 1950s $125

Lion Tamer
8" (20cm) hard plastic, 1990 $65

Lissy
11-1/2-12" (30-31cm) hard plastic, jointed knees and elbows, 1956-1958

Checked Coat with Dress and Hat, #1235, 1956 $475

Checked Dress with Cotton Pinafore, #1218, 1958
$375

Cotton Dress with Organdy Pinafore, #1240, 1956
$375

Dotted Skirt with Organdy Blouse and Hat, #1226, 1956
$400

Dotted Swiss Organdy Dress with Velvet Bonnet, #1227, 1956 $425

Nylon Dotted Party Dress, #1167, 1957 $425

Organdy Dress with Feather Stitching and Straw Hat, #1241, 1956 $425

Organdy Dress with Straw Hat, #1210, 1958 $400

Pink Taffeta Party Dress with Tulle Hat, #1250, 1956
$600

Sleeveless Cotton Dress with Bonnet, red, tangerine, light blue, dark blue, yellow, mauve, pink, purple, aqua, or green, #1222, 1956 $375

Taffeta Dress with Wide White Collar, #1151, 1957
$425

Trousseau Window Box Gift Set, #220, 1956 $1500 up

Wool Cardigan with Organdy Dress and Hat, #1234, 1956
$400

Basic Doll Wearing Chemise, #1100, 1957; #1200, 1958
$300

Coat and Hat $375

Cotton Dress $350 up

Cotton Dress with Cotton Pinafore $350 up

Faux Fur Coat and Hat $400

Long Organdy Party Dress $450 up

Nightgown $275

Organdy Dress $375 up

Robe $275

Sleeveless Cotton Dress $325 up

Sleeveless Organdy Dress $325 up

Striped Shirt with Skirt $375

21" (53cm) pink tulle dress, 1961 (Cissy) $1,500 up

21" (53cm) Portrait, pink dress with tiara, 1966 (Coco)
$2,300 up

Lithuania
8" (20cm) hard plastic, International Series, 1994
$65

Little Audrey
vinyl, 1954 $450

Little Betty
9-11" (23-28cm) composition, 1935-1943 $295

Little Bit Country
8" (20cm) hard plastic, MADC, 1997 (see Special Dolls)
$275

Little Bitsey
9" (23cm) vinyl, nurser, 1967-1968 $175

Little Bo Peep (see Bo Peep)

Little Boy Blue
7" (18cm) composition, 1937-1939 $400

Little Butch
9" (23cm) all vinyl, 1967-1968 $175

Late 1950s 12-inch (31cm) *Lissy* with original wardrobe. *Marge Meisinger Collection.*

Little Cherub
    11" (28cm) composition, 1945-1946 $325
    7" (18cm) all vinyl, 1960 $300

Little Colonel
    8-1/2-9" (22-23cm) composition, closed mouth (rare size)
    1935 $750
    11-13" (28-33cm) composition, closed mouth $600-$675
    14-17" (36-43cm) composition, open mouth $700-$800
    17" (43cm) composition, closed mouth $750
    18-23" (46-58cm) composition, open mouth $800-$900
    26-27" (66-69cm) composition, open mouth $1,200

Little Christmas Princess
    8" (20cm) hard plastic, 1995-1996 $70

Little Devil
    8" (20cm) hard plastic, *Americana Series*, 1992-1993
        $65

Little Doll Collector
    8" (20cm) hard plastic, Shirley's Dollhouse, 1999
    (see Special Dolls) $75

Little Dorrit
    16" (41cm) cloth, Dicken's character, 1934 $725

Little Edwardian
    7-1/2-8" (19-20cm) hard plastic, straight leg non-walker,
    #415, 1953-1954 $1,000
    7-1/2-8" (19-20cm) hard plastic, straight leg walker,
    1955 $1,000

Little Emily
    16" (41cm) cloth, Dicken's character, 1934 $725

Little Emperor
    8" (20cm) hard plastic, made for UFDC luncheon,
    1992 *(see Special Dolls)* $600

Little Genius
    12-14" (31-36cm) composition/cloth, 1935-1940,
    1942-1946 $250
    14" (36cm) composition in trunk with layette $375
    16-20" (42-51cm) composition/cloth, 1935-1937,
    1942-1946 $250 up
    18" (46cm) composition and latex, 1947 $300 up
    24-25" (61-64cm) composition/cloth, 1936-1940
        $275 up

    8" (20cm) hard plastic/vinyl, 1956-1964 *(also called
    Genius or Baby Genius)*
    Basic doll in box wearing panties and booties, #100, 1958;
    1960-1962; #200, 1959, 1963, 1964; #700, 1956
        $225
    Basic doll with molded hair wearing panties and booties,
    #210, 1964 $225
    Basic doll in box wearing sun suit, booties and bonnet,
    #200-1957 $225
    Checked cotton dress and bonnet, #740, 1956;
    #115, 1958 $275
    Christening gown, #765, 1956; #275, 1957;
    #141, 1958; #235, 1959, 1961; #135, 1960;
    #160, 1962; #250, 1963 $375 up
    Cotton dress, #121, 1962 $275
    Cotton and organdy dress with bonnet, #125, 1960
        $300
    Cotton dress and bonnet, #242, 1957; #216, 1959;
    #217, 1961; #230, 1963 $300
    Cotton dress with embroidery and bonnet, #226, 1961
        $300
    Cotton dress with gingham pinafore and bonnet,
    #248, 1957 $275
    Cotton dress with organdy pinafore and bonnet,
    #247, 1957; #135, 1958 $285
    Cotton dress with wool sacque and cap, #150, 1962
        $325
    Cotton jacket and panties set, #105, 1958 $275
    Cotton play suit with rocker, #228, 1961 $350
    Cotton romper and bonnet, #130, 1962 $275
    Cotton romper and pinafore with matching bonnet,
    #215, 1961 $275
    Crepe creeper set, #720, 1956 $250
    Crepe jacket and panties set, #110, 1958 $250

Doll in Sewing Basket, FAO Schwarz exclusive, 1965
$700 up

Embroidered organdy dress and bonnet, #742, 1956;
#244, 1957; #120, 1958; #126, 1960 $300
Flannel coat and bonnet, #265, 1957; #140, 1958
$275

Gabardine coat and bonnet, #780, 1956 $275
Jumper with leotard, #110, 1960 $300
Nude perfect doll $150
Nylon checked dress and bonnet, #220, 1959 $300
Organdy coat dress and bonnet, #240, 1963 $300
Organdy dress with bonnet, #755, 1956; #136, 1958;
#227, 1961; #140, 1962; #230, 1963 $300
Organdy dress with bonnet and wool shawl,
#767, 1956 $325
Organdy dress with coat and bonnet, #130, 1960 $325
Organdy dress with hooded cape, #775, 1956 $340
Organdy dress with lace ruffles, #243, 1957 $300
Organdy dress with wool sacque and cap, #766, 1956;
#260, 1957; #230, 1961 $325
Overalls and hat, #106, 1960 $300
Pastel organdy dress with feather stitching and bonnet,
#745, 1956 $300
Pin dot dress and bonnet, #741, 1956 $275
Pink and white organdy dress and bonnet, #123, 1958
$300
Robe, #220, 1963 $225
Romper, #225, 1963 $225
Romper or sun suit and coat dress, #215, 1959;
#116, 1960 $275
Rosebud cotton dress and bonnet, #743, 1956 $285
Sheets and pillows set $125
Striped cotton dress with white pinafore and bonnet,
#249, 1957 $300
Striped jersey and cotton romper with bonnet,
#730, 1956 $275
Train case with wardrobe, #190, 1960 $500 up
Layette box set, #790, 1956 $500 up
Two piece creeper set, #220, 1957 $275
White organdy dress with bonnet, #246, 1957 $300
White organdy dress with embroidery and bonnet,
#756, 1956 $300
NOTE: Most of the above outfits can be found boxed
without the doll. Deduct $175 from prices above for boxed
outfits only. In addition, there were many outfits that were
sold boxed that were not available on a doll. These boxed
outfits are priced from $35-$125.
7" (18cm) vinyl with painted eyes, various outfits,
1993-1995 $40-$50
Boxed outfits for 7" (18cm) vinyl with painted eyes,
1993-1994 $20-$30

Little Godey Lady
7-1/2-8" (19-20cm) hard plastic, straight leg walker,
1954 $1,150
7-1/2-8" (19-20cm) hard plastic, straight leg walker,
#491, 1955 $1,000 up

Little Granny
14" (36cm) plastic/vinyl, stripe gown, #1430, 1966
$240

14" (36cm) plastic/vinyl, floral gown, #1431, 1966
$260

Little Huggums (see Huggums, Little)
Little Jack Horner
7" (18cm) composition, 1937-1943 $350 up
Little Jumping Joan
8" (20cm) Storyland Dolls, 1989-1990 $70
Little Lady
21" (53cm) hard plastic, has braids and Colonial gown,
1949 $2,100
8" (20cm) hard plastic, gift set in frame with toiletries,
#1050, 1960 $1,200 up
8" (20cm) hard plastic, bent knee walker, doll only
$400

Little Lord Fauntleroy
16" (41cm) cloth, 1930s $725
13" (33cm) composition, 1936-1937 $700
Little Madeline
7-1/2-8" (19-20cm) hard plastic, straight leg non-walker,
1953 $700
8" (20cm) hard plastic, straight leg walker, Neiman
Marcus, doll in case with clothes, 1954 $1,200
8" (20cm) hard plastic, straight leg walker, Neiman Marcus
exclusive, doll only, 1954 $700
Little Maid
8" (20cm) straight legs, Storyland Dolls, 1987-1988
$70

Little Men (Nat, Stuffy and Tommy Bangs)
15" (38cm) hard plastic, circa 1952 $850 each
$2,700 set

Little Mermaid
10" (25cm) hard plastic, Portrette Series, 1992-1993
$105
8" (20cm) hard plastic, 1995 $65
Little Minister
8" (20cm) hard plastic, bent knee walker, #411, 1957
$2,500

Little Miss
8" (20cm) hard plastic, Storyland Dolls, 1989-1991
$65

Little Miss Godey
8" (20cm) hard plastic, MADC, 1992 (see Special Dolls)
$125

Little Miss Magnin
8" (20cm) hard plastic, made for I. Magnin, 1992
(see Special Dolls) $130
Little Miss Muffet (see Miss Muffet)
Little Nanny Etticoat
8" (20cm) hard plastic, 1986-1988 $75
Little Nell
16" (41cm) cloth, Dicken's character, 1934 $750
14" (36cm) composition, 1938-1940 $700
Little Orphan Annie
8" (20cm) hard plastic, includes plush dog, 1999
$50

Little Rascals
8" (20cm) FAO Schwarz, 1996 (see Special Dolls)
$350 set

Little Red Riding Hood (see Red Riding Hood)

Little Shaver

7" (18cm) cloth, 1940-1944	$525
10" (25cm) cloth, 1940-1944	$500
16" (41cm) cloth, 1940-1944	$575
22" (56cm) cloth, 1940-1944	$600 up
12" (31cm) plastic/vinyl, painted eyes	
Blue and white cardigan with romper, #2933, 1964	
	$275
Blue and white striped suit with hat, boy doll, #2942, 1963	$300
Blue and white striped suit with hat, girl doll, #2945, 1963	$275
Gingham dress with lace bib, #2935, 1964	$275
Lace panties with telephone #2930, 1963; #2930, 1964; #2950, 1965	$300
Lace trimmed dress with panties, #2940, 1963	$300
Pin dot cotton dress #2957, 1965	$300
Romper, #2932, 1963	$275
White dress with blue trim, #2945, 1964	$275
White suit with blue trim, boy doll, #2942, 1964	$300

Little Southern Boy/Girl

10" (25cm) latex/vinyl, 1950-1951	$175

Little Southern Girl

7 1/2-8" (19-20cm) hard plastic, 1953	$1,000

Little Thumbkins

8" (20cm) hard plastic, 1995	$65

Little Victoria

7-1/2-8" (19-20cm) straight leg non-walker, #376, 1953	$1,350
7-1/2-8" (19-20cm) straight leg walker, #328, 1954	$1,300

Little Women (Meg, Jo, Amy, Beth, Marme or Marmee)

16" (41cm) cloth, 1930-1936	$700 each
7" (18cm) composition, 1935-1944	$300 each
9" (23cm) composition, 1937-1940	$325 each
13-15" (33-38cm) composition, 1937-1946	$375 each
14-15" (36-38cm) hard plastic, 1947-1956	$475 each
14-15" (36-38cm) Amy with loop curls, 1947-1950	
	$525
14-15" (36-38cm) hard plastic, spread fingers, 1949-1952	$500 each
	matched set $2,600 set
11-1/2-12" (29-31cm) hard plastic, jointed elbow and knees, 1957-1958	$350 each
11-1/2-12" (29-31cm) hard plastic, one-piece arms and legs, 1959-1967	$275 each
7-1/2-8" (19-20cm) hard plastic, straight leg walker, 5 dolls, 1955	$400 each
8" (20cm) hard plastic, bent knee walker, 5 dolls, #609, 1956; #409, 1957; #581, 1958, #481, 1959	
	$275 each
8" (20cm) hard plastic, bent knee walker, 5 dolls, #381, 1960; #481, 1961; #381, 1962; #381, 1963; #781, 1964-1965	$175 each
Outfit only for 8" (20cm) doll, #0381, 1962-1963	
	$95 each

8" (20cm) hard plastic, bent knee, #781, 1965-1971; #7811 Amy, #7812 Beth, #7813 Jo, #7814 Meg, #7815 Marme, 1972	$110 each
8" (20cm) hard plastic, straight legs, "Alex Mold", #7811 to #7815, 1973, #411-#415, 1974-1975	$75 each
8" (20cm) hard plastic, straight legs, #411 to #415, 1976-1986	$60 each
8" (20cm) hard plastic, straight legs, #405 to #409, 1987-1990	$65 each
8" (20cm) hard plastic, straight legs, #411 to #415, 1991-1992	$75 each
8" (20cm) hard plastic, Amy with loop curls, #411, 1991	$90
8" (20cm) hard plastic, straight legs, #14523 to #14528, 1995-1996	$70 each
8" (20cm) hard plastic, Jo Goes to New York, trunk set, 1995	$175
8" (20cm) hard plastic, Meg in blue ball gown, 1995	$85
8" (20cm) hard plastic, Amy Goes to Paris, trunk set, 1996	$175
8" (20cm) hard plastic, straight legs, set of 5 dolls, FAO Schwarz, 1994 (see Special Dolls)	$700 set
8" (20cm) hard plastic, straight legs, FAO Schwarz, 1994 (see Special Dolls)	$125 each
8" (20cm) hard plastic, straight legs, 1999	$80 each
10" (25cm) hard plastic, Amy the Bride, 1995-1996	$90
10" (25cm) hard plastic, 1996 (no Marme)	$90 each
12" (31cm) plastic/vinyl, 1968-1989	$70 each
12" (31cm) set made for Sears, 1989-1990 (see Special Dolls)	$100 each
	$650 set
12" (31cm) hard plastic, 1993 (no Marme)	$100 each

Little Women Journals

16" (41cm) 1997-1999

Amy, Beth, Jo, Meg-doll only, 1997-1999	$100 each
Doll wearing Holiday dress, sold exclusively via Home Shopping Club, 1997	$150
Doll and book set, 1999	$110
Marme doll, 1999	$120
Additional Outfits	
Holiday Dresses, 1997-1999	$60 each
Hobby Outfits, 1997-1999	$50-$70 each
A Midsummer Nights Dream Costumes, 1998	
	$60 each
Nightgowns, 1997-1999	$30-$35 each
Picnic Outfits, 1999	$50 each
Winter Coats, 1997-1999	$40-$60 each
Marme's Winter Coat, 1999	$40
Accessories and Furniture	
A Midsummer Nights Dream Stage and Script, 1998	
	$220
Armoire, 1997-1999	$160
Baking Kit, 1999	$40
Bed with Journal, 1997-1999	$160
Bird Cage, 1997-1999	$10

Book, 1997-1999		$10
Brush and Comb Set, 1998-1999		$40
Carpet, 1997-1999		$10
Charm Bracelet, 1998-1999		$20
Christmas Tree, 1999		$25
Diary, 1997-1999		$40
Fireside Quilt, 1998		$80
Flower Basket, 1997-1999		$10
Lace Parasol, 1997-1999		$10
Lingerie, 1997-1999		$15
Magicloth Paper Dolls, 1998		$20
Mannequin, 1997		$30
Miss March's Doll Infirmary, 1998-1999		$50
School bag with glasses and inkwell, 1997-1999		$10
Sled, 1999		$20
Small Trunk with Necklace, 1997-1999		$40
Tea Set, 1998-1999		$65

Littlest Angel
9" (23cm) latex/vinyl, 1950-1957 — $195

Littlest Cherub
9" (23cm) latex, 1951 — $175

Littlest Kitten
8" (20cm), vinyl, 1963-1964, nude doll — $150

Dressed Dolls
Batiste Dress with Bib, #535-1963	$350
Check Dress, #830, 1964	$300
Check Organdy Dress, #845, 1964	$325
Christening Dress, #560, 1963; #895, 1964	$400
Cotton Dress, #530, 1963; #832, 1964	$300
Cotton Dress with Applique, #834, 1964	$325
Dress with Sweater, #551, 1963	$350
Leotard and Smock, #841, 1964	$350
Organdy Coat Dress, #550, 1963	$350
Organdy Dress, #540, 1963	$350
Romper, #225, 1963	$275
Rosebud Romper, #520, 1963; #800, 1964	$275
Tricot Denton, #815, 1964	$275
Velveteen Dress, #846, 1964	$400
White Cotton Dress with red leotard, #541, 1963	$350

NOTE: Most of the above outfits can be found boxed without the doll. Deduct $200 from prices above for boxed outfits only.

Additional Boxed Outfits
Booties #0502, 1963; #0802, 1964	$35
Batiste Dress #0505, 1963; #0805, 1964	$125
Blue or Pink Organdy Dress and Petti #0510, 1963; #0810, 1964	$150
Check Cotton Dress #0505, 1963; #0805, 1964	$125
Dotted Swiss Dress #0808, 1964	$135
Taffeta Coat and Bonnet #0515, 1963	$150
Doll in Sewing Basket or Gift Sets with wardrobes	$650 up

Lively Huggums (see Huggums)
Lively Kitten (see Kitten)
Lively Pussy Cat (see Pussy Cat)
Lola and Lollie Bridesmaid
7" (18cm) composition, 1938-1940 — $400 each

Lollie Baby
rubber/composition, 1941-1942 — $125

Lollipop Munchkin
8" (20cm) hard plastic, 1995 — $125

Looby Loo
15-1/2" (39cm) hard plastic, 1951-1954 — $700

Lord Fauntleroy
12" (31cm) *Portrait Children*, 1981-1983 — $90

Lord Valentine
8" (20cm) hard plastic, *Storyland Dolls*, 1994 — $60

Louisa
18" (46cm) hard plastic, *Fashions of the Century*, 1954-1955 — $1,700

Louisa (see Sound of Music)

Love
8" (20cm) hard plastic, Collector's United, 1994 (see *Special Dolls*) — $150

Love is in the Air
8" (20cm) Doll and Teddy Bear Expo West, 1999 (see *Special Dolls*) — $100

Lovey Dovey
19" (48cm) vinyl baby, closed mouth, molded or rooted hair, 1958-1959 — $175
12" (31cm) all hard plastic toddler, 1948-1951 — $375
16-19" (42-48cm) hard plastic/latex, 1950-1951 — $225
Doll with button to move head, "Answer" doll — $550

Lucinda
12" (31cm) plastic/vinyl, 1971-1982 — $325
14" (36cm) plastic/vinyl, blue gown, 1971-1982 — $95
14" (36cm) pink or peach gown, *Classic Dolls*, 1983-1986 — $85

Luck of the Irish
8" (20cm) *Americana Series*, 1992-1993 — $60

Lucy
8" (20cm) hard plastic, bent knee walker, *Americana Series*, #488, 1961 — $1,500

Lucy (Lucille Ball)
21" (53cm) plastic/vinyl, 1996 — $350
9" (23cm) hard plastic, wearing Vitametavegamin dress, 1996 — $100
9" (23cm) hard plastic, with *Ricky* doll, 1996 — $200 set
10" (25cm) hard plastic, polka dot dress, 1998-1999 — $160
10" (25cm) hard plastic, Italian Movie costume with wine vat, 1999 — $160

Lucy and Ethel at the Chocolate Factory
8" (20cm) FAO Schwarz, 1997 (see *Special Dolls*) — $175

Lucy Bride
14" (36cm) composition, 1937-1940 — $475
17" (43cm) composition, 1937-1940 — $575
21" (53cm) composition, 1942-1944 — $2,300
14" (36cm) hard plastic, 1949-1950 — $625
17" (43cm) hard plastic, 1949-1950 — $650

Lucy Locket
8" (20cm) hard plastic, 1986-1988 — $75
14" (36cm) plastic/vinyl, 1995 — $150

Lullaby Munchkin
8" (20cm) hard plastic, 1995 — $125

Lullaby League Munchkin
8" (20cm) hard plastic, 1999 — $70

Madame (Alexander)
21" (53cm) one-piece skirt in pink, 1984 $375
21" (53cm) pink with overskirt, 1985-1987 $300
21" (53cm) blue with full lace overskirt, 1988-1990
   $300
21" (53cm) pink silk and lace gown, limited to 500 dolls,
1995 $750
8" (20cm) hard plastic, pink gown, 1993 $125
8" (20cm) hard plastic, pink taffeta and lace gown, 1995
   $125
10" (25cm) hard plastic, with hard cover book and back
drop $250

Madame Butterfly
10" (25cm) made for Marshall Fields, 1990 *(see Special
Dolls)* $125
21" (53cm) plastic/vinyl, 1997 $350
8" (20cm) hard plastic, 1997-1998 $95

Madame Doll
21" (53cm) hard plastic/vinyl arms, pink brocade,
1966 only $2,400 up
14" (36cm) plastic/vinyl, *Classic Dolls*, 1967-1975
   $225

Madame Pompadour
21" (53cm) hard plastic/vinyl arms, pink lace overskirt,
1970 $1,000 up

Madame de Pompadour
10" (25cm) hard plastic, 1999 $160

Madelaine
14" (36cm) composition, 1940-1942 $600 up
18" (46cm) composition, 1940-1942 $650 up
21" (53cm) composition, 1940-1942 $800 up

Madelaine Du Bain
11" (28cm) composition, closed mouth, 1937 $500
14" (36cm) composition, 1938-1939 $500
14" (36cm) composition trunk set with wardrobe
   $800 up
17" (43cm) composition, 1939-1941 $625
21" (53cm) composition, 1939-1941 $800
14" (36cm) hard plastic, 1949-1951 $975

Madeline
17-18" (43-46cm) hard plastic, jointed elbows and knees,
1950-1953 $700 up
18" (46cm) hard plastic/vinyl head, jointed body, 1961
   $800

Mad Hatter
8" (20cm) hard plastic, 1995 $65

Madison, Dolly
14" (36cm) plastic/vinyl, 1st set, *First Ladies Series*,
1976-1978 $125

Madonna and Child
10" (25cm) hard plastic, 1995 $100

Maggie
15" (38cm) hard plastic, 1948-1954 $525
17-18" (43-46cm) hard plastic, 1949-1953 $675
20-21" (51-53cm) hard plastic, 1948-1954 $700 up
22-23" (56-58cm) hard plastic, 1949-1952 $775 up
17" (43cm) plastic/vinyl, *Elise* Face, 1972-1973 $160

Maggie Elf
8" (20cm) hard plastic, 1995 $55

Maggie Mixup
8" (20cm) hard plastic, 1960-1961
    Angel costume, #618, 1961 $750 up
    Basic doll in panties, #600, 1961 $400
    Checked cotton school dress and hat, #617, 1961
   $500
    Checked dress with pinafore and hat, #598, 1960
   $500
    Cotton beach pajamas, #596, 1960 $550
    Cotton dress with dog, #627, 1961 $500
    Ice skater, #626, 1961 $725
    Jumper with leotard, #611, 1961 $600
    Navy skirt with white leotard and navy beret,
    #597, 1960 $550
    Overalls with watering can, #610, 1961 $650
    Riding habit, 1960-1961 $575
    Roller skater, #593, 1960; #615, 1961 $700
16-1/2" (42cm) plastic/vinyl, 1960-1961
    Blue Gingham Dress with White Blouse, #1812, 1960
   $400
    Cotton and Organdy Party Dress, #1814, 1960 $450
    Skirt with Blouse, #1855, 1961 $450
    Slacks and Blouse Set, #1811, 1960 $400
    Slacks and Cardigan Set, #1850, 1961 $475
    8" (20cm) hard plastic, stamp doll, 1997-1998 $75

Maggie's First Doll
8" (20cm) Doll and Teddy Bear Expo, 1996 *(see Special
Dolls)* $125

Maggie Teenager
15-18" (38-46cm) hard plastic, 1951-1953 $450-$650
23" (58cm) 1951-1953 $700

Maggie Visits Rockerfeller Center
8" (20cm) hard plastic, MADC, 1999 *(see Special Dolls)*
   $75

Maggie Walker
15-18" (38-46cm) hard plastic, 1949-1953 $450 up
20-21" (51-53cm) 1949-1953 $575
23-25" (58-64cm) 1951-1953 $650

Magnolia
21" (53cm) rows of lace on pink gown, 1977 $525
21" (53cm) yellow gown, 1988 $275

Maid Marian
8" (20cm) hard plastic, *Storyland Dolls*, 1989-1991
   $75
21" (53cm) *Portrait Series*, 1992-1993 $350

Maid of Honor
18" (46cm) composition, 1940-1944 $750
18" (46cm) hard plastic, aqua, chartreuse, or red, *Beaux
Arts*, 1953 $1,500 up

Above: 1953 71/2-inch (19cm) *Little Madeline.* Very hard to find. *Marge Meisinger Collection. Photo by Carol J. Stover.*

1961 8-inch (20cm) *Maggie Mix-Up Angel.* Outfit was also sold separately. *Marge Meisinger Collection. Photo by Carol J. Stover.*

14" (36cm) plastic/vinyl, *Classic Dolls*, 1988-1989
$85

Majorette
14-17" (36-43cm) composition, 1937-1938 $900
8" (20cm) hard plastic, 1955 $925
8" (20cm) *Americana Series*, 1991-1992 $60

Mali
8" (20cm) hard plastic, 1996-1997 $65

Mambo
7-1/2-8" (19-20cm) hard plastic, *Wendy Loves the Mambo*, #481, 1955 $775

Mammy
8" (20cm) *Jubilee II* set, 1989 $80
8" (20cm) hard plastic, *Scarlett Series*, 1991-1992
$70
10" (25cm) hard plastic, 1996-1999 $95
In set with 10" (25cm) *Scarlett* and extra dress,
1996-1998 $230

Manet
21" (53cm) light brown with dark brown pinstripes,
1982-1983 $250
14" (36cm) *Fine Arts Series*, 1986-1987 $80

Man in the Moon Mobile
8" (20cm) hard plastic head on cloth body, 1996 $65

Marcella
13" (33cm) composition, 1936 $700
20-24" (51-61cm) composition, 1936 $800-$1000

March Hatter
cloth/felt, mid-1930s $800

Mardi Gras
10" (25cm) made for Spiegel, 1992 *(see Special Dolls)*
$125

Margaret
18" (46cm) hard plastic, *Fashions of the Century*,
1954-1955 $1,500 up

Margaret Ann
16" (41cm) porcelain, 1998-1999 $140

Margaret Rose *(see Princess Margaret Rose)*

Margot
10" (25cm) hard plastic, uses *Cissette* mold, has extra makeup,
1961 only
Bikini bathing suit, #900 $400
Black satin pants with white baby doll top, #905 $550
Purple satin gown with sequin bodice, #920 $600
Purple satin gown with matching cape, department store
exclusive $750
Satin dress with stole, #910 $550
Silver metallic gown with rhinestone straps, #921
$500
White satin gown and cloak, #925 $700
Boxed outfit only-gold brocade coat, #0966 $225
Boxed outfit only-gold brocade sheath gown, #0965
$225

Margot Ballerina
15-18" (38-46cm) hard plastic, red, yellow, white, pink or
blue tutu, 1953-1955 $650-$800
15-18" (38-46cm) hard plastic/vinyl arms, red, yellow,
white, pink or blue tutu, 1955 $650-$800

Maria *(see Sound of Music)*
Marie Antoinette
21" (53cm) composition, *Portrait Series*, 1940s $2,000 up
21" (53cm) floral print with pink insert, 1987-1988
$325

Marilla
10" (25cm) hard plastic, 1994 $80

Marine (Boy)
14" (36cm) composition, 1943-1944 $800 up

Marionettes, Tony Sarg
12"-14" (31-36cm) composition, 1934-1940 $350 up
*Alice in Wonderland, Ballet Dancer, Big Bad Wolf, Bones,
Dame, Fido the Dog, Grandmother, Gretchen, Gretel,
Hansel, Horse, Humpty Dumpty, Interlocutor, Judith,
Lawrence, Lucy Lavender, Margaret, Martin, Mr.
Archibald, Percival the Riding Master, Prince, Princess,
Pumpel the Gnome, Red Riding Hood, Rip Van Winkle,
Sambo, Tippytoes the Butler, Titania the Fairy, Tweedle-
dee, Tweedledum, Witch, ZaZa the Clown*

12" (31cm) composition, made for Disney, 1938
$375 up
*Donald Duck, Mickey Mouse, Minnie Mouse, Pluto, Seven
Dwarfs, Snow White*

Marley's Ghost
8" (20cm) hard plastic, 1996 $65

Marme *(see Little Women)*

Marm Liza
21" (53cm) composition, 1938, 1946 $3,000 up

Marta *(see Sound of Music)*

Martha
8" (20cm) hard plastic, *Bible Children Series*, 1953-1954
$7,000

Martin, Mary
14-17" (36-43cm) hard plastic, formal, 1948-1950
$800-$1,000
14-17" (36-43cm) in sailor suit, 1948-1950 $900-$1,100

Mary Ann
14" (36cm) plastic/vinyl, ballerina, pink or blue tutu,
#1412, 1965 $275
Tartan skirt with sweater and cap, #1410, 1965 $250
White pique dress, #1406, 1965 $275
14" (36cm) plastic/vinyl, *Classic Dolls*, 1994 $100

Mary Ann Dances for Grandma
14" (36cm) plastic/vinyl, Horchow, 1995 *(see Special
Dolls)* $250

Marybel
16" (41cm) rigid vinyl, *The Doll Who Gets Well*, 1959-1965
In case wearing romper, 1959, 1961, 1962 $325
In case with wardrobe, 1960 $500
In case, wearing robe, 1963-1964 $400
In case, wearing robe, long hair, #1570, 1965-67 $450
15" (38cm) vinyl, 1998 $155

Mary Cassatt
14" (36cm) plastic/vinyl child, *Fine Arts Series*, 1987
$100

Mary Cassatt Baby
14" (36cm) cloth/vinyl, 1969-1970 $175
20" (51cm) 1969-1970 $250

Above: 1949 hard plastic *Margaret O'Brien.* Very hard to find. *Benita Schwartz Collection.*

Above: Early 1950s 18-inch (46cm) *Margot* ballerina with clover wrist tag. *Benita Schwartz Collection.*

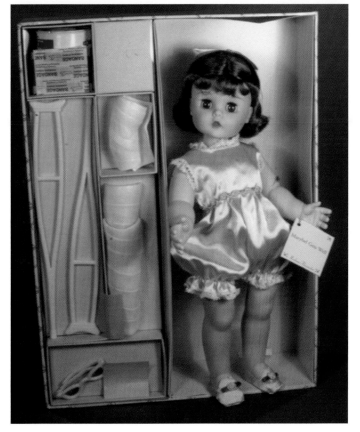

This 1998 reintroduction of the late 1950s doll *Marybell Gets Well* was a smash hit with collectors. *A. Glenn Mandeville Collection.*

Mary Ellen
      31" (79cm) hard plastic, 1954 $625
      31" (79cm) plastic/vinyl arms, 1955 $475
Mary Ellen Playmate
      16" (41cm) plastic/vinyl, Marshall Fields exclusive,
      1965 $375 up
Mary Gray
      14" (36cm) plastic/vinyl, *Classic Dolls*, 1988 $90
Mary Had a Little Lamb
      8" (20cm) hard plastic, 1996-1999 $70
Mary, Joseph and Baby Jesus
      8" (20cm) hard plastic, 1997-1999 $180 set
Mary Lennox
      14" (36cm) plastic/vinyl, 1993-1994 $95
      8" (20cm) hard plastic, 1997-1999 $80
Mary Louise
      21" (53cm) composition, 1938, 1946-1947 $2,500 up
      8" (20cm) hard plastic, same as 18" (46cm), straight leg
      walker, #0035D, 1954 $1,000 up
      18" (46cm) hard plastic, orange and green, *Me and My
      Shadow Series*, 1954 $1,250
Mary, Mary
      8" (20cm) hard plastic, bent knee walker, #751, 1965
                                                       $150
      8" (20cm) hard plastic, bent knee, *Storyland Dolls*,
      #751, 1965-1972 $110
      8" (20cm) hard plastic, straight legs, "Alex Mold",
      #0751, 1973; #451, 1974-1975 $75
      8" (20cm) hard plastic, straight legs, 1976-1987 $60
      8" (20cm) hard plastic, re-introduced, 1992 $60
      14" (36cm) plastic/vinyl, *Classic Dolls*, 1988-1990
                                                       $75
      14" (36cm) plastic/vinyl, *Classic Dolls*, 1994 $100
Mary, Mary Quite Contrary
      8" (20cm) hard plastic, 1996-1999 $70
      8" (20cm) hard plastic, TJ Maxx, 1998 *(see Special Dolls)*
                                                       $60
Mary, Mine
      21" (53cm) cloth /vinyl, 1977-1989 $125
      14" (36cm) cloth/vinyl, 1977-1979 $95
      14" (36cm) re-introduced 1989 $80
Mary Muslin
      19" (48cm) cloth, 1951 $550
      26" (66cm) 1951 $625
      40" (101cm) 1951 $900
Mary of Bethany
      8" (20cm) hard plastic, *Bible Children Series*, 1953-1954
                                                       $7,000
Mary Poppins
      10" (25cm) Disney Catalog, 1995 *(see Special Dolls)*
                                                       $150
Mary, Queen of Scots
      21" (53cm) 1988-1989 $350
Mary Rose Bride
      17" (43cm) hard plastic, 1951 $750
Mary Sunshine
      15" (38cm) plastic/vinyl, #4903, 1961 $385
Marzipan Dancer
      10" (25cm) hard plastic, 1995 $80

Matthew
      8" (20cm) hard plastic, 1995 $60
Mayor of Munchkinland
      8" (20cm) hard plastic, *Wizard of Oz*, 1994-1995 $80
Maypole Dance
      7 1/2-8" (19-20cm) hard plastic, straight leg walker or
      non-walker, 1953-1954 $650
      7 1/2-8" (19-20cm) hard plastic, straight leg walker,
      #458, 1955 $650
      8" (20cm) hard plastic, Shirley's Dollhouse, 1994 *(see
      Special Dolls)* $70
McElroy, Mary
      14" (36cm) plastic/vinyl, 4th set, *First Ladies Series*,
      1985-1987 $100
McGuffey Ana
      16" (41cm) cloth, 1935-1939 $700
      7" (18cm) composition 1935-1936 $350
      9" (23cm) composition, 1935-1939 $400
      11" (28cm) closed mouth, 1937-1939 $650
      11-13" (28-33cm) composition, 1937-1944 $600-$700
      13" (33cm) composition, 1938 $700
      14-16" (36-41cm) composition, 1937-1944 $625-$800
      14-1/2" (37cm) composition, coat, hat and muff, 1948
                                                       $900 up
      15" (38cm) composition, 1935-1937 $700
      17" (43cm) composition, 1937-1943 $825
      17-20" (43-51cm) composition, 1937-1942 $725-$875
      21-25" (53-64cm) composition, 1937-1942 $800-$1000
      28" (71cm) composition $1,100 up
      13" (33cm) composition doll in trousseau box with
      wardrobe, 1942 $1,000 up
      8" (20cm) hard plastic, bent knee walker, #616, 1956
                                                       $800
      18" (46cm), 25" (64cm), 31" (79cm) flat feet, 1955-1956
                                                       $500-$1,000
      14" (36cm), 18" (46cm), 21" (53cm) hard plastic,
      1948-1950 $600-$1,100
      8" (20cm) hard plastic, bent knee or bent knee walker,
      (was *American Girl* 1962-1964) #788, 1965 $375
      14" (36cm) plastic/vinyl, plaid dress, eyelet apron,
      Classic Dolls, 1968-1969 $135
      14" (36cm) plastic/vinyl, plaid dress, *Classic Dolls*,
      1977-1986 $80
      14" (36cm) plastic/vinyl, mauve stripe pinafore, *Classic
      Dolls*, 1987-1988 $90
      14" (36cm) plastic/vinyl, 1995 $85
      8" (20cm) *Storyland*, 1990-1991 $70
      12" (31cm) hard plastic, very rare doll, 1963 $1,800
      29" (74cm) cloth/vinyl, 1952 $675
      15" (38cm) porcelain, 1999 $165
McGuffey Baby
      14" (36cm) composition/cloth, 1937 $375
      18" (46cm) composition/cloth, 1937 $425
      22" (56cm) composition/cloth, 1937 $475
McGuffey Butch
      22" (56cm) composition/cloth, 1940-1941 $475
McKee, Mary
      14" (36cm) plastic/vinyl, 4th set, *First Ladies Series*,
      1985-1987 $100

1953 7 1/2-inch (19cm) *Maypole Dance. Sara Tondini Collection. Photo by Zehr Photography.*

McKinley, Ida
  14" (36cm) plastic/vinyl, 5th set, *First Ladies Series*, 1988
  $100

Meagan
  14" (36cm) vinyl, 1999 $75-$85

Medici, Catherine De
  21" (53cm) porcelain, 1990-1991 $500

Meg *(see Little Women)*

Melanie
  21" (53cm) composition, 1945-1947 $2,500 up
  8" (20cm) hard plastic, bent knee walker, #633, 1956
  $1,100
  21" (53cm) hard plastic/vinyl arms, #2235, 1961 *(Cissy)*
  $1,200 up
  21" (53cm) blue gown, wide lace down sides, 1966
  $2,500
  10" (25cm) yellow multi-tiered skirt, #1182, 1970
  $450
  21" (53cm) blue, white rick-rack around hem ruffle, blonde, 1967 $600
  21" (53cm) rust faille gown, braid trim, brown velvet hat, 1968 $550
  21" (53cm) blue gown, white trim, multi-rows of lace, bonnet, 1969 $525

Late 1930s 11-inch (28cm) *McGuffey Ana.* Rare color combination (necklace not original to doll). *Veronica Jochens Collection.*

  21" (53cm) white gown, red ribbon trim, 1970 $550
  21" (53cm) blue gown, white sequin trim, 1971 $475
  21" (53cm) white gown, red jacket and bonnet, 1974
  $500
  21" (53cm) white nylon gown with pink trim, 1979-1980
  $350
  21" (53cm) pink nylon with blue ribbon, 1981 $350
  12" (31cm) green gown, brown trim, *Portrait Children Series*, 1987 $85
  10" (25cm) all royal blue, black trim, *Jubilee II*, 1989
  $100
  10" (25cm) hard plastic, Sewing Circle dress, 1996
  $90
  8" (20cm) lavender, lace, *Scarlett Series*, 1990 $75
  8" (20cm) peach gown, bonnet with lace, 1992 $70
  21" (53cm) all orange with lace shawl, 1989 $300

Melinda
  14" (36cm) plastic/vinyl, Cotton Gingham Dress, #1412, 1963 $300

The last doll made in the last decade of 1999, the 16-inch (41cm) *Millennium Spectacular* doll is a very limited edition of 2,000. #26080. *A. Glenn Mandeville Collection.*

16" (41cm) plastic/vinyl, Cotton Gingham Dress, #1612, 1963 $350
16" (41cm) plastic/vinyl, Dotted Cotton Dress with Straw Hat, #1510, 1962 $350
22" (56cm) plastic/vinyl, Dotted Cotton Dress with Straw Hat, #1910, 1962 $400
14" (36cm) plastic/vinyl, Organdy Dress with Red Velvet Bodice, #1415, 1963 $375
16" (41cm) plastic/vinyl, Organdy Dress with Red Velvet Bodice, #1512, 1962; #1615, 1963 $400
22" (56cm) plastic/vinyl, Organdy Dress with Red Velvet Bodice, #1912, 1962 $450
14" (36cm) plastic/vinyl, Organdy Party Dress with Lace Ruffles, #1420, 1963 $325
16" (41cm) plastic/vinyl, Organdy Party Dress with Lace Ruffles, #1620, 1963 $375
22" (56cm) plastic/vinyl, Organdy Party Dress with Lace Ruffles, #2020, 1963 $450

10" (25cm) hard plastic, blue gown with white trim, #1173, 1968 $400
10" (25cm) pink multi-tiered skirt, #1182, 1969 $425

Melody and Friend
8" (20cm) hard plastic with a 26" (66cm) porcelain Günzel doll, 1991 $700

Merlin
8" (20cm) hard plastic, 1999 $80

Merry Angel
8" (20cm) hard plastic, made for Spiegel, 1991
(see Special Dolls) $140

Mexico (Mexican)
7" (18cm) composition, 1936 $300
9" (23cm) composition, 1938-1939 $325
8" (20cm) hard plastic, bent knee walker, #776, 1964-1965 $150
8" (20cm) hard plastic, bent knee, #776, 1965-1972 $95
8" (20cm) hard plastic, straight legs, "Alex Mold", #0776, 1973; #576, 1974-1975 $70
8" (20cm) hard plastic, straight legs, 1976-1991 $60
8" (20cm) hard plastic, 1995 $60
8" (20cm) hard plastic, 1997-1998 $75

Michael
11" (28cm) plastic/vinyl, with teddy bear, 1969 (*Peter Pan* set) $350
8" (20cm) *Storyland Dolls*, 1992-1993 $70

Midnight
21" (53cm) dark blue, black, 1990 $300

Millennium Masquerade
10" (25cm) also available as African American, 1999 $200

Millennium Spectacular
16" (41cm) also available as African American, 1999 $450

Mimi
30" (76cm) multi-jointed body, wearing tulle party dress, #3030, 1961 $575
Long Ruffled Dress, #3035, 1962 $900
Red sweater, plain skirt $550
Romper suit with skirt, #3006, 1961 $475
Slacks, stripe top, straw hat, #3010, 1961 $550
Tyrolean outfit, #3025, 1961 $925
14" (36cm) *Opera Series*, 1983-1986 $90
21" (53cm) hard plastic/vinyl arms, pink cape and trim on white gown, *Portrait Series*, 1971 $500

Miracle on 131st Street
10" (25cm) Santa and 8" (20cm) *Wendy* in set, 1996 $150

Miracle Santa
10" (25cm) hard plastic, 1996 $80

Miracle Wendy
8" (20cm) hard plastic, 1996 $65

Miss America
14" (36cm) composition, 1941-1943 $800

Miss Eliza Doolittle
10" (25cm) hard plastic, 1995-1997 $90

Miss Flora McFlimsey
    15" (38cm) vinyl head, #1502, 1953 $625

Miss Gulch
    10" (25cm) hard plastic, comes with bicycle and Toto,
    1997-1999 $120

Miss Judy's Grand Tour
    21" (53cm) *Jacqueline* doll in trunk set with wardrobe,
    FAO Schwarz exclusive, 1962 $1,000 up

Miss Leigh
    8" (20cm) hard plastic, CU Gathering, 1989 *(see Special Dolls)* $200

Miss Liberty
    10" (25cm) MADC, 1991 *(see Special Dolls)* $125

Miss Magnin
    10" (25cm) made for I. Magnin, 1991 *(see Special Dolls)* $150

Miss Millennium
    8" (20cm) made for Lillian Vernon, 1999 *(see Special Dolls)* $75

Miss Muffet
    8" (20cm) hard plastic, bent knee walker, #752, 1965 $150
    8" (20cm) hard plastic, bent knee, *Storyland Dolls,*
    #752, 1965-1972 $125
    8" (20cm) hard plastic, straight legs, "Alex Mold",
    #0752, 1973; #452, 1974-1975 $75
    8" (20cm) straight legs, 1976-1986 $65
    8" (20cm) hard plastic, *Storyland Dolls,* 1986-1988 $65
    8" (20cm) straight legs, 1987-1988 $65
    8" (20cm) hard plastic, 1993-1994 $65
    8" (20cm) hard plastic, 1998-1999 $90
    8" (20cm) hard plastic, TJ Maxx, 1997 *(see Special Dolls)* $60

Miss Scarlett
    14" (36cm) plastic/vinyl, made for Belk & Leggett,
    1988 *(see Special Dolls)* $150

Miss Smarty
    8" (20cm) hard plastic, 1999 $70

Miss Tennessee Waltz
    8" (20cm) hard plastic, CU Nashville, 1997 *(see Special Dolls)* $125

Miss Unity
    10" (25cm) hard plastic, UFDC, 1991 *(see Special Dolls)* $350

Miss U.S.A.
    8" (20cm) hard plastic, bent knee, *Americana Series,*
    #728, 1966-1968 $350

Miss Victory
    20" (51cm) composition, magnetic hands, 1944-1946 $800

Misterioso
    10" (25cm) hard plastic, 1996 $90

Mistress Mary
    7" (18cm) composition, 1937-1941 $325

Molly
    14" (36cm) *Classic Dolls,* 1988 $80

Molly Cottontail
    cloth/felt, 1930s $650

Mommy and Me
    14" (36cm) and 7" (18cm) composition, matching outfits,
    1940-1943 $1,600 set
    10" (25cm) and 8" (20cm) hard plastic set, At Home or On
    The Go, 1996-1998 $155

Mommy's Pet
    14-20" (36-51cm) cloth/vinyl, 1977-1986 $55-$100

Mona Lisa
    8" (20cm) hard plastic, 1997 $80

Monet
    21" (53cm) hard plastic, black and white check gown
    with red jacket, 1984-1985 $300

Monique
    8" (20cm) Disneyland Teddy Bear & Doll Classic,
    1993 *(see Special Dolls)* $475

Monroe, Elizabeth
    14" (36cm) plastic/vinyl, 1st set, *First Ladies Series,*
    1976-1978 $100

Mop Top Annie
    8" (20cm) hard plastic, 1995 $70

Mop Top Baby
    12" (31cm) vinyl and cloth, boy doll, 1997 $55
    12" (31cm) vinyl and cloth, girl doll, 1997-1998 $55

Mop Top Billy
    8" (20cm) hard plastic, *Storyland Dolls,* 1994-1996,
    1998-1999 $75

Mop Top Wendy
    8" (20cm) hard plastic, *Storyland Dolls,* 1994-1996,
    1998-1999 $80

Morgan Le Fay
    10" (25cm) Disney World Doll and Teddy Bear
    Convention, 1995 *(see Special Dolls)* $225

Morisot
    21" (53cm) plastic/vinyl, lime green gown with white lace,
    1985-1986 $300

Morning Glory
    14" (36cm) plastic/vinyl, 1995 $140

Morocco
    8" (20cm) hard plastic, bent knee, #762, 1968-1970 $300
    8" (20cm) hard plastic, 1996-1997 $70

Moss Rose
    14" (36cm) *Classic Dolls,* 1991 $160

Mother and Me
    15" (38cm) and 9" (23cm) composition, gift set with
    wardrobe, 1942 $1,500 up

Mother Goose
    8" (20cm) straight legs, *Storyland Dolls,* 1986-1992 $65
    8" (20cm) hard plastic, 1997-1999 $70

Mother Hubbard
    8" (20cm) *Classic Dolls,* 1988-1989 $65

Mother Superior
    10" (25cm) hard plastic, *Sound of Music Set,* 1997-1999 $115

Extremely rare 1928 *My Betty*. Composition shoulder plate, arms, legs. Marked on shoulder plate "Fiboroid." Dress tagged "Madame Alexander." Wrist tag states all the details. *Veronica Jochens Collection.*

Mother's Day
    8" (20cm) hard plastic, 1995 $65
Mouseketeer
    8" (20cm) made for Disney, 1991 $125
    8" (20cm) hard plastic, pair made for Disney Theme Parks, 1999 (see Special Dolls) $175
Mr. O'Hara
    8" (20cm) *Scarlett Series,* 1993 $75
Mr. And Mrs. Frankenstein
    8" (20cm) hard plastic, sold as a pair only, 1996 $160
Mrs. Buck Rabbit
    cloth/felt, mid-1930s $650
Mrs. Claus
    8" (20cm) hard plastic, mid-year release, 1993 $75
    14" (36cm) plastic/vinyl, 1995 $100
Mrs. Darling
    10" (25cm) hard plastic, 1993-1994 $140
Mrs. Fezziwig
    8" (20cm) hard plastic, 1996 $65
Mrs. Inky
    14" (36cm) cloth, poodle, 1954 $375
Mrs. March Hatter
    cloth/felt, mid-1930s $650
Mrs. Molloy's Millinery Shop
    10" (25cm) *Portrette* trunk set, 1994 $225
Mrs. O'Hara
    8" (20cm) hard plastic, *Scarlett Series,* 1992-1993
        $75
Mrs. Quack-A-Field
    cloth/felt, mid-1930s $675
Mrs. Smoky Tail
    cloth/felt, 1930s $675
Mrs. Snoopie Goes-A-Marketing
    cloth/felt, 1930s $675
Muffin
    19" (48cm) cloth, 1966 $135
    14" (36cm) cloth, 1963-1977 $100
    14" (36cm) cloth, African American, 1965-1966 $125
    12" (31cm) all vinyl, various outfits, 1989-1990 $70
    12" (31cm) vinyl, Ballerina, pink or blue tutu, 1989-1990
        $70
    12" (31cm) in trunk, wardrobe, 1990 $175
Munchkin Herald
    8" (20cm) hard plastic, *Wizard of Oz Series,* 1994
        $80
Munchkin Peasant
    8" (20cm) hard plastic, *Wizard of Oz Series,* 1994
        $80
Music Box Stand
    For 8" (20cm) and 10" (25cm) dolls, 1997-1998
        $40
My Betty
    composition, 1928 $600 up
My Little Sweetheart
    8" (20cm) also available in African American, made for A Child at Heart, 1992 *(see Special Dolls)* $75-$125

Nan McHare
   cloth/felt, 1930s $700
Nana Governess
   8" (20cm) hard plastic, bent knee walker, #433, 1957
                                                        $1,250 up
Nana
   6" (16cm) plush stuffed dog, 1993 only $45
Nancy Ann
   17" (43cm) hard plastic, 1950 $1,000
Nancy Dawson
   8" (20cm) hard plastic, *Storyland Dolls,* 1988-1989
                                                        $70
Nancy Drew
   12" (31cm) plastic/vinyl, white coat, #1262, 1967
                                                        $600
   Tweed suit, pink or blue, #1264 $725
Nancy Jean
   8" (20cm) hard plastic, Made for Belk & Leggett,
   1990 *(see Special Dolls)* $75
Napoleon
   12" (31cm) plastic/vinyl, *Portraits of History,* 1980-1986
                                                        $75
Nat *(see Little Men)*
Natasha
   21" (53cm) brown and paisley brocade, 1989-1990
                                                        $350
National Velvet
   12" (31cm) plastic/vinyl, *Romance Series,* 1991 $80
   8" (20cm) hard plastic, 1996 $80
Nativity Set
   8" (20cm) hard plastic, 1997-1999 $900
Navaho Woman
   8" (20cm) hard plastic, MADC, 1994 *(see Special Dolls)*
                                                        $300
Neiman Marcus
   8" (20cm) hard plastic, party trunk, 1990 *(see Special
   Dolls)* $275
Nelson, Lord
   12" (31cm) plastic, vinyl, *Portraits of History,* 1984-1986
                                                        $75
Netherlands Boy
   8" (20cm) hard plastic, straight legs, "Alex Mold",
   #577, 1974-1975 $75
   8" (20cm) hard plastic, straight legs, #577, 1976-1989
                                                        $60
Netherlands Girl
   8" (20cm) hard plastic, straight legs, "Alex Mold",
   #591, 1974-1975 $75
   8" (20cm) hard plastic, #591, 1976-1992 $60
Nicole
   10" (25cm) hard plastic, *Portrette Series,* 1989-1990
                                                        $70

Nigeria
   8" (20cm) hard plastic, 1995 $65
Nightingale, Florence
   14" (36cm) *Classic Dolls,* 1986-1987 $70
Nighty Night
   Outfit only for 14" (36cm) doll, 1996 $45
Nina Ballerina
   7" (18cm) composition, 1940 $325
   9" (23cm) composition, 1939-1941 $375
   14" (36cm) hard plastic, 1949-1950 $550
   15" (38cm) hard plastic, 1951 $625
   17" (43cm) hard plastic, 1949-1950 $650
   18" (46cm) hard plastic, 1949-1950 $700
   23" (58cm) hard plastic, 1951 $850
Nixon, Pat
   14" (36cm) plastic/vinyl, *First Ladies Series,* 1994
                                                        $125
Noel
   12" (31cm) porcelain, New England Collector's Society,
   1989-1991 *(see Special Dolls)* $250
Normandy
   7" (18cm) composition, 1935-1938 $300
Norway
   8" (20cm) hard plastic, bent knee, #784, 1968-1972
                                                        $100
   8" (20cm) hard plastic, straight legs, "Alex Mold",
   #0784, 1973; #584, 1974-1975 $70
   8" (20cm) hard plastic, straight legs, 1976-1987 $60
   8" (20cm) hard plastic, straight legs, 1996-1997 $80
Norwegian
   7" (18cm) composition, 1936-1940 $300
   9" (23cm) composition, 1938-1939 $325
Now I'm Nine
   8" (20cm) hard plastic, CU Nashville, 1999 *(see Special
   Dolls)* $65
Nurse *(see Red Cross Nurse for additional listings)*
   16" (41cm) cloth, 1930s $600 up
   7" (18cm) composition, 1936-1939 $300
   13" (33cm) composition, Dionne Nurse, 1936-1937
                                                        $800
   15" (38cm) composition, 1939-1943 $550
   36" (91cm) plastic/vinyl, all white uniform, 1960 *(Joanie)*
                                                        $450
   36" (91cm) plastic/vinyl, colored dress, white pinafore,
   #3610, 1961 *(Joanie)* $450
   8" (20cm) hard plastic, bent knee walker, white uniform,
   #563, 1956; #363, 1957 $550 up
   8" (20cm) hard plastic, bent knee walker, has baby,
   #429, 1961; #363, 1962; #460, 1963; #660,1964
                                                        $500 up
   8" (20cm) hard plastic, bent knee or bent knee walker,
   has baby, #624, 1965 $475
   8" (20cm) hard plastic, white uniform (striped not
   produced), *Americana Series,* 1990-1991 $65
   8" (20cm) hard plastic, World War II costume, 1999
                                                        $70

Nutcracker *(see Ballerinas)*
Nutcracker Prince
   8" (20cm) hard plastic, 1995 $65

O

O'Brien, Margaret
14-1/2" (37cm) composition, 1946-1948 $800
17-19" (43-48cm) composition, 1946-1948 $900-$1000
21-24" (53-61cm) composition, 1946-1948 $1,000-$1,275
14" (36cm) composition in window box with wardrobe,
1947 $1,000 up
18" (46cm) composition in suitcase with wardrobe,
1947 $1,000 up
14" (36cm) hard plastic, 1949-1951 $950 up
17-18" (43-46cm) hard plastic, 1949-1951 $1,000 up
21-22" (53-56cm) hard plastic, 1949-1951 (very rare)
    $1,300 up

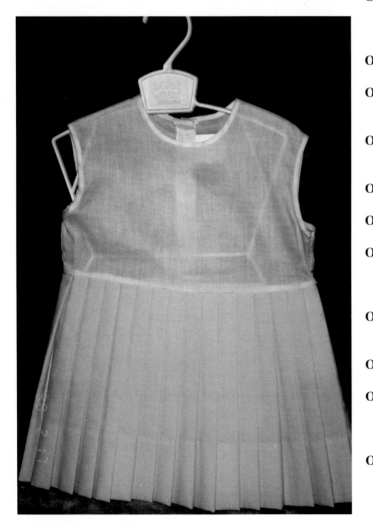

Matching dress for the child. The Madame Alexander name was on the hang tag for these rare outfits. *Marge Meisinger Collection.*

8" (20cm) hard plastic, MADC, 1998 *(see Special Dolls)*
    $80
Pin workshop kit, MADC exclusive, 1998 $15

Oktoberfest
8" (20cm) Greenville Show, 1992 *(see Special Dolls)*
    $100

Oktoberfest (Boy)
8" (20cm) Greenville Show, 1992 *(see Special Dolls)*
    $150

Old Fashion Girl
13" (33cm) composition, 1945-1947 $600
20" (51cm) composition $700
14" (36cm) hard plastic, 1948 $700
20" (51cm) hard plastic, 1948 $775

Olive Oyl
10" (25cm) hard plastic, 1996 $95

With 8" (20cm) *Popeye* and *S'wee Pea* in set, 1996
    $175

Oliver Twist
16" (41cm) cloth, Dickens character, 1934 $700
7" (18cm) composition, 1935-1936 $400
8" (20cm) *Storyland Dolls,* 1992 $55

Oliver Twistail
cloth/felt, 1930s $750

Olympia
8" (20cm) hard plastic, Collector's United, 1996
(see Special Dolls) $125

One Enchanted Evening
16" (41cm) plastic/vinyl, UFDC Convention, 1999
(see Special Dolls) $250

One, Two, Buckle My Shoe
14" 36cm) plastic/vinyl, 1995 $90

Opening Night
10" (25cm) *Portrette,* 1989 $80

Ophelia
12" (31cm) *Romance Collection, Nancy Drew* Face,
1992 $100
12" (31cm) #1312, *Lissy* Face, 1993 $120

Orange Blossom
10" (25cm) hard plastic, MADC, 1999 *(see Special Dolls)*
    $225

Orchard Princess
21" (53cm) composition, 1939, 1946-1947 $2,500

Orphan Annie
14" (36cm) plastic/vinyl, *Literature Series,* #1480,
1965-1966 $350
Window box gift set, #1485, 1965 $650

Out and About
8" (20cm) outfit only, exclusive for MADC Friendship
Luncheon, 1999 $40

Pakistan
8" (20cm) hard plastic, *International Dolls*, 1993
$60

Pamela
12" (31cm) hard plastic, with wigs, window box, 1963
$900 up
In case, hard plastic, 1962-1963 $950 up
In case, hard plastic, FAO Schwarz exclusive, 1962-1964
$950 up
12" (31cm) vinyl, in case, FAO Schwarz exclusive,
1966-1971 $700 up

Pamela Plays Dress Up at Grandma's
12" (31cm) hard plastic, made for Horchow, 1993
(see Special Dolls) $250

Pan American-Pollera
7" (18cm) composition, 1936-1938 $325

Panama
8" (20cm) hard plastic, 1985-1987 $75

Pandora
8" (20cm) hard plastic, made for dolls 'n bearland,
1991 *(see Special Dolls)* $125

Parisian Chic
10" (25cm) hard plastic, *Through the Decades Collection*,
1999 $120

Park Avenue Wendy
8" (20cm) hard plastic, 1998 $80
In set with *Alex the Bellhop*, 1997-1999 $160

Parlor Maid
8" (20cm) hard plastic, bent knee walker, #579, 1956
$975 up

Pat-A-Cake
8" (20cm) hard plastic, 1995 $60

Patchity Pam
15" (38cm) cloth, #65, 1966 $200

Patchity Pepper
15" (38cm) cloth, #60, 1966 $200

Patterson, Martha Johnson
14" (36cm) plastic/vinyl, 3rd set, *First Ladies Series*,
1982-1984 $100

Patty
18" (46cm) plastic/vinyl, 1965 $250

Patty Pigtails
14" (36cm) hard plastic, 1949 $700

Paulette
10" (25cm) *Portrette*, 1989-1990 $100

Pearl (June)
10" (25cm) *Birthstone Collection*, 1992 $75

Pearl of the 20's
10" (25cm) hard plastic, 1998 $200

Peasant
7' (18cm) composition, 1936-1937 $300
9" (23cm) composition, 1938-1939 $325

Peggy Bride
14-18" (36-46cm) hard plastic, 1950-1951 $650
21" (53cm) hard plastic, 1950 $850

Penny
7" (18cm) composition, 1936-1938 $300
34" (86cm) cloth/vinyl, 1951 $500
42" (106cm) 1951 $750

Peppermint Twist
8" (20cm) hard plastic, 1995 $60

Peron, Eva
10" (25cm) hard plastic, 1997 $100

Persia
7" (18cm) composition, 1936-1938 $325

Peru
8" (20cm) hard plastic, 1985-1987 $80
8" (20cm) hard plastic, *International Dolls*, 1993
$60

Peruvian Boy
8" (20cm) hard plastic, bent knee walker, #770, 1965
$475
8" (20cm) hard plastic, bent knee, #770, 1965-1966
$450

Peter Pan
7 1/2-8" (19-20cm) hard plastic, straight leg non-walker,
Quiz-Kins, 1953 $950
15" (38cm) hard plastic, #1505, 1953-1954 $800
14" (36cm) plastic/vinyl, 1969 $300
8" (20cm) hard plastic, *Storyland Dolls*, re-introduced,
1991-1994 $60
8" (20cm) hard plastic, 1999 $70
Complete set of four dolls (*Peter, Michael, Wendy,
Tinkerbell*), 1969 $1,200 up

Phantom of the Opera-Christine
10" (25cm) hard plastic, 1997 $100

Piano *(see Furniture)*

Picnic Day
18" (46cm) hard plastic, *Glamour Girls Series*, 1953
$1,500 up

Phillippines
8" (20cm) straight legs, 1985-1986 $85
Yellow gown, 1987 $100

Pierce, Jane
14" (36cm) plastic/vinyl, 3rd set, *First Ladies Series*,
1982-1984 $100

Pierrot Clown
8" (20cm) hard plastic, bent knee walker, #561, 1956
$1,000 up
14" (36cm) *Classic Dolls*, 1991-1992 $80

Pilgrim
7" (18cm) composition, 1935-1938 $300
8" (20cm) hard plastic, *American Series*, 1994-1995
$60

Pilgrim Girl
8" (20cm) hard plastic, QVC, 1998 *(see Special Dolls)*
$75

Pink Champagne
18" (46cm) hard plastic, 1950-1951 $5,000 up
Pink Pristine Angel
10" (25cm) hard plastic, 1997-1999 $110
Pink Sparkle Princess
15" (38cm) porcelain, 1999 $170
Pink Victorian Tree Topper (see Tree Topper)
Pinkie or Pinky
16" (41cm) cloth, 1940s $500
14-18" (36-46cm) composition, cloth baby, 1937-1939
    $250-$300
20-23" (51-58cm) composition, cloth baby, 1937-1939
    $275-$325
13-19" (33-48cm) vinyl baby, 1954 $95-$150
12" (31cm) plastic/vinyl, *Portrait Children Series*,
1975-1987 $75
8" (20cm) hard plastic, 1997-1998 $70
Pinocchio
8" (20cm) *Storyland Dolls*, 1992-1994 $70
Pip
all cloth, *Dicken's character*, early 1930s $ 900
7" (18cm) composition, 1935-1936 $325
Pippi Longstocking
18" (46cm) cloth, 1996, not produced
Pisces
8" (20cm) hard plastic, 1997-1998 $85
Pitty Pat
16" (41cm) cloth, 1950s $500
Pitty Pat Clown
1950s $450
Playmates
29" (74cm) cloth, 1940s $475 up
Pocahontas
8" (20cm) hard plastic, bent knee, *Americana* and
Storyland Dolls, #721, 1967-1970 $400
8" (20cm) hard plastic, *Americana Series*, re-introduced
1991-1992 $65
8" (20cm) hard plastic, *Americana Series*, complete
costume change, 1994-1996 $55
14" (36cm) plastic/vinyl, 1995-1996 $90
Polish (Poland)
7" (18cm) composition, 1935-1936 $300
8" (20cm) hard plastic, bent knee walker, #780,
1964-1965 $175
8" (20cm) hard plastic, bent knee, #780, 1965-1972
    $100
8" (20cm) hard plastic, straight legs, "Alex Mold",
#0780, 1973; #580, 1974-1975 $70
8" (20cm) hard plastic, straight legs, 1976-1988 $60
8" (20cm) hard plastic, re-introduced, 1992-1994
    $65
Polk, Sarah
14" (36cm) plastic/vinyl, 2nd set, *First Ladies Series*,
1979-1981 $100
Pollera (Pan American)
7" (18cm) composition, 1936-1937 $300
Polly
17" (43cm) plastic/vinyl, 1965 only, wearing orange cotton
ruffled dress, #1715 $275

Wearing pink empire formal, #1722 $400
Wearing white lace dress with blue lining, #1724 $275
Wearing red velveteen suit, #1731 $300
Wearing turquoise satin and velvet gown, #1732 $450
Wearing mauve pleated tulle formal, #1751 $400
Wearing pink chiffon formal, #1752 $425
Wearing white brocade bridal gown, #1754 $450
Wearing white tulle bridal gown, #1765 $325
Dressed as a ballerina, pink or blue tutu, #1725 $275
plastic/vinyl, in trunk with wardrobe, FAO Exclusive,
1965 $1,000 up
Polly Flinders
8" (20cm) *Storyland Dolls*, 1988-1989 $80
Polly Pigtails
14" (36cm) hard plastic, 1949-1951 $525
17" (43cm) 1949-1951 $650
21" (53cm) hard plastic, 1949-1951 $750 up
8" (20cm) hard plastic, MADC, 1990 (see Special Dolls)
    $125
Polly Put the Kettle On
7" (18cm) composition, 1936-1937 $300
8" (20cm) hard plastic, 1998-1999 $80
Pollyana
16" (41cm) rigid vinyl, 1960-1961 $400
22" (56cm) 1960-1961 $475
14" (36cm) *Classic Dolls*, 1987-1988 $95
8" (20cm) *Storyland Dolls*, 1992-1993 $70
14" (36cm) *Classic Dolls*, 1994 $100
8" (20cm) hard plastic, QVC, 1999 (see Special Dolls)
    $75
Polynesian Princess
8" (20cm) hard plastic, Collector's United, 1998 (see
Special Dolls) $175
Poodle
14-17" (36-43cm) plush, 1940s-1950s $375
Poor Cinderella (see Cinderella)
Poor Scarlett (see Scarlett)
Pop (see Snap, Crackle, Pop)
Popeye
8" (20cm) hard plastic, 1996 $80
With 10" (25cm) *Olive Oyl* and *S'wee Pea* in set, 1996
    $175
Poppy
9" (23cm) vinyl, 1953 $125
Portrait Elise
17" (43cm) plastic/vinyl, 1972-1973 $225
Portrait Scarlett (see Scarlett)
Portugal
8" (20cm) hard plastic, bent knee, #785, 1968-1972
    $100
8" (20cm) hard plastic, straight legs, "Alex Mold",
#0785, 1973; #585, 1974-1975 $70
8" (20cm) straight legs, 1976-1987 $65
8" (20cm) *International Dolls*, 1993-1994 $65
Posey Pets
15" (38cm) cloth, plush animals, 1940s $450
Pram
For baby dolls, 1997 $120

Precious
    12" (31cm) composition/cloth baby, 1937-1940 $250
    12" (31cm) all hard plastic toddler, 1948-1951 $375

President's Wives *(see First Ladies)*

Prince Charles
    8" (20cm) hard plastic, bent knee walker, #397, 1957
                                  $800

Prince Charming
    16-17" (41-43cm) composition, 1947 $750
    14-15" (36-38cm) hard plastic, 1948-1950 $750
    17-18" (43-46cm) hard plastic, 1948-1950 $900
    21" (53cm) hard plastic, 1949-1951 $1,100
    12" (31cm) hard plastic, *Romance Collection*, 1990-1991
                                  $90
    8" (20cm) hard plastic, *Storyland Dolls*, 1993-1994
                                  $70
    8" (20cm) hard plastic, 1995 $60

Prince Phillip
    18" (46cm) hard plastic, 1953 $900
    21" (53cm) 1953 $1,000

Princess
    13-15" (33-38cm) composition, 1940-1942 $575
    24" (61cm) composition, 1940-1942 $900
    14" (36cm) plastic/vinyl, 1990-1991 $125
    12" (31cm) plastic/vinyl, *Romance Collection*, 1990-1992
                                  $90

Princess Alexandria
    24" (61cm) cloth, composition, 1937 $375

Princess and the Pea
    8" (20cm) hard plastic, made for Dolly Dears, 1993
    (see Special Dolls) $100

Princess and the Pea
    mattress, made for Dolly Dears, 1993 *(see Special Dolls)*
                                  $60

Princess Ann
    8" (20cm) hard plastic, bent knee walker, #396, 1957
                                  $850

Princess Buddir-al-Buddoor
    8" (20cm) *Storyland Dolls*, 1993-1994 $70

Princess Diana
    10" (25cm) hard plastic, 1998-1999 $170

Princess Elizabeth
    7" (18cm) composition, 1937-1939 $400
    8" (20cm) with Dionne head, 1937 (rare) $425 up
    9-11" (23-25cm) composition, 1937-1941 $375-$450
    13" (33cm) composition, with closed mouth, 1937-1941
                                  $675
    14" (36cm) composition, 1937-1941 $650
    15-16" (38-41cm) composition, open mouth, 1937-1941
                                  $650
    17-19" (43-48cm) composition, open mouth, 1937-1941
                                  $800
    24" (61cm) composition, open mouth, 1938-1939
                                  $950
    28" (71cm) composition, open mouth, 1938-1939
                                  $1,100

Princess Flavia
    21" (53cm) composition, 1939, 1946-1947 $1,900 up

Princess Margaret Rose
    15-18" (38-46cm) composition, 1937-1938 $850 up
    21" (53cm) composition, 1938 $1,000 up
    14-18-21" (36-46-53cm) hard plastic, 1949-1953 $900 up
    18" (46cm) hard plastic, pink taffeta gown and tiara,
    Beaux Art Series, 1953 $1,800 up
    15" (38cm) Ashton-Drake Galleries, 1998 *(see Special
    Dolls)* $200

Princess Rosetta
    21" (53cm) composition, 1939, 1946-1947 $2,000 up

Priscilla
    18" (46cm) cloth, mid-1930s $650
    7" (18cm) composition, 1935-1938 $300
    8" (20cm) hard plastic, bent knee, #789, 1965;
    #729, 1966-1970 $350

Prissy
    8" (20cm) *Scarlett Series*, 1990 $70
    8" (20cm) re-introduced 1992-1993 $95
    8" (20cm) hard plastic, 1995 $65

Pristine Angel
    10" (25cm) hard plastic, *Anniversary Collection*,
    1995 $100

Prom Queen
    8" (20cm) MADC, 1992 *(see Special Dolls)* $225
    10" (25cm) hard plastic, TJ Maxx, 1998 *(see Special
    Dolls)* $70

Psycho
    10" (25cm) hard plastic, 1998, not produced

Puddin'
    14" (36cm) cloth/vinyl, 1966-1997 $85-$95
    18" (46cm) cloth/vinyl 1966-1993 $85-$110
    21" (53cm) cloth/vinyl 1966-1993, 1995-1996 $100-125

Puerto Rico
    8" (20cm) hard plastic, 1998-1999 $75

Pumpkin
    22" (56cm) cloth/vinyl, 1967-1976 $140
    22" (56cm) with rooted hair, 1976 $175

Puss 'n Boots
    8" (20cm) hard plastic, 1995 $70

Pussy Cat
    14" (36cm) cloth/vinyl, 1965-1985, 1987-1999 $80-$100
    14" (36cm) cloth/vinyl, African American, 1970-1976,
    1985, 1989-1998 $85-$110
    18" (46cm) cloth/vinyl, 1989-1997 $110-$125
    20" (51cm) cloth/vinyl, 1965-1984, 1987-1988 $95-$125
    20" (51cm) cloth/vinyl, African American, 1970-1984
                                  $95-$125
    24" (61cm) cloth/vinyl, 1965-1985 $100-$165
    14" (36cm) in basket with layette, FAO Schwarz exclusive,
    1966-1971 $350 up
    14" (36cm) in trunk with layette, FAO Schwarz exclusive,
    1976 $325 up
    14" (36cm) in vinyl trunk with layette, FAO Schwarz
    exclusive, 1980 $350 up
    18" (46cm) made for FAO Schwarz, 1987 *(see Special
    Dolls)* $125
    14" (46cm) made for Horchow, 1993 *(see Special Dolls)*
                                  $125
    Lively, 14" (36cm), 20" (51cm), 24" (61cm) head and
    limbs move, 1966-1969 $100-$200

Left: 1930s all composition 16-inch (41cm) *Princess Elizabeth*. Veronica Jochens Collection.

Late 1930s rare 13-inch (33cm) all composition *Princess Elizabeth*. This deluxe model came with a jeweled tiara and human hair. *Veronica Jochens Collection.*

Q

Queen (also Queen Elizabeth II)

18" (46cm) hard plastic, white gown, long cape trimmed with fur, *Beaux Arts Series*, 1953 $1,500 up

18" (46cm) hard plastic, same gown, tiara as above but no cape, *Glamour Girl Series,* 1953 $1,000

18" (46cm) hard plastic, white gown, short orlon cape, *Me and My Shadow Series*, 1954 $1,000

7-1/2-8" (19-20cm) hard plastic, orlon cape, straight leg walker, #0030A, 1954 $1,050

20" (51cm) hard plastic/vinyl arms, white brocade, *Dream Come True Series*, #2099, 1955 $1,200 up

20" (51cm) hard plastic/vinyl arms, white brocade, *Fashion Parade Series*, #2042, 1956 $1,000

20" (51cm) hard plastic/vinyl arms, gold brocade, *Formal Gown Series,* #2171, 1957 $900

7-1/2-8" (19-20cm) hard plastic, straight leg walker, velvet robe, #499, 1955 $800

10" (25cm) hard plastic, gold gown, blue sash, # 971, 1957 $450

10" (25cm) gold gown, panels on back of dress, #879, 1958 $475

10" (25cm) white gown, blue sash, #742, 1959 $425

10" (25cm) gold gown, blue sash, #842, 1960-1961 $425

10" (25cm) gold gown, #763, 1962 $425

10" (25cm) white gown, #765, 1963 $425

10" (25cm) in vinyl case with wardrobe, FAO Schwarz exclusive, 1959 $1,200 up

18" (46cm) white gown, red sash, #1780, 1963 *(Elise)* $750

With vinyl *Marybel* head $800

21" (53cm) gold gown, 1958, 1961-1963 $850

18" (46cm) vinyl head, gold brocade gown, 1966 *(Elise)* $950

21" (53cm) hard plastic/vinyl arms, gold brocade gown, 1965 $800

21" (53cm) gold gown, 1968 $775

10" (25cm) hard plastic, white gown, red sash, 1972-1973 $350

14" (36cm) *Classic Dolls*, 1990 $95

8" (20cm) 40th Anniversary, mid-year release, 1992 $150

16" (41cm) porcelain, 1998 $200

Queen Alexandrine

21" (53cm) composition, 1939-1941 $2,000

Queen Charlotte

10" (25cm) MADC, 1991 *(see Special Dolls)* $275

Queen Elizabeth I

10" (25cm) made for My Doll House, 1990 *(see Special Dolls)* $150

8" (20cm) hard plastic, 1999 $85

Queen Esther

8" (20cm) hard plastic, *Bible Children Series*, 1953-1954 $7,000

8" (20cm) hard plastic, 1995 $90

Queen Isabella

8" (20cm) hard plastic, 1992 $125

Queen of Hearts

8" (20cm) straight legs, *Storyland Dolls,*1987-1990 $70

10" (25cm), Disney World Doll and Teddy Bear Convention, 1992 *(see Special Dolls)* $350

8" (20cm) hard plastic, 1995-1996 $80

Queen of the Roses

10" (25cm) hard plastic, 1999 $110

Quintuplets (so called Fisher Quints)

hard plastic, 1964 $450 set

Quiz-Kins

8" (20cm) hard plastic, straight leg non-walker, in romper, #312, 1953 $525

Bride, 1953-1954 $650

Girl with wig wearing dress, 1953-1954 $650

Groom, 1953-1954 $475

Peter Pan, caracul wig, 1953 $950

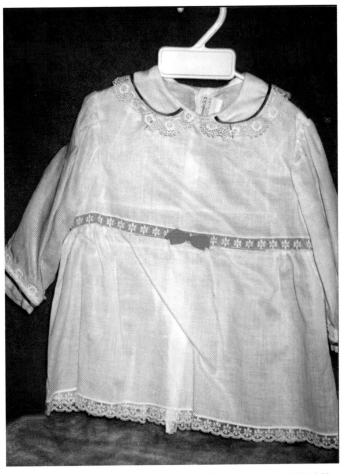

Another child's dress bearing the Madame Alexander name. Mid 1960s. *Marge Meisinger Collection.*

Rachel
  8" (20cm) a few tagged *Rachael*, made for Belk & Leggett, 1989 *(see Special Dolls)* — $85

Raincoat
  8" (20cm) outfit only, exclusive for MADC Travel Doll Party, 1998 — $30

Rainy Day
  14" (36cm) outfit only, 1996 — $45

Randolph, Martha
  14" (36cm) plastic/vinyl, 1st set, *First Ladies Series,* 1976-1978 — $100

Rapunzel
  10" (25cm) *Portrette*, 1989-1992 — $120
  8" (20cm) hard plastic, 1995-1999 — $75
  14" (36cm) plastic/vinyl, 1996 — $130

Rapunzel & Mother Gothel
  14" (36cm), 8" (20cm) *Classic Dolls*, 1993-1994 — $225

Really Ugly Stepsister
  8" (20cm) hard plastic, 1997-1998 — $80

Rebecca
  14-17" (36-43cm), 21" (53cm) composition, 1940-1941 — $750 up
  14" (36cm) hard plastic, 1948-1949 — $900
  14" (36cm) plastic/vinyl, two-tiered skirt in pink, *Classic Dolls*, 1968-1969 — $125
  one-piece skirt, pink dotted or checked dress, 1970-1985 — $75
  blue dress with striped pinafore, 1986-1987 — $80

Rebecca of Sunnybrook Farm
  8" (20cm) hard plastic, 1996 — $65
  8" (20cm) hard plastic, TJ Maxx, 1998 *(see Special Dolls)* — $70

Record
  With stories narrated by Madame Alexander, 1978 — $30

Red Boy
  8" (20cm) hard plastic, bent knee, #740, 1972 — $100
  8" (20cm) hard plastic, straight legs, "Alex Mold", #0740, 1973; #440, 1974-1975 — $70
  8" (20cm) hard plastic, straight legs, 1976-1988 — $60

Red Cross Nurse
  7" (18cm) composition, 1937, 1941-1943 — $325
  9" (23cm) composition, 1939, 1942-1943 — $350
  14" (36cm) composition — $600

Red, Gold and Green Tree Topper *(see Tree Topper)*
Red Lace *(see Tree Topper)*
Red Queen
  8" (20cm) hard plastic, 1996-1999 — $115
  In set with 8" (20cm) *White King*, 1996-1997 — $200

Red Riding Hood
  16" (41cm) cloth/felt, 1930s — $650
  7" (18cm) composition, 1936-1942 — $300
  9" (23cm) composition, 1939-1940 — $325
  9-11" (23cm-28cm), vinyl/latex, 1952 — $350
  7-1/2-8" (19-20cm) hard plastic, straight leg walker, #471, 1955 — $725
  8" (20cm) hard plastic, bent knee walker, #608, 1956 — $550
  8" (20cm) hard plastic, bent knee walker, #382, 1962-1963; #782, 1964-1965 — $135
  Outfit only for 8" (20cm) doll, #0382, 1962-1963 — $95
  8" (20cm) hard plastic, bent knee, #782, 1965-1972 — $100
  8" (20cm) hard plastic, straight legs, "Alex Mold", #0782, 1973; #482, 1974-1975 — $75
  8" (20cm) hard plastic, various costumes, 1976-1999 — $55-75
  8" (20cm) hard plastic, topsy turvy with Grandmother and wolf, 1996 — $130
  14" (36cm) plastic/vinyl, 1995 — $95
  14" (36cm) plastic/vinyl, 1996 — $95

Red Shoes
  8" (20cm) hard plastic, 1995 — $70

Red Velvet Tree Topper *(see Tree Topper)*
Renaissance Bride
  10" (25cm) hard plastic, 1999 — $130

Renoir
  21" (53cm) composition, 1945-1946 — $2,500
  14" (36cm) hard plastic, 1950 — $1,000
  21" (53cm) hard plastic/vinyl arms, 1961 *(Cissy)* — $950
  18" (46cm) hard plastic/vinyl arms, vinyl head, #1765, 1963 — $750
  21" (53cm) hard plastic/vinyl arms, pink gown, 1965 — $750
  21" (53cm) blue gown with black trim, 1966 — $2,300
  21" (53cm) navy blue gown, red hat, 1967 — $675
  21" (53cm) yellow gown, full lace overdress, 1969-1970 — $700
  21" (53cm) yellow gown, 1971 — $675
  21" (53cm) pink gown, black jacket, 1972 — $600
  21" (53cm) yellow gown with black ribbon trim, 1973 — $600
  10" (25cm) hard plastic, navy with red hat, #1175, 1968 — $425
  10" (25cm) hard plastic, blue dress with pleated trim, #1175, 1969 — $450
  10" (25cm) pale blue gown, short jacket, stripe or dotted skirt, #1180, 1970 — $450

Renoir Child
  12" (31cm) plastic/vinyl, *Portrait Children Series*, 1967 — $175
  14" (36cm) plastic/vinyl, 1968 — $200

Renoir Girl
  14" (36cm) plastic/vinyl, white dress with red ribbon, 1967-1968 — $175

Pink dress, white pinafore, 1969-1971 $125
Pink multi-tiered lace gown, 1972-1986 $75
Pink pleated nylon dress, 1986 $80
14" (36cm) plastic/vinyl, with watering can, 1985-1987
$85
8" (20cm) hard plastic, with watering can, 1997 $75
14" (36cm) plastic/vinyl, with hoop, 1986-1987 $85

Renoir's On The Terrace
8" (20cm) hard plastic, 1999 $80

Rhett
12" (31cm) plastic/vinyl, *Portrait Children Series*,
1981-1985 $75
8" (20cm) hard plastic, *Jubilee II*, 1989 $95
8" (20cm) hard plastic, *Scarlett Series*, various costumes,
1991-1994 $80
10" (25cm) hard plastic, 1996-1997 $100

Rhoda
8" (20cm) hard plastic, *Bible Children's Series*,
1953-1954 $7,000

Ricky
9" (23cm) hard plastic, 1996 $95

Riding Habit
8" (20cm) hard plastic, bent knee walker, #571, 1956;
#373G, 1957; #355, 1962; #441, 1963; #641, 1964
$475
8" (20cm) hard plastic, bent knee walker, boy doll,
#373B, 1957 $475
8" (20cm) hard plastic, bent knee walker, Devon Horse
Show, #541, 1958 $700
8" (20cm) hard plastic, bent knee or bent knee walker,
#623, 1965 $400
8" (20cm) *Americana Series*, 1990 $80

Riley's Little Annie
14" (36cm) plastic/vinyl, *Literature Series*, #1481, 1967
$225

Ring Around the Rosey
8" (20cm) hard plastic, 1995 $65
8" (20cm) hard plastic, 1998-1999 $80

Ring Bearer
14" (36cm) hard plastic, 1951 $600

Ring Master
8" (20cm) hard plastic, CU Gathering, 1991 *(see Special
Dolls)* $175

Riverboat Queen-Lena
8" (20cm) hard plastic, MADC, 1990 *(see Special Dolls)*
$325

Roaring 20's Bride
10" (25cm) hard plastic, 1999 $150

Roaring 20's Catherine
16" (41cm) porcelain, 1999 $215

Robin Hood
8" (20cm) hard plastic, *Storyland Dolls*, 1988-1990
$70

Rock and Roll Group
8" (20cm) hard plastic, set of 4 dolls, 1997 $300

Rococo Bride
10" (25cm) hard plastic, 1998-1999 $140

Rococo Catherine
16" (41cm) porcelain, 1998-1999 $300

Rodeo
7-1/2-8" (19-20cm) hard plastic, *Wendy Goes to a Rodeo*,
#483, 1955 $950

Rodeo Rosie
14" (36cm) plastic/vinyl, 1996 $120

Roller Skating
7-1/2-8" (19-20cm) hard plastic, straight leg walker,
#426, 1955 $625
8" (20cm) hard plastic, bent knee walker, #556, 1956;
#356, 1957; #358, 1962 $600

Romance
21" (53cm) composition, 1945-1946 $1,950 up

Romeo
18" (46cm) composition, 1949 $1,300
7-1/2-8" (19-20cm) hard plastic, straight leg walker,
#474, 1955 $1,000
8" (20cm) hard plastic, *Storyland Collection*, mid-year
release, 1994 $95
12" (31cm) plastic/vinyl, *Portrait Children Series*,
1978-1987 $70
12" (31cm) re-introduced, *Romance Series*, 1991-1992
$90

Roosevelt, Edith
14" (36cm) plastic/vinyl, 5th set, *First Ladies Series*,
1988 $100

Roosevelt, Eleanor
14" (36cm) plastic/vinyl, 6th set, *First Ladies Series*,
1989-1990 $110

Rosamund Bridesmaid
15" (38cm) hard plastic, 1951 $625
17-18" (43-46cm) hard plastic, 1951 $700

Rose
9" (23cm) early vinyl toddler, pink organdy dress and
bonnet, 1953 $140

Rosebud
13" (33cm) cloth/vinyl, 1953 $165
15" (38cm) cloth/vinyl, in Christening dress, FAO Schwarz
exclusive, 1953 $225
16-18" (41-46cm) cloth/vinyl, 1952-1953 $165
22-25" (56-64cm) 1953 $190
14-20" (36-51cm) cloth/vinyl, 1986 $65
14" (46cm) cloth/vinyl, African American, 1986 $75

Rose Fairy
8" (20cm) hard plastic, bent knee walker, #622, 1956
$1,500
8" (20cm) hard plastic, 1999 $80

Rose Queen
8" (20cm) hard plastic, MADC, 1998 *(see Special Dolls)*
$250

Rose Splendor
16" (41cm) plastic/vinyl, 1998 $550

Rosette
10" (25cm) *Portrette Series*, 1987-1989 $85

Rosey Posey
14" (36cm) cloth/vinyl, 1976 $80
21" (53cm) cloth/vinyl, 1976 $110

Rosie the Riveter
  8" (20cm) hard plastic, 1999 $80
Ross, Betsy
  8" (20cm) hard plastic, bent knee, *Americana Series*,
  #731, 1967-1972 $135
  8" (20cm) hard plastic, straight legs, "Alex Mold",
  #0731, 1973; #431, 1974-1975 $70
  8" (20cm) hard plastic, Bicentennial gown with star print,
  1976 $100
  8" (20cm) hard plastic, straight legs, 1976-1987 $65
  8" (20cm) hard plastic, white face, 1986 $60
  8" (20cm) hard plastic, 1991-1992 $65
  8" (20cm) hard plastic, QVC, 1998 *(see Special Dolls)*
                                                   $75
Rosy
  14" (36cm) 1988-1990 $80
Round Up Day Mouseketeer
  8" (20cm) made for Disney, 1992 *(see Special Dolls)*
                                                   $125
Row, Row, Row Your Boat
  8" (20cm) hard plastic, 1998-1999 $100
Roxanne
  8" (20cm) hard plastic, *Storyland Dolls*, 1994 $70
Royal Evening
  18" (46cm) hard plastic, 1953 $2,500 up
Royal Wedding
  21" (53cm) composition, 1947 $2,100 up
Rozy
  12" (31cm) plastic/vinyl, 1969 $350
Rub-a-Dub Baby
  11" (28cm) vinyl, 1996 $75
Ruby (July)
  10" (25cm) hard plastic, *Birthstone Collection*, 1992
                                                   $80
Ruffles Clown
  21" (53cm) cloth, 1954 $450

Rumania
  8" (20cm) hard plastic, bent knee, #786, 1968-1972
                                                   $100
  8" (20cm) hard plastic, straight legs, "Alex Mold",
  #0786, 1973; #586, 1974-1975 $70
  8" (20cm) hard plastic, straight legs, 1976-1987 $65
  8" (20cm) hard plastic, white face, 1986 $60
Rumbera, Rumbero
  7" (18cm) composition, 1938-1943 $325
  9" (23cm) composition, 1939-1941 $350
Rumpelstiltskin & Miller's Daughter
  8" (20cm) and 14" (36cm) limited to 3,000 sets, 1992
                                                   $275
Russia
  8" (20cm) hard plastic, bent knee walker, #774, 1965
                                                   $135
  8" (20cm) hard plastic, bent knee, #774, 1965-1972
                                                   $100
  8" (20cm) hard plastic, straight legs, "Alex Mold",
  #0774, 1973; #574, 1974-1975 $70
  8" (20cm) hard plastic, straight legs, 1976-1988 $65
  8" (20cm) hard plastic, re-introduced, 1991-1992
                                                   $65
  8" (20cm) hard plastic, *International Series*, 1994
                                                   $65
  8" (20cm) hard plastic, 1999 $150
Russian
  7" (18cm) composition, 1935-1938 $300
  9" (23cm) composition, 1938-1942 $350
Rusty
  20" (51cm) cloth/vinyl, 1967-1968 $325
Ruth
  8" (20cm) hard plastic, *Bible Children's Series*,
  1953-1954 $7,000

Sagittarius
  8" (20cm) hard plastic, 1998 $85
Sailing with Sally
  8" (20cm), Collector's United, 1998 *(see Special Dolls)*
                                                   $70
Sailor
  14" (36cm) composition, 1942-1945 $800
  17" (43cm) composition, 1943-1944 $950
  8" (20cm) hard plastic, boy UFDC, 1990 *(see Special
  Dolls)* $700
  8" (20cm) hard plastic, boy, made for FAO Schwarz,
  1991 *(see Special Dolls)* $100

  12" (31cm) hard plastic, *(Lissy)*, see *Columbian Sailor*,
  UFDC, 1993 *(see Special Dolls)* $225
Sailorette
  10" (25cm) hard plastic, *Portrette Series*, 1988 $75
Saks Own Christmas Carol
  8" (20cm), made for Saks Fifth Avenue, 1993 *(see Special
  Dolls)* $100
Sally Bride
  14" (36cm) composition, 1938-1939 $500
  18-21" (46-53cm) composition, 1938-1939 $575-$700
Salome
  14" (36cm) *Opera Series,* 1984-1986 $95
Salute to the Century
  8" (20cm) hard plastic, 1999 $100
Samantha
  14" (36cm) made for FAO Schwarz, 1989 *(see Special
  Dolls)* $175
  10" (25cm) hard plastic, Bewitched, 1997 $110

Samantha Gold
    14" (36cm) gold ruffled gown, *Classic Dolls*, 1991-1992
        $170

Samson
    8" (20cm) hard plastic, 1995 $90

Sandy McHare
    cloth/felt, 1930s $700

Santa Claus
    8" (20cm) hard plastic, mid-year release, 1993 $80
    14" (36cm) plastic/vinyl, 1995 $95

Santa's Little Helper
    8" (20cm) hard plastic, 1998-1999 $100

Sapphire (September)
    10" (25cm) hard plastic, *Birthstone Collection*, 1992
        $75

Sardinia
    8" (20cm) hard plastic, 1989-1991 $60

Sargent
    14" (36cm) plastic/vinyl, dressed in lavender, *Fine Arts Series*, 1984-1985 $80

Sargent's Girl
    14" (36cm) plastic/vinyl, dressed in pink, *Fine Arts Series*, 1986 $85

Scarecrow
    8" (20cm) hard plastic, *Wizard of Oz Series*, 1993-1999
        $70

Scarlett O'Hara
(Pre-Movie, 1937-1938)
    7" (18cm) composition, 1937-1939 $500
    9" (23cm) composition, 1938-1941 $550
    11" (28cm) composition, 1937-1942 $675
    14-15" (36-38cm) composition, 1941-1943 $825
    18" (46cm) composition, 1939-1946 $1,000
    21" (53cm) composition, 1942-1946 $1,500
    7-1/2-8" (19-20cm) hard plastic, straight leg walker, white gown with red flowers, 1953-1954 $1,300
    7-1/2-8" (19-20cm) hard plastic, straight leg walker, #485, yellow, blue or pink floral, 1955 $1,400
    8" (20cm) hard plastic, bent knee walker, # 631, pink, yellow or blue floral gown, 1956 $1,400
    8" (20cm) hard plastic, bent knee walker, white with red ribbon, #431, 1957 (extremely rare) $1,500
    8" (20cm) hard plastic, bent knee or bent knee walker, white or cream gown, #785, 1965 $650
    8" (20cm) hard plastic, bent knee, flowered gown, #725, 1966-1972 $350
    8" (20cm) hard plastic, bent knee, bright pink floral trim, 1971 only $400
    8" (20cm) hard plastic, straight legs, white gown, "Alex Mold", #0725, 1973; #425, 1974-1975 $75
    8" (20cm) hard plastic, in white gown, 1976-1985
        $65
    8" (20cm) hard plastic, white gown with red sash, MADC, 1986 *(see Special Dolls)* $275
    8" (20cm) hard plastic, white face, blue dot gown, 1987 (rare) $175

8" (20cm) hard plastic, straight legs, flowered gown, 1986-1989 $70
8" (20cm) hard plastic, *Jubilee II,* all green velvet gown, 1989 $125
8" (20cm) hard plastic, MADC, 1990 *(see Special Dolls)*
    $150
8" (20cm) hard plastic, straight legs, tiny floral print, *Scarlett Series*, 1990 $75
8" (20cm) hard plastic, four-tier white gown, curly hair, 1991 only $70
8" (20cm) hard plastic, rose floral print, oversized bonnet, 1992 $70
8" (25cm) hard plastic, green and white stripe gown, 1993
    $75
8" (20cm) hard plastic, in trunk, *Honeymoon in New Orleans*, 1993-1994 $200
8" (20cm) hard plastic, 70th Anniversary, mid-year release, 1993 $125
8" (20cm) hard plastic, Bride, 1994 $70
8" (20cm) hard plastic, picnic, 1994 $65
8" (20cm) hard plastic, white organdy with red trim, 1995-1996 $80
8" (20cm) hard plastic, picnic dress with organdy overskirt, 1995 $90
8" (20cm) hard plastic, green velour and taffeta, Anniversary Collection, 1995 $100
8" (20cm) hard plastic, floral dress, *Tomorrow is Another Day*, 1995-1996 $80
8" (20cm) hard plastic, maroon gown, *Ashley's Farewell*, 1996 $80
8" (20cm) hard plastic, red velvet gown, *Ashley's Birthday*, 1996 $100
8" (20cm) hard plastic, picnic dress with red rose print, 1996-1998 $80
8" (20cm) hard plastic, *Poor Scarlett*, 1998-1999
    $95
8" (20cm) hard plastic, white ruffle dress, *Sweet Sixteen Scarlett*, 1999 $90
10" (25cm) hard plastic, lace trim in bonnet, green taffeta gown, black braid trim, #1174, 1968 $450
10" (25cm) hard plastic, green taffeta gown, white braid trim, #1174, 1969 $475
10" (25cm) hard plastic, green taffeta gown, black braid trim, #1181, 1970-1972; #1180, 1973 $425
10" (25cm) hard plastic, *Jubilee II,* burgundy and white gown, 1989 $135
10" (25cm) hard plastic, floral print gown, *Scarlett Series,* 1990-1991 $100
10" (25cm) hard plastic, *Scarlett at the Ball*, all in black, 1992 $150
10" (25cm) hard plastic, green velvet with gold trim, 1993-1994 $125
10" (25cm) hard plastic, red dress and boa, 1994 $125
10" (25cm) hard plastic, blue and white dress, 1995
    $120
10" (25cm) hard plastic, black mourning dress, with or without hat box, 1996-1997 $110

1956 8-inch (20cm) *Scarlett*, green rosebuds. *Sara Tondini Collection. Photo by Zehr Photography.*

1956 8-inch (20cm) hard plastic *Scarlett. Sara Tondini Collection. Photo by Zehr Photography.*

1955 8-inch (20cm) *Scarlett* with yellow rosebuds. *Sara Tondini Collection. Photo by Zehr Photography.*

1957 8-inch (20cm) hard plastic *Scarlett. Sara Tondini Collection. Photo by Zehr Photography.*

10" (25cm) hard plastic, black mourning dress, in set with *Rhett* doll, 1996 $200

10" (25cm) hard plastic, in hoop and petti, 1996-1998 $100

10" (25cm) hard plastic, in hoop and petti, in set with *Mammy* and picnic dress, 1996-1998 $230

10" (25cm) hard plastic, blue gown, *Portrait Scarlett*, 1998-1999 $130

12" (31cm) hard plastic, green taffeta gown and bonnet, 1963 (rare) $1,400

12" (31cm) plastic/vinyl, green gown with braid trim, 1981-1985 $90

14" (36cm) hard plastic, 1950s $1,500

14" (36cm) plastic/vinyl, floral gown, 1968 $450

14" (36cm) plastic/vinyl, white gown with rows of lace, *(also called Gone With The Wind)* 1968-1986 $90

14" (36cm) plastic/vinyl, *Jubilee I*, all green velvet, 1986 $175

14" (36cm) plastic/vinyl, blue or green floral print, 1987-1989 $150

14" (36cm) plastic/vinyl, tiny floral print, *Scarlett Series*, 1990 $150

14" (36cm) plastic/vinyl, white ruffles, green ribbon, *Scarlett Series*, 1991-1992 $150

14" (36cm) plastic/vinyl with 8" (20cm) hard plastic *Bonnie Blue, Stroll Down Peachtree Lane,* limited to 2500 sets, 1995 $250

16" (41cm) hard plastic, 1950s $1,600

18" (46cm) hard plastic/vinyl arms, pale blue organdy gown, #1760, 1963 only *(Elise)* $950

20" (51cm) hard plastic, 1950s $1,850

20" (51cm) jointed arms, *Cissy,* deep green velvet gown, 1958 (rare) $2,500

21" (53cm) *Cissy,* straight arms, white gown with green ribbons on skirt, 1961 (rare) $2,500

21" (53cm) *Cissy,* straight arms, blue taffeta gown with black trim, #2240, 1961 $1,700

21" (53cm) hard plastic/vinyl arms, red gown, 1962 $1,000 up

21" (53cm) hard plastic/vinyl arms, green taffeta gown, 1965 $1,800

21" (53cm) plastic/vinyl, all white gown, red sash and roses variations, 1966 *(Coco)* $2,500

21" (53cm) plastic/vinyl, green taffeta gown with black trim, 1967 $650

21" (53cm) plastic/vinyl, floral print gown with wide white hem, 1968 $1,000

21" (53cm) plastic/vinyl, green taffeta gown white braid trim, 1969 $675

21" (53cm) plastic/vinyl, green taffeta, white trim on jacket, 1970 $675

21" (53cm) plastic/vinyl, all green taffeta, white lace at cuffs, 1975-1977 $400

21" (53cm) plastic/vinyl, silk floral gown, green parasol, white lace, 1978 $450

21" (53cm) plastic/vinyl, green velvet, 1979-1985 $375

21" (53cm) plastic/vinyl, floral gown, green parasol, 1986 $350

21" (53cm) plastic/vinyl, layered all over white gown, 1987-1988 $350

21" (53cm) plastic/vinyl, red birthday party gown, 1989 $425

21" (53cm) plastic/vinyl, Bride, *Scarlett Series*, 1990-1993 $350

21" (53cm) plastic/vinyl, green on white, three ruffles around skirt, 1991-1992 $325

21" (53cm) plastic/vinyl, green gown with bustle, *Scarlett Series*, 1994 $325

21" (53cm) plastic/vinyl, pink floral picnic dress, 1996 $325

21" (53cm) plastic/vinyl, red rose picnic dress, 1997 $325

21" (53cm) plastic/vinyl, black mourning dress, 1999 $500

21" (53cm) porcelain, green velvet, gold trim, limited to 1500 dolls, 1991 $550

School Girl
    7" (18cm) composition, 1936-1939 $300

School Girl
    14" (36cm) outfit only, 1996 $45

Scorpio
    8" (20cm) hard plastic, 1998 $85

Scotch Bunny
    16" (41cm) cloth, late 1930s $700

Scotland Boy
    8" (20cm) hard plastic, *International Series,* 1994 $60

Scottish (Scotland, Scots Lass or Scotch)
    7" (18cm) composition, 1936-1939 $300
    9" (23cm) composition, 1939-1940 $325
    8" (20cm) hard plastic, bent knee walker, #496, 1961; #396, 1962-1963; #796, 1964-1965 $135
    Outfit only for 8" (20cm) doll, #0396, 1962-1963 $95
    8" (20cm) hard plastic, bent knee walker, *Maggie* smile face, 1962-1963 $150
    8" (20cm) hard plastic, bent knee, #796, 1965-1972 $95
    8" (20cm) hard plastic, straight legs, "Alex Mold", #0796, 1973, #596, 1974-1975 $70
    8" (20cm) hard plastic, straight legs, 1976-1993 $65

Scouting
    8" (20cm) hard plastic, *Americana Series,* 1991-1992 $70

Scrooge
    14" (36cm) plastic/vinyl, 1996 $120

Secret Garden Trunk Set
    8" (20cm) FAO Schwarz, 1994 *(see Special Dolls)* $195
    14" (36cm) plastic/vinyl, 1995 $200

September
    14" (36cm) plastic/vinyl, *Classic Dolls,* 1989 $80

Setting Sail for Summer
    8" (20cm) MADC, 1994 *(see Special Dolls)* $125

Seven Dwarfs
    9" (23cm) composition, 1937 $500 each
75th Anniversary Huggable Huggums
    12" (31cm) vinyl/cloth, 1998 $80
75th Anniversary Print
    Limited to 1500 framed prints, 1998 $500
75th Anniversary Wendy
    8" (20cm) hard plastic, 1998 $100
Sewing Basket
    8" (20cm) hard plastic, has Alexander-kin included, FAO
    Schwarz exclusive, 1962, 1963, 1966-1971 $800 up
    8" (20cm) hard plastic/vinyl, has *Little Genius* included,
    FAO Schwarz exclusive, 1964-1965 $700 up
Shadow Jackie *(see Jackie)*
Shadow Madame Butterfly *(see Madame Butterfly)*
Shadow of Madame
    8" (20cm) Doll and Teddy Bear Expo, 1994 *(see Special Dolls)* $200
Shadow Polka Dot Lucy *(see Lucy)*
Shadow Stepmother *(see Wicked Stepmother)*
Shaharazad
    10" (25cm) hard plastic, *Portrette Series*, 1992-1993
                                                    $90
Shea
    8" (20cm) hard plastic, elf, CU Gathering, 1990
    (see Special Dolls) $200
Shepherd and Drummer Boy
    8" (20cm) hard plastic, sold as a pair, 1997-1999
                                                    $150
Shepherdess with Lamb
    8" (20cm) hard plastic, 1999 $85
She Sells Seashells
    8" (20cm) hard plastic, 1996 $70
Shimmering 30's Catherine
    16" (41cm) porcelain, 1999 $200
Shoe Accessory Pak
    For 8" (20cm) doll, 1999 $22
Shoe Bag
    Cloth bag, available for 8" (20cm), 10" (25cm),
    21" (53cm) $100 each
    Workshop kit for 8" (20cm), MADC exclusive, 1997
                                                    $15
Shoemaker's Elf
    8" (20cm) hard plastic, boy or girl, 1996 $65
Showgirl
    10" (25cm) hard plastic, MADC, 1996 *(see Special Dolls)*
                                                    $250
    10" (25cm) hard plastic, wearing black costume, MADC,
    1996 *(see Special Dolls)* $400
    Pin workshop kit, MADC exclusive, 1996 $15
Sicily
    8" (20cm) hard plastic, 1989-1990 $75
Silver Sensation Tree Topper
    10" (25cm) made for Disneyland, 1999 *(see Special Dolls)*
                                                    $135
Simone
    21" (53cm) hard plastic/vinyl arms, in trunk, 1968 (same
    doll as *Jacqueline*) $2,000

Singin' in the Rain
    8" (20cm) FAO Schwarz, 1996 *(see Special Dolls)*
                                                    $260
Sir Lancelot *(see Lancelot)*
Sir Lapin O'Hare
    cloth/felt, 1930s $675
Sitting Pretty
    18" (46cm) cloth body, 1965 (rare) $425
Skater's Waltz
    15-18" (38-46cm) hard plastic/vinyl, 1955-1956
                                                    $550-$650
Skate with Wendy
    8" (20cm) hard plastic, MADC, 1998 *(see Special Dolls)*
                                                    $80
Skating Doll
    16" (41cm) composition, 1947-1950 $675
Sleeping Beauty
    7-9" (18-23cm) composition, 1941-1944 $375-$475
    14-1/2" (37cm) composition, 1941 $500
    15-16" (38-41cm) composition, 1938-1940 $450
    18-21" (46-53cm) composition, 1941-1944 $600-$850
    16-1/2" (42cm) hard plastic, 1959 $625
    21" (53cm) hard plastic, 1959 $900
    10" (25cm) hard plastic, 1959-1960 $400
    14" (36cm) plastic/vinyl, gold gown, *Classic Dolls*,
    1971-1985 $85
    14" (36cm) plastic/vinyl, blue gown, *Classic Dolls*,
    1986-1990 $85
    14" (36cm) plastic/vinyl, pink gown, 1996 $120
    10" (25cm) hard plastic, *Portrette Series*, 1991-1992
                                                    $95
    8" (20cm) hard plastic, 1995 $75
    8" (20cm) hard plastic, 1997-1999 $70
    14" (36cm) plastic/vinyl, gift set, Disney Catalog,
    1995 *(see Special Dolls)* $250
    8" (20cm) hard plastic, Disney Store Gallery, 1999
    (see Special Dolls) $80
Sleeping Beauty's Prince
    8" (20cm) hard plastic, 1999 $80
Slumbermate
    11-12" (28-31cm) cloth/composition, 1930s-1940s
                                                    $275
    21" (53cm) composition/cloth, 1940s $400
    13" (33cm) vinyl/cloth, 1951 $175
Smarty
12" (31cm) plastic/vinyl, 1962-1963
    Blue and Red Suit, #1155, 1963 $325
    Blue Smock Dress, #1137, 1962 $350
    Cotton Sun Dress with Watering Can and Bonnet,
    #1135, 1962 $300
    Dress with Hat and Basket, #1140, 1962 $325
    Floral Nylon Dress with Bonnet, #1136, 1962 $325
    Gingham Dress, #1130, 1962 $300
    Nightgown with Baby, #1160, 1963 $400
    Sweater and Pants Set, #1162, 1963 $350
    White Cotton Dress with Floral Ruffle, #1141, 1962
                                                    $325

In case with Artie, FAO Schwarz exclusive, 1962
$1,000

Boxed Outfits for 12" (31cm) 1962-1963
    Dress with Bloomers $100
    Dress with Bloomers and Bonnet $100
    Nylon Nightgown $50
    Nylon Robe $50
    Smock with Bloomers $100

Smee
    8" (20cm) hard plastic, *Storyland Dolls*, 1993-1994
$60

Smokey Tail
    cloth/felt, 1930s $675

Snap, Crackle, Pop
    8" (20cm) all three dolls sold as a set, 1998-1999
$240
    8" (20cm) each doll sold individually, 1998 $80

Snowflake
    8" (20cm) hard plastic, MADC, 1995 *(see Special Dolls)*
$150

Snow Queen
    10" (25cm) hard plastic, *Portrette Series*, 1991-1992
$95
    8" (20cm) hard plastic, 1995 $75

Snow White
    12" (31cm) composition, 1939-1940 $425
    13" (33cm) composition, painted eyes, 1937-1939
$450
    13" (33cm) composition, sleep eyes, 1939-1940 $450
    16-17" (41-44cm) composition, 1938-1942 $525
    18" (46cm) composition, 1939-1940 $700
    20" (51cm) composition, 1938 $700
    24" (61cm) composition, 1938 $800
    28" (71cm) composition, 1938 $850
    15" (38cm) hard plastic, 1952 $750
    18" (46cm) hard plastic, 1952 $850
    23" (58cm) hard plastic, 1952 $1,000
    21" (53cm) hard plastic, early 1950s $1,100
    14" (36cm) plastic/vinyl, white gown, *Classic Dolls*, 1968-1986 $100
    14" (36cm) ecru and gold gown, red cape, 1986-1992
$100
    14" (36cm) plastic/vinyl, 1995 $150
    14" (36cm) plastic/vinyl, trunk set with wardrobe, 1996 $300
    14" (36cm) plastic/vinyl, Disney license, 1967-1977
$375
    14" (36cm) plastic/vinyl, gift set, Disney Catalog, 1996 *(see Special Dolls)* $250
    8" (20cm) hard plastic, Disney Colors, 1972-1976 *(see Special Dolls)* $450
    12" (31cm) plastic/vinyl, made for Disney 1990 *(see Special Dolls)* $200
    8" (20cm) *Storyland Dolls*, 1990-1992 $65
    8" (20cm) hard plastic, 1995-1999 $60
    12" (31cm) vinyl/cloth, baby doll, 1997 $55
    10" (25cm) Disneyland/Disney World, 1993 *(see Special Dolls)* $150

    8" (20cm) hard plastic, made for Disney Store Gallery, 1999 *(see Special Dolls)* $80

Snow White's Prince
    8" (20cm) hard plastic, 1996-1997 $70

So Big
    22" (56cm) cloth/vinyl, painted eyes, 1968-1975
$250

Soccer Boy
    8" (20cm) hard plastic, 1997 $60

Soccer Girl
    8" (20cm) hard plastic, 1997-1998 $60

Sock Hop
    8" (20cm) hard plastic, *Through the Decades Collection*, 1999 $75
    8" (20cm) M. Pancner's House of Collectibles *(see Special Dolls)* $75

So Lite Baby or Toddler
    10" (25cm) cloth, 1930s-1940s $325
    12" (31cm) cloth, 1930s-1940s $325
    14" (36cm) cloth, 1930s-1940s $350
    18" (46cm) cloth, 1930s-1940s $375
    20" (51cm) cloth, 1930s-1940s $375
    24" (61cm) cloth, 1930s-1940s $400

Soldier
    14" (36cm) composition, 1943-1944 $775
    17" (43cm) composition, 1942-1945 $875

Sound of Music
    all in same outfit: red skirt, white attached blouse, black vest that ties in front with gold thread, ca. 1965 (very rare) $475 up each

Dressed in Sailor Suits & Tagged, Ca 1965
    10" (25cm) *Friedrich*, *Gretl*, or *Marta* $350 each
    12" (31cm) *Brigitta* with *Lissy* Face $600
    14" (36cm) *Louisa* $475
    14" (36cm) *Brigitta*, *Liesl* $425 each
    17" (43cm) *Maria* $525

Large Set 1965-1970
    10" (25cm) *Friedrich* #1107 $225
    10" (25cm) *Marta* #1102, 10" (25cm) *Gretl* #1101
$200 each
    14" (36cm) *Brigitta* #1403, 14" (36cm) *Liesl* #1405
$200 each
    14" (36cm) *Louisa* #1404 $300
    17" (43cm) *Maria* #1706, has *Polly* or *Elise* face $325

Small Set, 1971-1973
    8" (20cm) *Marta*, 8" (20cm) *Friedrich*, 8" (20cm) *Gretl*
$200 each
    10" (25cm) *Brigitta* $185
    10" (25cm) *Liesl* $200
    10" (25cm) *Louisa* $250
    12" (31cm) *Maria* $300

Re-introduced 1992-1993
    8" (20cm) *Brigitta* $85
    8" (20cm *Gretl* and *Kurt* (boy in sailor suit) $85 each
    10" (25cm) *Maria* $100
    12" (31cm) *Maria Bride* $125

1993 (continuation of set)
    8" (20cm) *Friedrich* $85

8" (20cm) *Marta*	$125
10" (25cm) *Liesl*	$100
10" (25cm) *Maria* at the Abbey	$100

1997-1999 Set

8" (20cm) *Gretl Von Trapp* or *Marta Von Trapp*, 1998-1999	$100 each
9" (23cm) *Brigitta Von Trapp*, or *Friedrich Von Trapp*, 1998-1999	$100 each
10" (25cm) *Kurt Von Trapp*, *Liesl Von Trapp*, or *Louisa Von Trapp*, 1998-1999	$100 each
10" (25cm) *Captain Von Trapp*, 1998-1999	$125
10" (25cm) *Maria at the Abbey* or *Maria Travel Ensemble*, 1997-1999	$125 each
10" (25cm) *Mother Superior*, 1997-1999	$115

South American
| 7" (18cm) composition, 1938-1943 | $300 |
| 9" (23cm) composition, 1939-1941 | $325 |

Southern Belle or Girl
7-1/2-8" (19-20cm) hard plastic, straight leg walker and non-walker, 1953-1954	$1,000
8" (20cm) hard plastic, 1955	$800
8" (20cm) hard plastic, bent knee walker, #410, 1956	$950
8" (20cm) hard plastic, bent knee walker, #385, 1963; #785, 1964	$525
Outfit only for 8" (20cm) doll, #0385, 1963	$175
8" (20cm) hard plastic, TJ Maxx, 1998 *(see Special Dolls)*	$60
12" (31cm) hard plastic, 1963	$1,500
21" (53cm) hard plastic/vinyl arms, blue gown with wide pleated hem, 1965	$1,000
21" (53cm) White gown with green ribbon trim, 1967	$650
10" (25cm) hard plastic, white gown with rows of lace and green ribbon, #1170, 1968	$400
10" (25cm) hard plastic, white gown with pink sash, #1170, 1969	$400
10" (25cm) hard plastic, white gown with red sash, #1185, 1970	$400
10" (25cm) hard plastic, white gown with green sash, #1185, 1971-1972; #1184, 1973	$400
10" (25cm) made for My Doll House, 1989 *(see Special Dolls)*	$150

Southern Boy
| 9" (23cm) vinyl/latex Cherub, 1952 | $350 |

Southern Girl
9" (23cm) vinyl/latex Cherub, 1952	$350
11-14" (28-36cm) composition, 1940-1943	$425-$525
17-21" (43-53cm) composition, 1940-1943	$700-$825

Spanish Boy
| 8" (20cm) hard plastic, bent knee walker, #779, 1964-1965 | $400 |
| 8" (20cm) hard plastic, bent knee, #779, 1965-1968 | $375 |

Spanish Girl
7 (18cm) composition, 1935-1939	$300
9" (23cm) composition, 1936-1940	$325
8" (20cm) hard plastic, bent knee walker, #495, 1961; #395, 1962-1963; #795, 1964-1965	$130

Outfit only for 8" (20cm) doll, #0395, 1962-1963	$95
8" (20cm) hard plastic, bent knee, three-tiered skirt, #795, 1965-1972	$100
8" (20cm) hard plastic, straight legs, "Alex Mold", #0795, 1973; #595, 1974-1975	$70
8" (20cm) hard plastic, straight legs, three-tiered skirt, 1976-1982	$65
8" (20cm) hard plastic, straight legs, two-tiered skirt, 1983-1985	$65
8" (20cm) hard plastic, straight legs, white with red polka dots, 1986-1989	$65
8" (20cm) hard plastic, straight legs, all red tiered skirt, 1990-1992	$65
8" (20cm) hard plastic, *International Series*, 1994-1995	$65
8" (20cm) hard plastic, 1999	$90

Spanish Matador
| 8" (20cm) hard plastic, 1992-1993 | $60 |

Special Event Doll
| 8" (20cm) hard plastic, 1994 *(see Special Dolls)* | $100 |

Special Girl
| 24" (61cm) cloth/composition, 1942-1946 | $525 |

Spring
| 14" (36cm) plastic/vinyl, *Classic Dolls*, 1993 | $140 |

Spring Break
| 8" (20cm) hard plastic, made for Metroplex Doll Club, 1992 *(see Special Dolls)* | $275 |

Spring Flowers
| 14" (36cm) plastic/vinyl, *Classic Dolls*, 1994 | $120 |
| 8" (20cm) hard plastic, QVC, 1999 *(see Special Dolls)* | $70 |

Springtime
| 8" (20cm) hard plastic, made for MADC, 1991 *(see Special Dolls)* | $200 |

Springtime Bride
| 10" (25cm) hard plastic, QVC, 1999 *(see Special Dolls)* | $100 |

Springtime Darling
| 8" (20cm) hard plastic, MADC, 1999 *(see Special Dolls)* | $75 |

Starlett Glamour
| 10" (25cm) hard plastic, MADC, 1999 *(see Special Dolls)* | $130 |

Starlight Angel
| 10" (25cm) hard plastic, 1999 | $110 |

Statue of Liberty
| 14" (36cm) plastic/vinyl, 1986, not produced | |

Stilts
| 8" (20cm) hard plastic, clown on stilts, 1992-1993 | $70 |

Story Princess
| 8" (20cm) hard plastic/vinyl, 1956 | $1,250 |
| 15-18" (38-46cm) hard plastic, 1954-1956 | $650-$800 |

Stuffy *(see Little Men)*

Suellen
| 14-17" (36-43cm) composition, 1937-1938 | $1,000 |
| 12" (31cm) yellow, multi-tiered skirt, *Scarlett Series*, 1990 | $80 |

1940s 21-inch (53cm) all composition *Southern Girl. Veronica Jochens Collection.*

12" (31cm) made for Jean's Dolls, 1992 *(see Special Dolls)* $150
8" (20cm) hard plastic, *Scarlett Series*, 1994-1995 $65
8" (20cm) hard plastic, 1999 $80

Suffragette
10" (25cm) hard plastic, *Through the Decades Collection*, 1999 $110

Sugar and Spice
8" (20cm) hard plastic, 1998-1999 $90

Sugar Darlin'
14-18" (36-46cm) cloth/vinyl, 1964 $100-$150
14" (36cm), 18" (46cm), 23" (58cm) *Lively*, knob makes head and limbs move, 1964 $160-$225
23" (58cm) 1964 $175
14" (36cm) *Musical Lively*, 1964 $200

Sugar Plum Fairy
8" (20cm) hard plastic, bent knee walker, #544, 1958 $425
10" (25cm) *Portrette Series*, 1992-1993 $95

8" (20cm) hard plastic, 1999 $80

Sugar Tears
14" (36cm) vinyl baby, 1964 $125
14" (36cm) vinyl baby in window box with layette,
1964 $175
14" (36cm) vinyl baby in basket with layette, FAO
Schwarz exclusive, 1964 $250

Sulky Sue
8" (20cm) hard plastic, 1988-1990 $80

Summer
14" (36cm) *Classic Dolls*, 1993 $150

Summer Blossom
8" (20cm) hard plastic, MADC, 1999 *(see Special Dolls)*
     $75

Summer Cherry Picker
8" (20cm) hard plastic, QVC, 1998 *(see Special Dolls)*
     $100

Summer Skies
14" (36cm) *Classic Dolls*, 1994 $120

Sunbeam
11" (28cm) vinyl/cloth, 1951 $85
16" (41cm) vinyl/cloth, 1950-1951 $110
19-20" (48-51cm) vinyl/cloth, 1950-1951 $125-$150
23-24" (58-61cm) vinyl/cloth, 1950-1951 $135-$175

Sunbonnet Sue
9" (23cm) composition, 1937-1940 $325

Sunflower Clown
40" (101cm) all cloth, flower eyes, 1951 $875

Sunny
8" (20cm) hard plastic, CU Nashville, 1996 *(see Special
Dolls)* $125

Sun pin workshop kit
MADC exclusive, 1999 $15

Super Genius
8" (20cm) plastic/vinyl, 1995 $45

Susanna
8" (20cm) made for Dolly Dears, 1992 *(see Special Dolls)*
     $250

Susie Q
16" (41cm) cloth, 1938-1942 $675
8" (20cm) hard plastic, 1995 $65

Suzy 12" (31cm) plastic/vinyl, 1970 $375

Swan Lake *(see Ballerinas)*

Swan Princess
10" (25cm) hard plastic, 1995 $80

Sweden (Swedish)
7" (18cm) composition, 1936-1940 $300
9" (23cm) composition, 1937-1941 $325
8" (20cm) hard plastic, bent knee walker, #492, 1961;
#392, 1962-1963; #792,1964-1965 $135
Outfit only for 8" (20cm) doll, #0392, 1962-1963
     $95
8" (20cm) hard plastic, bent knee walker, *Maggie* smile
face, 1962-1963 $150
8" (20cm) hard plastic, bent knee, #792, 1965-1972
     $100
8" (20cm) hard plastic, straight legs, "Alex Mold",
#0792, 1973; #592, 1974-1975 $70

8" (20cm) hard plastic, straight legs, 1976-1989 $60
8" (20cm) hard plastic, straight legs, white face,
1985-1987 $60
8" (20cm) hard plastic, straight legs, re-introduced
1991 only $65

Sweet Baby
18-1/2-20" (47-51cm) cloth/latex, 1948 $65-$90
14" (36cm) 1983-1984 $70
14" (36cm) 1987-1994 $75-$85
14" (36cm) in carry case, 1990-1992 $125

Sweet Dreams
12" (31cm) vinyl/cloth, 1996 $60
12" (31cm) vinyl/cloth, with layette, 1996 $75

Sweet Silk Victorian
8" (20cm) hard plastic, 1999 $65

Sweet Sixteen
14" (36cm) *Classic Dolls,* 1991-1992 $130
10" (25cm) hard plastic, African American available,
1997 $80

Sweet Sixteen Scarlett *(see Scarlett)*

Sweet Tears
9" (23cm) vinyl, 1965-1974 $80
9" (23cm) vinyl, with layette in box, 1965-1973 $150
14" (36cm) 1965-1982 $70
14" (36cm) in window box, 1965-1974 $150
14" (36cm) in trunk, trousseau, 1967-1974 $175
14" (36cm) with layette, 1974-1979 $150
16" (41cm) 1965-1971 $85
16" (41cm) in basket with trousseau, FAO Schwarz
exclusive, 1965 $225
16" (41cm) in window box with trousseau, FAO Schwarz
exclusive, 1965-1966 $200

Sweet Violet
18" (46cm) hard plastic, jointed, 1954 only $800 up

Sweetie Baby
22" (56cm) all plastic, 1962 $150

Sweetie Walker
23" (58cm) all plastic, 1962 $300

Swiss (Switzerland)
7" (18cm) composition, 1936 $300
9" (23cm) composition, 1935-1938 $325
8" (20cm) hard plastic, bent knee walker, #494, 1961;
#394, 1962-1963; #794, 1964-1965 $135
Outfit only for 8" (20cm) doll, #0394, 1962-1963
     $95
8" (20cm) hard plastic, bent knee walker, *Maggie* smile
face, 1962-1963 $150
8" (20cm) hard plastic, bent knee, #794, 1965-1972
     $95
8" (20cm) hard plastic, straight legs, "Alex Mold",
#0794, 1973; #594, 1974-1975 $70
8" (20cm) hard plastic, straight legs, 1976-1990 $60
8" (20cm) hard plastic, straight legs, white face,
1985-1987 $55

Sylvester the Jester
14" (36cm) plastic/vinyl, 1992-1993 $100

Former Madame Alexander Doll Club president Tanya McWhorter was honored by the factory with an 8-inch (20cm) limited edition doll in her likeness in 1999.

Taft, Helen
  14" (36cm) plastic/vinyl, 5th set, *First Ladies Series*,
  1988 $100
Tanya
  8" (20cm) hard plastic, Colonial Southwest, Inc. exclusive,
  1999 *(see Special Dolls)* $65
Tara
  Gone With The Wind House, 1998-1999 $190

Taurus
  8" (20cm) hard plastic, 1998 $85
Team Canada
  8" (20cm) hard plastic, 1998-1999 $90
Teapot pin workshop kit
  MADC exclusive, 1997 $15
Teeny Twinkle
  cloth, flirty eyes, 1946 $600
Tennis
  7-1/2-8" (19-20cm) hard plastic, straight leg walker,
  #415, 1955 $450
  8" (20cm) hard plastic, bent knee walker, #527, 1956;
  #327,1957 $425
  8" (20cm) hard plastic, boy or girl doll, 1997 $55 each
Texas
  8" (20cm) hard plastic, *Americana Series*, 1991 $65
Texas Shriner
  8" (20cm) hard plastic, Shriner's National Convention,
  1993 *(see Special Dolls)* $400
Thailand
  8" (20cm) hard plastic, bent knee, #767, 1966-1972
                                                            $100
  8" (20cm) hard plastic, straight legs, "Alex Mold",
  #0767, 1973; #567, 1974-1975 $70
  8" (20cm) hard plastic, straight legs, 1976-1989 $60
Thank You
  8" (20cm) hard plastic, 1997-1998 $60
There Was a Little Girl
  14" (36cm) plastic/vinyl, 1995 $100
There's No Place Like Home
  Wizard of Oz House, 1997-1999 $150
Thinking of You
  8" (20cm) hard plastic, 1998-1999 $80
Thomas, Marlo
  17" (43cm) plastic/vinyl, red velvet formal,
  #1793, 1967 $650
  Blue and green mini dress with white boots,
  #1789, 1967 $675
  Black and purple mini dress with white boots,
  #1789, 1967 $700
Thoroughly Modern Wendy
  8" (20cm) hard plastic, made for Disney Theme Parks,
  1992 *(see Special Dolls)* $100
Three Little Pigs
  16" (41cm) cloth, 1930s $550 each
  12" (31cm) composition, 1938-1939 $700 each
  12" (31cm) plastic/vinyl, 1996-1997 $80 each
                                                       $250 set
Three Wise Men
  8" (20cm) hard plastic, set of 3 dolls, 1997-1999 $330 set
Thumbelina & Her Lady
  (name was changed, see Her Lady and Child)
Tibet
  8" (20cm) hard plastic, *International Dolls*, 1993
                                                            $60

Tiger Lily
    8" (20cm) hard plastic, 1992-1993 $75

Timmy Toddler
    23" (58cm) plastic/vinyl, 1960-1961 $175
    30" (76cm) 1960 $225

Timothy
    8" (20cm) hard plastic, *Bible Children Series*, 1953-1954
    $7,000

Tin Woodsman
    8" (20cm) hard plastic, *Wizard of Oz Series*, 1993-present
    $70

Tinkerbell
    10" (25cm) hard plastic, 1969 (and possibly later)
    $475
    8" (20cm) hard plastic, Disney exclusive, 1973 $900 up
    8" (20cm) hard plastic, magic wand, *Storyland Dolls*,
    1991-1999 $75
    14" (36cm) plastic/vinyl, 1996 $100

Tinkles
    8" (20cm) hard plastic, 1995 $50

Tiny Betty
    7" (18cm) composition, 1934-1943 $300 up

Tiny Tim
    cloth, 1934 $700
    7" (18cm) composition, 1934-1937 $350
    14" (36cm) composition, 1938-1940 $600
    8" (20cm) hard plastic, 1996 $65

Tiny Tinkle
    12" (31cm) hard plastic, molded hair baby, 1948 $225

Tiny Twinkle
    cloth doll, 1930s $450

Tippi
    8" (20cm) hard plastic, CU Gathering, 1988 *(see Special Dolls)* $375

Tippy Toe
    16" (41cm) cloth, 1940s $625

Today I Feel Silly
    16" (41cm) cloth, FAO Schwarz, 1999 *(see Special Dolls)*
    $45

To Madame, With Love
    8" (20cm) Doll and Teddy Bear Expo, 1995 *(see Special Dolls)* $125

Tomorrow is Another Day *(see Scarlett)*

Tom Sawyer
    8" (20cm) hard plastic, *Storyland Dolls*, 1989-1990
    $65

Tommy
    12" (31cm) hard plastic, made for FAO Schwarz 100th
    Anniversary, 1962 $1,300

Tommy Bangs *(see Little Men)*

Tommy Snooks
    8" (20cm) hard plastic, *Storyland Dolls*, 1988-1991
    $55

Tommy Tittlemouse
    8" (20cm) hard plastic, *Storyland Dolls*, 1988-1991
    $55

Tony Sarg Marionettes *(see Marionettes)*

Tooth Fairy
    10" (25cm) *Portrette*, 1994 $80

    8" (20cm) hard plastic, 1995 $60
    8" (20cm) hard plastic, 1999 $80

Topsy-Turvy
    7-9" (18-23cm) composition, with *Tiny Betty* heads,
    1935 $225
    7" (18cm) with *Dionne Quints* heads, 1936 $325

Toto
    8" (20cm) hard plastic, Disney World Doll and Teddy Bear
    Convention, 1997 *(see Special Dolls)* $150

Toulouse-Lautrec
    21" (53cm) plastic/vinyl, black and pink, 1986-1987
    $275

Toy Soldier
    8" (20cm) hard plastic, *Storyland Dolls*, 1993-1994
    $60

Trapeze Artist
    10" (25cm) hard plastic, *Portrette Series*, 1990-1991
    $95

Tree Topper
    10-11" (25-28cm) hard plastic, dolls in cones without legs
    Merry Angel, made for Spiegel, 1991 *(see Special Dolls)*
    $140
    Joy Noel, made for Spiegel, 1992 *(see Special Dolls)*
    $125
    Blue Fairy, made for Disney Catalog, 1995 *(see Special Dolls)* $165
    Golden Holiday, made for Bloomingdales by Mail,
    1999 *(see Special Dolls)* $120
    White Tree Topper, made for QVC, 1999 *(see Special Dolls)* $90
    Silver Sensation, made for Disneyland, 1999 *(see Special Dolls)* $135
    Cream Lace, Ivory Lace, Angel Lace, 1992-1994
    $90
    Red Lace, 1992 $90
    Pink Victorian, 1993-1995 $95
    Red, Gold & Green, Red Velvet, 1993-1994 $90
    White Antique, 1994-1995 $90
    Florentine Angel, 1995 $90
    Yuletide Angel, 1995-1997 $95
    Christmas Angel, 1995-1996 $90
    Glorious Angel, 1996-1998 $100
    Heavenly Angel, 1997-1998 $100
    Glistening Angel, 1998-1999 $120
    Winter Lights, 1999 $135

Treena Ballerina
    15" (38cm) hard plastic, pink, yellow, or red tutu,
    1952 $775
    18-21" (46-53cm) hard plastic, pink, yellow, or red tutu,
    1952 $900

Trick and Treat
    8" (20cm) hard plastic, made for A Child at Heart,
    1993 *(see Special Dolls)* $145

Truman, Bess
    14" (36cm) plastic/vinyl, 6th set, *First Ladies Series*,
    1989-1990 $100

Trunk
    Fits 8" (20cm) and 10" (25cm) dolls, blue box logo,
    1998 $70

Navy fabric, 1999 $80
Tunsia
  8" (20cm) hard plastic, 1989 $75
Turkey
  8" (20cm) hard plastic, bent knee, #787, 1968-1972
    $100
  8" (20cm) hard plastic, straight legs, "Alex Mold",
  #0787, 1973; #587, 1974-1975 $70
  8" (20cm) hard plastic, straight legs, 1976-1986 $60
Tweedledee & Tweedledum
  14" (36cm) cloth, 1930-1931 $750 each
  8" (20cm) Disney World Doll and Teddy Bear Convention,
  1994 *(see Special Dolls)* $250 pair
  8" (20cm) hard plastic, sold as a pair, 1998-1999
    $160 pair
  8" (20cm) hard plastic, sold individually, 1998 $80 each
20's Bride
  10" (25cm) hard plastic, 1995 *(see Brides)* $95
20's Traveler
  10" (25cm) hard plastic, *Portrette Series*, 1992 only
    $95
Twilight Angel
  8" (20cm) hard plastic, 1998-1999 $100
Twinkle, Twinkle, Little Star
  8" (20cm) hard plastic, 1997 $60

Tyler, Julia
  14" (36cm) plastic/vinyl, 2nd set, *First Ladies Series*,
  1979-1981 $100
Tyrolean Boy*
  8" (20cm) hard plastic, bent knee walker, #399,
  1962-1963; #799, 1964-1965 $175
  Outfit only for 8" (20cm) doll, #0399, 1962-1963
    $100
  8" (20cm) hard plastic, bent knee, #799, 1965-1972
    $100
  8" (20cm) hard plastic, straight legs, "Alex Mold",
  #0799, 1973 $70
Tyrolean Girl*
  8" (20cm) hard plastic, bent knee walker, #398,
  1962-1963; #798, 1964-1965 $175
  Outfit only for 8" (20cm) doll, #0398, 1962-1963
    $100
  8" (20cm) hard plastic, bent knee walker, *Maggie*
  smile face, 1962-1963 $185
  8" (20cm) hard plastic, bent knee, #798, 1965-1972
    $100
  8" (20cm) hard plastic, straight legs, "Alex Mold",
  #0798, 1973 $70

*Became Austria in 1974.

U.S.A.
  8" (20cm) hard plastic, *International Dolls*, 1993-1994
    $60
  8" (20cm) hard plastic, astronaut, 1999 $85
U.S. Armed Forces Set
  8" (20cm) 4 doll set with flags, African American
  available, 1997-1998 $340
  Individual dolls-Air Force, Army, Marines, Navy, African
  American available, 1997-1998 $85 each
Ugly Stepsister
  10" (25cm) hard plastic, 1997-1998 $85
Ultimate Angel
  21" (53cm) plastic/vinyl, 1998-1999 $550
Uncle Sam
  8" (20cm) hard plastic, 1995 $70

Undergarment Doll
  8" (20cm) hard plastic, MADC, 1998 *(see Special Dolls)*
    $40
Underwear Accessory Package
  For 8" (20cm) doll, 1999 $20
Union Officer
  12" (31cm) hard plastic/vinyl, *Scarlett Series*, 1990-1991
    $80
Union Soldier
  8" (20cm) hard plastic, *Scarlett Series*, 1991 $85
United States
  8" (20cm) hard plastic, straight legs, "Alex Mold",
  #559, 1974-1975 $75
  8" (20cm) hard plastic, misspelled Untied States
    $95
  8" (20cm) hard plastic, straight legs, #559, 1976-1987
    $65
  8" (20cm) hard plastic, 1988-1992 $60
  8" (20cm) hard plastic, Statue of Liberty, 1996-1998
    $75
  8" (20cm) hard plastic, TJ Maxx, 1997 *(see Special Dolls)*
    $65

Valentine Prince and Princess
  8" (20cm) hard plastic, Collector's United, 1997
  (see Special Dolls) $135

Van Buren, Angelica
  14" (36cm) plastic/vinyl, 2nd set, *First Ladies Series*,
  1979-1981 $100

Velvet Party Dress
  8" (20cm) hard plastic, #389, 1957 $550

Vermont Maiden
  8" (20cm) made for Enchanted Doll House, 1990
  (see Special Dolls) $100

Victoria
  21" (53cm) composition, 1939, 1941 $1,875 up
  21" (53cm) composition, 1945-1946 $1,850 up
  14" (36cm) hard plastic, 1950-1951 $975
  8" (20cm) hard plastic, matches 18" (46cm) doll, straight
  leg walker, #0030C, 1954 $1,100
  18" (46cm) hard plastic, blue gown, *Me and My Shadow
  Series,* 1954 $1,650

Victoria (Baby)
  18" (46cm) cloth/vinyl, baby, 1966 $75
  20" (51cm) cloth/vinyl, baby, 1967-1989 $90
  14" (36cm) cloth/vinyl, baby, 1975-1988, 1990-1997
  $85-110
  14" (36cm) cloth/vinyl, baby, African American,
  1996 $100

20" (51cm) cloth/vinyl, baby, in dress, jacket, bonnet,
1986 $95
14" (36cm) cloth/vinyl, baby, made for Lord & Taylor,
1989 *(see Special Dolls)* $95
18" (46cm) cloth/vinyl, baby, re-introduced, 1991-1993,
1995-1997 $85-$100
14" (36cm) cloth/vinyl, "Lifelike" baby, 1999 $75
18" (46cm) cloth/vinyl, "Lifelike" baby, African American
available, 1998-1999 $110

Victorian "so-called"
  18" (46cm) hard plastic, pink taffeta and black velvet
  gown, *Glamour Girl Series*, 1953 $1,600

Victorian Bride
  10" (25cm) hard plastic, *Portrette Series*, 1992 *(see Brides)*
  $95
  10" (25cm) hard plastic, 1998-1999 *(see Brides)* $135

Victorian Catherine
  16" (41cm) porcelain, 1998-1999 $300

Victorian Christmas
  8" (20cm) hard plastic, 1999 $95

Victorian Skater
  10" (25cm) hard plastic, *Portrette Series*, 1993-1994
  $100

Vietnam
  8" (20cm) hard plastic, #788, 1968-1969 $285
  8" (20cm) hard plastic, *Maggie* smile face, 1968-1969
  $300
  8" (20cm) hard plastic, re-introduced in 1990-1991
  $60

Violet (Nutcracker Ballerina)
  10" (25cm) *Portrette Series*, 1994 $75

Violetta
  10" (25cm) hard plastic, 1987-1988 $65

Virgo
  8" (20cm) hard plastic, 1998 $85

W.A.A.C. (Army)
  14" (36cm) composition, 1943-1944 $800

W.A.A.F. (Air Force)
  14" (36cm) composition, 1943-1944 $800

W.A.V.E (Navy)
  14" (36cm) composition, 1943-1944 $800

Waltz
  16" (41cm) plastic/vinyl, 1999 $190

Want *(see Ghost of Christmas Present)*

Washington, George and Martha
  8" (20cm) hard plastic, sold as a pair, 1998 $180

Washington, Martha
  14" (36cm) plastic/vinyl, 1st set, *First Ladies Series*,
  1976-1978 $200

Watchful Guardian Angel
  10" (25cm) hard plastic, 1998-1999 $180
  In set with 8" (20cm) *Forrest* and *Heather*, 1998-1999
  $380

Weeping Princess of Korea
  8" (20cm) hard plastic, *Maggie* face, 1995 $60

Welcome Home (Desert Storm)
  8" (20cm) hard plastic, boy or girl, African American or
  white, blonde or brunette, mid-year release, 1991
  $55 each

Well Dressed Bears
  7" (18cm) plush, 1993-1994 $30 each

Wendy *(see also Alexander-kins)*
  14"-22" (36-56cm) composition, 1944-1945 $450 up
  8" (20cm) hard plastic, trousseau suitcase, FAO Schwarz
  exclusive, 1953 $1,000 up

15" (38cm) hard plastic, 1955-1956 (Bride) $625
18" (46cm) hard plastic, 1955-1956 (Bride) $800
25" (64cm) hard plastic, 1955 (Bride) $925
8" (20cm) hard plastic, first MADC doll, 1989 *(see Special Dolls)* $150
8" (20cm) hard plastic, pink coat and dress, *Anniversary Collection*, 1995 $100

Wendy (From Peter Pan)
15" (38cm) hard plastic, #1506, 1953-1954 $700
14" (36cm) plastic/vinyl, 1969 $300
8" (20cm) hard plastic, slippers with pompons, no faces, *Storyland Dolls*, 1991-1994 $60
8" (20cm) hard plastic, 1999 $60

Wendy Angel *(see Angel)*

Wendy Ann *(see also Alexander-Kins)*
9" (23cm) composition, painted eyes, 1936-1940 $375
11-16" (28-41cm) composition, 1935-1948 $550
11" (28cm) composition in case with wardrobe $900 up
14" (36cm) composition, in riding habit, 1938-1939 (some wigged) $450
16" (41cm) composition with trousseau, 1941 $1,100 up
17-21" (43-53cm) composition, 1938-1944 $700-$900
14-1/2-17" (37-43cm) hard plastic, 1948-1949 $675-$900
16-22" (42-56cm) hard plastic, 1948-1950 $725-$900
23-25" (58-64cm) hard plastic, 1949 $875
8" (20cm) hard plastic, trousseau suitcase, FAO Schwarz exclusive, 1954 $1,000 up
20" (51cm) hard plastic, 1956 $575

Wendy Ballerina
8" (20cm) hard plastic, 1997-1999 $80

Wendy Cheerleader *(see also Cheerleader)*
8" (20cm) hard plastic, 1998-1999 $80

Wendy Elf
8" (20cm) hard plastic, 1995 $65

Wendy Goes to Summer Camp
8" (20cm) hard plastic, CU Nashville, 1998 *(see Special Dolls)* $100

Wendy Goes to the Circus
8" (20cm) hard plastic, 1996 $60

Wendy Goes to the Fair
8" (20cm) outfit only, exclusive for MADC Travel Doll Party, 1997 $35

Wendy Honors Margaret Winson
8" (20cm) hard plastic, MADC, 1996 *(see Special Dolls)* $80

Wendy Honors Madame
8" (20cm) hard plastic, mid-year release, 1993 $125

Wendy Joins MADC
8" (20cm) hard plastic, MADC, 1995 *(see Special Dolls)* $125

Wendy Loves Being A Prom Queen
8" (20cm) hard plastic, 1994 $60

Wendy Loves Being Best Friends
8" (20cm) hard plastic, MADC, 1993 *(see Special Dolls)* $90

Wendy Loves Being Just Like Mommy
8" (20cm) hard plastic, 1993-1994 $75

Wendy Loves Being Loved
8" (20cm) hard plastic doll and wardrobe, mid-year release, 1992 $125

Wendy Loves Fashions
Outfits for 8" (20cm)
Cherry Romper, 1993-1994 $25
Organdy Dress, 1993-1994 $20
Pajamas, 1993 $20

Wendy Loves Her ABC's
8" (20cm) hard plastic, made for ABC Unlimited Productions, 1993 *(see Special Dolls)* $100

Wendy Loves Her First Day of School
8" (20cm) hard plastic, 1994 $60

Wendy Loves Her Sunday Best
8" (20cm) hard plastic, 1994 $65

Wendy Loves Learning to Sew
8" (20cm) hard plastic, Suitcase Sewing Kit, 1994 $90

Wendy Loves Summer
8" (20cm) hard plastic, box set, 1993-1994 (doll and wardrobe) $90

Wendy Loves Her Sun Dress
8" (20cm) hard plastic, 1993-1994 $45

Wendy Loves the County Fair
8" (20cm) hard plastic, 1993-1994 $60

Wendy Loves Winter
8" (20cm) hard plastic, box set, 1994 $90

Wendy Makes It Special
8" (20cm) hard plastic, 1997-1998 $80
With customized hat box $80

Wendy On Safari
8" (20cm) outfit only, exclusive for MADC Travel Doll Party, 1999 $30

Wendy Plays Masquerade
8" (20cm) outfit only, exclusive for MADC Friendship Luncheon, 1998 $35

Wendy's Best Friend Maggie
8" (20cm) MADC, 1994 *(see Special Dolls)* $80

Wendy's Dollhouse Trunk Set
8" (20cm) hard plastic, 1996 $200

Wendy's Dollhouse Trunk Set
Additional Outfits for 8" (20cm) 1996
Artist, Ballet, Goes to the Farm, Sunday Best $35 each

Wendy's Favorite Pastime
8" (20cm) Disney Theme Parks, 1994 *(see Special Dolls)* $90

Wendy 75th Anniversary 8" (20cm) hard plastic, 1998 $100

Wendy's Special Cheer *(see also Cheerleader)*
8" (20cm) hard plastic, customized sweater, 1998-1999 $80

Wendy's Tea Party
8" (20cm) hard plastic, MADC, 1997 *(see Special Dolls)* $125

Wendy Salutes the Olympians
8" (20cm) hard plastic, 1996 $110

1953 7 1/2-inch (19cm) *Wendy's Favorite Outfit. Sara Tondini Collection. Photo by Zehr Photography.*

Below: 1953 7 1/2-inch (19cm) *Little Southern Girl. Sara Tondini Collection. Photo by Zehr Photography.*

1955 8-inch (20cm) *Wendy Helps Mummy Serve Luncheon. Sara Tondini Collection. Photo by Zehr Photography.*

1964 12-inch (31cm) *Little Shaver* dolls. *Tanya McWhorter Collection.*

1955 8-inch (20cm) *Wendy Goes to Sunday School. Sara Tondini Collection. Photo by Zehr Photography.*

1955 8-inch (20cm) *Wendy Goes to Matinee. Sara Tondini Collection. Photo by Zehr Photography.*

1955 8-inch (20cm) *Wendy Garden Party. Sara Tondini Collection. Photo by Zehr Photography.*

1956 8-inch (20cm) *Wendy's First Long Dancing Dress. Marge Meisinger Collection. Photo by Carol J. Stover.*

1956 8-inch (20cm) *Wendy Goes Calling with Mother.* Very hard to find. *Sara Tondini Collection. Photo by Zehr Photography.*

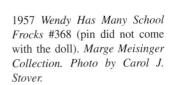

1957 *Wendy Has Many School Frocks* #368 (pin did not come with the doll). *Marge Meisinger Collection. Photo by Carol J. Stover.*

1957 8-inch (20cm) *Wendy's
Graduation Dress. Marge
Meisinger Collection.*

1963 8-inch (20cm) *Cousin
Marie* hard plastic *Wendy.
Marge Meisinger Collection.*

1962-65 8-inch (20cm) *Wendy* in a party dress. The *Wendy* and *Wendy-kin* named dolls would cease production in 1965. *Sara Tondini Collection. Photo by Zehr Photography.*

1955 8-inch (20cm) hard plastic *Wendy Visits Auntie. Sara Tondini Collection. Photo by Zehr Photography.*

Wendy Shops at FAO
  8" (20cm) hard plastic, made for FAO Schwarz, 1993
  (see Special Dolls) $80

Wendy Starts Her Collection
  8" (20cm) Jacobsen's, 1994 *(see Special Dolls)* $100

Wendy Starts Her Travels
  8" (20cm) hard plastic, trunk set, MADC, 1996
  (see Special Dolls) $175

Wendy Tap Dancer
  8" (20cm) hard plastic, 1998 $80

Wendy The Gardener
  8" (20cm) hard plastic, 1998-1999 $90

Wendy The Witch
  8" (20cm) hard plastic, 1999 $80

Wendy Tours the Factory
  8" (20cm) hard plastic, MADC, 1996 *(see Special Dolls)*
       $160

Wendy Visits the World's Fair 1893
  8" (20cm) Shirley's Doll House, 1993 *(see Special Dolls)*
       $80

Wendy Walks Her Dog
  8" (20cm) Jean's Dolls, 1995 *(see Special Dolls)*
       $75

Wendy Works Construction
  8" (20cm) hard plastic, 1998-1999 $90

White Rabbit
  14"-17" (36-43cm) cloth/felt, 1940s $550-$650
  8" (20cm) hard plastic, 1995 $80

White Rabbit in Court
  8" (20cm) hard plastic, 1996-1997 $65

White Tree Topper
  10" (25cm) made for QVC, 1999 *(see Special Dolls)*
       $90

White Antique Tree Topper *(see Tree Topper)*
White Christmas
  10" (25cm) hard plastic, 1995 $90
  10" (25cm) hard plastic, pair from movie, 1997 $225

White Iris
  10" (25cm) hard plastic, 1998-1999 $140

White King
  8" (20cm) hard plastic, 1996-1998 $95
  With Red Queen, sold as a set, 1996-1997 $200

Wicked Stepmother
  8" (20cm) hard plastic, 1996-1997 $80
  8" (20cm) hard plastic, topsy turvy doll, 1996 $175
  21" (53cm) plastic/vinyl, 1996 $350

Wicked Witch of the West
  8" (20cm) hard plastic, *Wizard of Oz Series,* mid-year
  release, 1994 $80
  10" (25cm) hard plastic, 1997-1999 $100

Wilder, Laura Ingalls *(see Ingalls, Laura)*
Wilson, Edith
  14" (36cm) plastic/vinyl, 5th set, *First Ladies Series,*
  1988 $100

Wilson, Ellen
  14" (36cm) plastic/vinyl, 5th set, *First Ladies Series,*
  1988 $100

Winged Monkey
  8" (20cm) hard plastic, *Wizard of Oz Series,* 1994
       $175

Winnie Walker
  15" (38cm) hard plastic, navy or gray coat with red dress,
  #1536, 1953 $450
  18" (46cm) hard plastic, navy coat or gray with red dress,
  #1836, 1953 $550
  25" (53cm) hard plastic, navy coat or gray with red dress,
  #2540, 1953 $700
  15" (46cm) hard plastic, organdy dress with bonnet,
  #1536, 1953 $475
  18" (46cm) hard plastic, organdy dress with bonnet,
  #1836, 1953 $575
  25" (46cm) hard plastic, organdy dress with bonnet,
  #2537, 1953 $750
  25" (46cm) hard plastic, blue taffeta coat, bonnet with pink
  dress, FAO Schwarz exclusive, 1953 $800
  In trunk with trousseau, FAO Schwarz exclusive,
  1953 $900 up

Winter
  14" (36cm) plastic/vinyl, *Classic Dolls,* 1993 $150

Winter Angel
  8" (20cm) hard plastic, factory altered doll for Shirley's
  Doll House, 1993 *(see Special Dolls)* $85

Winter Fun Skater
  8" (20cm) hard plastic, 1995 $60

Winter Lights Tree Topper *(see Tree Topper)*
Winter Rain
  14" (36cm) plastic/vinyl, *Classic Dolls,* 1994 $120

Winter Sports
  8" (20cm) hard plastic, made for Shirley's Doll House,
  1991 *(see Special Dolls)* $75

Winter Wonderland
  8" (20cm) made for Nashville Show, 1991 *(see Special
  Dolls)* $185
  8" (20cm) hard plastic, Lillian Vernon, 1997 *(see Special
  Dolls)* $100
  10" (25cm) hard plastic, 1999 $120

Winter Wonderland II
  8" (20cm) made for Nashville Show, 1992 *(see Special
  Dolls)* $95

Wintertime
  8" (20cm) hard plastic, MADC Premiere, 1992
  (see Special Dolls) $195

Witch
  8" (20cm) hard plastic, *Americana Series,* 1992-1993
       $65

Withers, Jane
  12-13-1/2" (31-34cm) composition, closed mouth,
  1937 $1,000
  15-17" (38-43cm) 1937-1939 $1,000
  17" (43cm) cloth body, 1939 $1,350
  18-19" (46-48cm) composition, open mouth, 1937-1939
       $1,300
  19-20" (48-51cm) composition, closed mouth version
       $1,450

20-21" (51-53cm) composition, open mouth, 1937
$1,850

With Love
8" (20cm) hard plastic, African American available, 1995-1997 $75

Wizard, The
8" (20cm) hard plastic, *Wizard of Oz Series,* mid-year release, 1994 $130
8" (20cm) hard plastic, 1998-1999 $95
8" (20cm) hard plastic, with balloon, 1998-1999 $150

Wizard of Oz
doll stand kit, exclusive for Disney World Doll and Teddy Bear Convention, 1997 $50

Workin' Out with Wendy
8" (20cm) hard plastic, *Through the Decades Collection,* 1999 $65

World War II Nurse
8" (20cm) hard plastic, 1999 $70

Wynken, Blynken & Nod
8" (20cm) hard plastic, set of three dolls and a wooden shoe, 1993-1994 $200

1988 *Tanya Dear.* This 14-inch (36cm) doll was designed by Madame Alexander and presented to Tanya McWhorter. One other doll exists, which was Madame's personal doll. *Tanya McWhorter Collection.*

A stunning
all original
composition
1937 *Jane
Withers*.
*Marge Meisinger
Collection.*
*Photo by Carol
J. Stover.*

1952 15-inch (38cm) hard
plastic *Cynthia*. *Tanya
McWhorter Collection.*

Yes, Virginia, There is a Santa Claus
8" (20cm) hard plastic, 1999 $80
Yolanda
12" (31cm) hard plastic/vinyl, slim teenage body,
1965, nude doll $165
Turquoise evening gown with white lace bodice,
#1010, 1965 $375
Pink tulle bridesmaid, #1020, 1965 $425
Bride, #1030, 1965-1967 $375
Yugoslavia
8" (20cm) hard plastic, bent knee, #789, 1968-1972
                                                               $100
8" (20cm) hard plastic, straight legs, "Alex Mold",
#0789, 1973; #589, 1974-1975 $70
8" (20cm) hard plastic, straight legs, 1976-1986
                                                               $60
8" (20cm) hard plastic, CU Gathering, 1987 FAD
(see Special Dolls) $100
Yuletide Angel Tree Topper *(see Tree Topper)*

Zodiac Calendar
1997-1998 $15
Zorina Ballerina 17" (43cm) composition, 1937-1938
                                                               $1,800

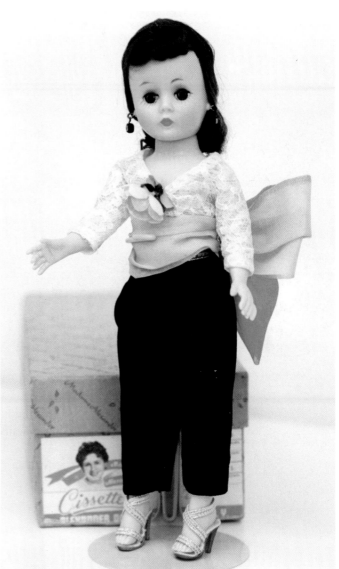

1957 10-inch (25cm) *Cissette. Tanya McWhorter Collection.*

Left: 19631963 12-inch (31cm) *Lissy Scarlett,* all hard plastic. *Tanya McWhorter Collection.*

About the Author

Bordentown, New Jersey based collector-dealer-author A. Glenn Mandeville is no stranger to the doll world.

"I have always been attracted to perfect miniature things," says Glenn.

As a teenager, this love translated into model trains and later to dolls.

"The same elements exist in dolls and trains . . . The flawless miniaturization of life," is often quoted by the author.

In the mid-1980s Glenn began writing doll articles and books for Hobby House Press, Inc. At the time, he was the head of the foreign language department for a local school system. During the summer, he would prowl the flea markets for rare doll finds.

This hobby soon became a full-time business. serving as Regional Director for United Federation of Doll Clubs, Inc. and as the first Chairman of Judges, Modern Division, Glenn has left an indelible mark on the collector's world.

More books followed on collectible dolls and Glenn became a frequent guest on the talk show circuit including CBS's "Regis & Kathie Lee," CNBC's "Smart Money," NBC's "Eddie Huggins," and the RKO Radio network.

Glenn's personal appearances at leading doll shops and collector's gatherings led him to the Presidency of the Madame Alexander Doll Club for 1992.

"I can honestly say I was overwhelmed," says Glenn, when referring to the Madame Alexander Doll Club. "Collectors are really eager to learn the most that they can about their hobby."

It was the collector outreach that led Glenn to compile the first *Madame Alexander Dolls Value Guide* and to continue with a second and third edition.

"Shared knowledge is my goal," quotes Glenn, and as collector's agree, this book has it all!